THE ROCK DIARY 1983

THE ROCK DIARY 1983

DAVID FUDGER
&
PETER SILVERTON

PROTEUS BOOKS
LONDON AND NEW YORK

PROTEUS BOOKS is an imprint of The Proteus Publishing Group

United States
PROTEUS PUBLISHING CO., INC.
733 Third Avenue
New York, N.Y. 10017

Distributed by:
THE SCRIBNER BOOK COMPANIES, INC.
597 Fifth Avenue
New York, N.Y. 10017

United Kingdom
PROTEUS (PUBLISHING) LIMITED
Bremar House
Sale Place
London, W2 1PT

ISBN 0 86276 020 8

First published in U.S. 1982
First published in U.K. 1982

Design: Dave Fudger
Editor: Nicky Hodge
Typeset by Laura Beck and Lynne Shippam at Portobello Typesetting
Printed in Great Britain by The Anchor Press Ltd

THE ROCK DIARY 1983

Written by
Peter Silverton

Designed by
Dave Fudger

CONTENTS

THE ROCK DIARY 1983

For Chloë and Daniel

THE ROCK DIARY 1983

THANKS to my bank manager who never ceased to remind me how little money was in my account; to anyone who's ever written about rock'n'roll; to anyone who's ever answered a record company phone (yes, that was me on the other end, requesting the precise date your least favourite pop star released his seventh single); to all of you who'll write, care of the publishers, pointing out the inevitable errors; to everyone who created the events contained herein — because without them...And, finally, to the three voices which have helped remind me why I started on the project in the first place — Elvis Presley, Elvis Costello and Elvis, my dog.
Peter Silverton
London, April 1982

&THANKS To the following record companies for the use of record covers and promotional material which provided the bulk of the photographs that appear in the book — A&M, Arista, Beggars Banquet, Bronze, Carrere, CBS, Columbia, Charisma, Charly, Chiswick, Chrysalis, Decca, E G, EMI, Ensign, Factory, Faulty Products, Island, Magnet, MCA, Motown, Old Gold, Phonogram, Polydor, Rak, RCA, Riva, Rough Trade, RSO, Safari, Stiff, Swansong, 2 Tone, Virgin and WEA. Special thanks also to Alf Martin of Record Mirror for demonstrating how easy it can be to be a gentleman, and gratitude to the trustees of the Nel Collection for allowing me to plunder their archives. Thanks a million Lesley, for your patience and the Index.
Dave Fudger May 1982

THE ROCK DIARY 1983

BANK & PUBLIC HOLIDAYS

Dates in italics are not general holidays

Australia 1983
New Year holiday — 1 January
Australia Day holiday — 31 January
Good Friday — 1 April
Easter Eve — 2 April
Easter Monday — 4 April
Anzac Day — 25 April
Christmas holiday — 27 December
Boxing Day (except SA) — 26 December

Belgium
New Year holiday — 1 January
Easter Monday — 4 April
Labour Day holiday — 2 May
Ascension Day — 12 May
Whit Monday — 23 May
National Feast — 21 July
Assumption Day — 15 August
All Saints — 1 November
Armistice Day holiday — 11 November
King's Name Day — 11 November
(schools, govt offices) — 15 November
Christmas holiday — 26 December

Canada
New Year holiday — 1 Janury
Good Friday — 1 April
Easter Monday — 4 April
Victoria Day — 23 May
Dominion Day holiday — 1 July
Labour Day — 5 September
Thanksgiving Day — 10 October
Remembrance Day holiday — 11 November
Christmas holiday — 26 December

Denmark
New Year's Day — 1 January
Maundy Thursday — 31 March
Good Friday — 1 April
Easter Monday — 4 April
National Day (schools) — 16 April
General Prayer Day — 29 April
Ascension Day — 12 May
Whit Monday — 23 May
Constitution Day — —
Christmas Day — —
Boxing Day — 26 December

England & Wales
Bank holiday — 3 January
Good Friday — 1 April
Easter Monday — 4 April
May Day holiday — 2 May
Spring Bank Holiday — 30 May
Summer Bank Holiday — 29 August
Christmas Day — —
Boxing Day — 26 December
Bank holiday — 27 December

France
New Year's Day — 1 January
Easter Monday — 4 April
Labour Day — —
Ascension Day — 12 May
Whit Monday — 23 May
National Day — 14 July
Assumption Day — 15 August
All Saints — 1 November
Armistice Day — 11 November
Christmas Day — —

Germany, West
New Year's Day — 1 January
Good Friday — 1 April
Easter Monday — 4 April
Labour Day — —
Ascension Day — 12 May
Whit Monday — 23 May
Day of Unity — 17 June
Repentance Day — 16 November
Christmas holiday — 26 December

Italy
New Year's Day — 1 January
Easter Monday — 4 April
Liberation Day — 25 April
Labour Day — —
Assumption Day — 15 August
All Saints Day — 1 November
Immaculate Conception Day — 8 December
Christmas Day — —
Boxing Day — 26 December

Netherlands
New Year holiday — 1 January
Good Friday — 1 April
Easter Monday — 4 April
Queen's Day (civil service) — 30 April
Ascension Day — 12 May
Whit Monday — 23 May
Christmas holiday — 26,27 December

N. Ireland
Bank holiday — 3 January
St Patrick's Day holiday — *17 March*
Good Friday — *1 April*
Easter Monday — 4 April
May Day holiday — 2 May
Spring Bank holiday — *30 May*
Orangeman's Day — 12 July
Summer Bank holiday — *29 August*
Christmas Day — —
Boxing Day — 26 December
Bank holiday — 27 December

Republic of Ireland
Bank holiday — 3 January
St Patrick's Day holiday — 17 March
Good Friday — *1 April*
Easter Monday — 4 April
June holiday — 6 June
August holiday — 1 August
October holiday — 31 October
Christmas Day — —
St Stephen's Day — 26 December
Bank Holiday — 27 December

Scotland
Bank holiday — 3 January
Bank holiday — 4 January
Good Friday — *1 April*
Spring Bank holiday — *2 May*
Bank holiday — *30 May*
Summer Bank holiday — *1 August*
Christmas Day — —
Boxing Day — 26 December
Bank holiday — *27 December*

Sweden
New Year's Day — 1 January
Epiphany — 6 January
Good Friday — 1 April
Easter Monday — 4 April
Labour Day — —
Ascension Day — 12 May
Whit Monday — 23 May
Midsummer holiday — 25 June
All Saints holiday — 5 November
Christmas Day — —
Boxing Day — 26 December

Switzerland
New Year's holiday — 1, 2 January
Good Friday — 1 April
Easter Monday — 4 April
Ascension Day — 12 May
Whit Monday — 23 May
Christmas — 26 December

USA
New Year holiday — 1 January
Washington's Birthday holiday — 21 February
Memorial Day — 30 May
Independence Day — 4 July
Labour Day — 5 September
Columbus Day — 10 October
Veterans Day holiday — 11 November
Thanksgiving Day — 24 November
Christmas holiday — 26 December

FESTIVALS & ANNIVERSARIES 1983

Circumcision — Jan 1
Epiphany — 6
Conversion of St Paul — 25
Purification — Feb 2
St Valentine — 14
Shrove Tuesday — 15
Ash Wednesday — 16
First Sunday in Lent — 20
St David — Mar 1
Mothering Sunday — 13
St Patrick — 17
St Joseph — 19
Annunciation — 25
Palm Sunday — 27
Maundy Thursday — 31
Good Friday — Apr 1

Easter Day — 3
St George — 23
St Mark — 25
St Philip and St James — May 1
Ascension Day — 12
St Matthias — 14
Sunday after Ascension — 15
Pentecost — 22
Trinity Sunday — 29
Corpus Christi — Jun 2
St Barnabas — 11
Fathers Day — 19
St. John, Baptist — 24
St Peter — 29
St Thomas — Jul 3
St Swithin — 15

St Mary Magdalene — 22
St James — 25
Transfiguration — Aug 6
Assumption — 15
St Bartholomew — 24
Blessed Virgin Mary — Sep 8
St Mattnew — 21
St Michael — 29
Muslim New Year, 1404 — Oct 8
St Luke — 18
United Nations Day — 24
St Simon and St Jude — 28
All Saints — Nov 1
Remembrance Sunday — 13
First Sunday in Advent — 27
St Andrew — 30
Christmas (Sunday) — Dec 25
St Stephen, Boxing Day — 26
S. John, Evangelist — 27
Holy Innocents — 28

JEWISH FESTIVALS

AM5742
Passover — 29 March
Pentecost — 18 May
Fast of Ab — 19 July

AM5744
New Year — 8 September
Day of Atonement — 17 September
Tabernacles — 22 September
Rejoicing of the Law — 30 September
Dedication of the Temple — 1 December

THE ROCK DIARY 1983

BEWARE!

A warning from Jonathan King

I'M NOT SURE that I approve of all this.
I mean, it's all very well having a diary to hand including various trivial or vital facts about the previous dates of the ROCK era, but it makes one feel a trifle old, don't you know, to read about anniversaries long dead and gone.

For instance, I turn to FEB. 22nd and I'm reliably informed that the first GENESIS single was released on that date in 1968! Since I discovered, named and produced the band, that set me off on a wave of nostalgia and memories that lasted all day and into part of the next. There was I, an innocent teenager fresh out of school and into my first year at Cambridge University, when I wrote a song ('Everyone's Gone to the Moon') and recorded it and WHAM it was an international hit and I was on 'Ready, Steady, Go' and 'Top of the Pops' and 'Hullaballoo' in the USA and all the rest of it.

The sixties were a great collection of years to grow through one's teens and twenties. I remember being introduced to a new, young American guitarist by Chas Chandler at the Scotch club in London on the day JIMI HENDRIX arrived — unknown — in Britain.

I still have somewhere his 'Thank you' letter for my music paper column predicting stardom for the young sprout.

Come to that, I still have my 1966 column predicting the same for DAVID BOWIE.

Then we moved on, through the times of peace, flowers and drugs; beads and meditation; Monterey and Woodstock (I was sitting with Paul Simon beside the pool at the Beverly Wilshire hotel in L.A. when he said to me — rather dreamily — 'I wonder if one could do a FREE concert'); James Bond, Carnaby Street and Vietnam until the SEVENTIES arrived. They were an interesting decade for me. I was Top Record Producer of the year in Britain, I launched and found such diverse talents as 10CC, The Bay City Rollers and The Rocky Horror Show, whilst having dozens of hits myself, under my own and assumed names, ranging from 'Una Paloma Blanca' to One Hundred Ton and a Feather. But the big musical movement of the time was the advent of PUNK — rapidly followed by NEW WAVE MUSIC.

The Police, Elvis Costello, The Boomtown Rats — and, of course, the vastly under rated SEX PISTOLS — bringing the voices and sounds of a new generation to the music world. It's all memories, isn't it? Whether for you the names and events of the following pages merely trigger reminiscences of friends and lovers long faded, or revive — as they do for me — faces and personalities out of the past, it's virtually guaranteed that you won't be able to turn from day to day without opening a closet door packed with skeletons, though I could have put that better.

For the next year, then, you and I will have much to muse on as the hours pass by. 'Lunch with Shirley' our DIARY will tell us. But will we arrive on time for lunch with Shirley? Or will we sit gazing into the air, spinning off on a whirl of memories until the darkness falls and Shirley has gone home starving?

'Business meeting with merchant bank' our own handwriting will declare, but the danger is that, enrapt and hypnotised by the spectres of past events, we will miss our meeting and fail to tie up that multi-billion dollar deal.

Can you afford to take these awful risks? Perhaps you'd better not buy this temptress nestling like a snake in your hand. Oh! It's too late?

Well, in that case, never mind. Sit back, give in to temptation, relax and let your mind wander through the maze of mirrors conjured up by the facts contained herein.

CALENDARS

1982

	January	February	March	April	May	June
M	4 11 18 25	1 8 15 22	1 8 15 22 29	5 12 19 26	3 10 17 24 31	7 14 21 28
T	5 12 19 26	2 9 16 23	2 9 16 23 30	6 13 20 27	4 11 18 25	1 8 15 22 29
W	6 13 20 27	3 10 17 24	3 10 17 24 31	7 14 21 28	5 12 19 26	2 9 16 23 30
T	7 14 21 28	4 11 18 25	4 11 18 25	1 8 15 22 29	6 13 20 27	3 10 17 24
F	1 8 15 22 29	5 12 19 26	5 12 19 26	2 9 16 23 30	7 14 21 28	4 11 18 25
S	2 9 16 23 30	6 13 20 27	6 13 20 27	3 10 17 24	1 8 15 22 29	5 12 19 26
S	3 10 17 24 31	7 14 21 28	7 14 21 28	4 11 18 25	2 9 16 23 30	6 13 20 27

	July	August	September	October	November	December
M	5 12 19 26	2 9 16 23 30	6 13 20 27	4 11 18 25	1 8 15 22 29	6 13 20 27
T	6 13 20 27	3 10 17 24 31	7 14 21 28	5 12 19 26	2 9 16 23 30	7 14 21 28
W	7 14 21 28	4 11 18 25	1 8 15 22 29	6 13 20 27	3 10 17 24	1 8 15 22 29
T	1 8 15 22 29	5 12 19 26	2 9 16 23 30	7 14 21 28	4 11 18 25	2 9 16 23 30
F	2 9 16 23 30	6 13 20 27	3 10 17 24	1 8 15 22 29	5 12 19 26	3 10 17 24 31
S	3 10 17 24 31	7 14 21 28	4 11 18 25	2 9 16 23 30	6 13 20 27	4 11 18 25
S	4 11 18 25	1 8 15 22 29	5 12 19 26	3 10 17 24 31	7 14 21 28	5 12 19 26

1983

	January	February	March	April	May	June
M	3 10 17 24 31	7 14 21 28	7 14 21 28	4 11 18 25	2 9 16 23 30	6 13 20 27
T	4 11 18 25	1 8 15 22	1 8 15 22 29	5 12 19 26	3 10 17 24 31	7 14 21 28
W	5 12 19 26	2 9 16 23	2 9 16 23 30	6 13 20 27	4 11 18 25	1 8 15 22 29
T	6 13 20 27	3 10 17 24	3 10 17 24 31	7 14 21 28	5 12 19 26	2 9 16 23 30
F	7 14 21 28	4 11 18 25	4 11 18 25	1 8 15 22 29	6 13 20 27	3 10 17 24
S	1 8 15 22 29	5 12 19 26	5 12 19 26	2 9 16 23 30	7 14 21 28	4 11 18 25
S	2 9 16 23 30	6 13 20 27	6 13 20 27	3 10 17 24	1 8 15 22 29	5 12 19 26

	July	August	September	October	November	December
M	4 11 18 25	1 8 15 22 29	5 12 19 26	3 10 17 24 31	7 14 21 28	5 12 19 26
T	5 12 19 26	2 9 16 23 30	6 13 20 27	4 11 18 25	1 8 15 22 29	6 13 20 27
W	6 13 20 27	3 10 17 24 31	7 14 21 28	5 12 19 26	2 9 16 23 30	7 14 21 28
T	7 14 21 28	4 11 18 25	1 8 15 22 29	6 13 20 27	3 10 17 24	1 8 15 22 29
F	1 8 15 22 29	5 12 19 26	2 9 16 23 30	7 14 21 28	4 11 18 25	2 9 16 23 30
S	2 9 16 23 30	6 13 20 27	3 10 17 24	1 8 15 22 29	5 12 19 26	3 10 17 24 31
S	3 10 17 24 31	7 14 21 28	4 11 18 25	2 9 16 23 30	6 13 20 27	4 11 18 25

1984

	January	February	March	April	May	June
M	2 9 16 23 30	6 13 20 27	5 12 19 26	2 9 16 23 30	7 14 21 28	4 11 18 25
T	3 10 17 24 31	7 14 21 28	6 13 20 27	3 10 17 24	1 8 15 22 29	5 12 19 26
W	4 11 18 25	1 8 15 22 29	7 14 21 28	4 11 18 25	2 9 16 23 30	6 13 20 27
T	5 12 19 26	2 9 16 23	1 8 15 22 29	5 12 19 26	3 10 17 24 31	7 14 21 28
F	6 13 20 27	3 10 17 24	2 9 16 23 30	6 13 20 27	4 11 18 25	1 8 15 22 29
S	7 14 21 28	4 11 18 25	3 10 17 24 31	7 14 21 28	5 12 19 26	2 9 16 23 30
S	1 8 15 22 29	5 12 19 26	4 11 18 25	1 8 15 22 29	6 13 20 27	3 10 17 24

	July	August	September	October	November	December
M	2 9 16 23 30	6 13 20 27	3 10 17 24	1 8 15 22 29	5 12 19 26	3 10 17 24 31
T	3 10 17 24 31	7 14 21 28	4 11 18 25	2 9 16 23 30	6 13 20 27	4 11 18 25
W	4 11 18 25	1 8 15 22 29	5 12 19 26	3 10 17 24 31	7 14 21 28	5 12 19 26
T	5 12 19 26	2 9 16 23 30	6 13 20 27	4 11 18 25	1 8 15 22 29	6 13 20 27
F	6 13 20 27	3 10 17 24 31	7 14 21 28	5 12 19 26	2 9 16 23 30	7 14 21 28
S	7 14 21 28	4 11 18 25	1 8 15 22 29	6 13 20 27	3 10 17 24	1 8 15 22 29
S	1 8 15 22 29	5 12 19 26	2 9 16 23 30	7 14 21 28	4 11 18 25	2 9 16 23 30

JANUARY
SATURDAY

1

1977 THE ROXY CLUB, the first place that punks could call home, opened in London's Covent Garden. After a trial run just before Christmas, The Clash played at this, the official, gala opening of the premises punk entrepreneur, gold-toothed, badly dressed Andrew Czeczowski had taken over from a gay soul disco. A suitably fetid basement, the Roxy immediately became the one venue every new punk band aspired to play. A casual visitor could be forgiven for assuming that the audience were more interested in cramming into the ladies toilet to take drugs and play with each other than they were in the music. Tiny, neatly groomed girls would disappear into the lavatory, emerging twenty minutes later with a couple of yards of dog chain draped from an ear and a rivet through a nostril. Although the Roxy was only in Czeczowski's capable hands for a few months of emphetamine psychosis, it was ensured an immortality of a sort with the relese of the Live At The Roxy compilation later that year.

1967 MOON MULLICAN, 'king of the hillbilly piano players' and a little league rockabilly cult, died in Beaumont, Texas. His heart gave out.

1964 TOP OF THE POPS' first edition. The weekly tradition of BBC1's swift run through the charts began in a BBC Manchester studio converted from a deconsecrated church (demolished in the seventies). Hosting the first show was Jimmy Saville, a club DJ brought in by producer Johnny Stewart for an air of freshness — and strange as it might seem now it's Jimmy Saville OBE — street credibility. Making his TV debut, Saville introduced a show which included Dusty Springfield, The Rolling Stones and, at number one, The Dave Clark Five with 'Glad All Over'.

1962 THE BEATLES' audition for Decca Records. Despite A&R man Mike Smith's enthusiasm for Harrison's rendition of 'The Sheik Of Araby' and Lennon's 'Please Mr. Postman', head of A&R Dick Rowe declined the offer and opted instead for Brian Poole And The Tremeloes, commenting 'Groups of guitars are on the way out.'

1957 COOL FOR CATS, an 'intimate record programme' with dancers working out to new releases, first broadcast by British TV.

1953 HANK WILLIAMS, the singer who took country music out of its Southern hill country ghetto, died in the back of his Cadillac on his way to a show in West Virginia. The certificate said 'Heart attack'. Nearer the truth would be too many heartaches, too many pills and too much booze. An illiterate raised in abject poverty in Alabama, Williams kept with him a morbid, even savage Pentacostal view of life which gave his songs a desparate, poetic heart closer to the blues than the domestic platitudes of most country. Even his gospels sound racked with doubt. Paradoxically for one who existed on the fringes of society, his best songs have become mainstream standards. Every Las Vegas schlock trader has recorded 'Your Cheatin' Heart' and 'Lovesick Blues' while The Carpenters desecrated the memory of his happiest tune, 'Jambalaya'. His soul can be no more at rest now than it was while he lived.

1948 THE AMERICAN MUSICIANS UNION started a recording strike.

1942 COUNTRY JOE McDONALD born, El Monte, California.

1941 ASCAP, the American songwriters' organisation, imposed a ban on any of its songs being played on the radio. A small cartel of Broadway writers, ASCAP had excluded entry to both black and country songwriters, keeping their songs off the radio. As the strike was announced, a new organisation, BMI (Broadcast Music of America) was formed which did admit blacks, Southerners and new writers. Although the strike was settled by October, ASCAP had forever lost its dominance and BMI's open-door policy brought the voices of the disenfranchised on to the airwaves, directly paving the way for the emergence of both R&B and white rock'n'roll.

#1 US 45
1966
'Sounds Of Silence'
Simon & Garfunkel

SUNDAY

2

1980 LARRY WILLIAMS, fifties rocker and composer of those two epiphanies of alliteration 'Short Fat Fannie' and 'Dizzie Miss Lizzie', shot himself in his Los Angeles home.

#1 UK 45
1972
'Long Haired Lover From Liverpool'
Little Jimmy Osmond

THE ROXY CLUB
41-43 Neal Street, Covent Garden, WC2

Wednesday 18th January	Saturday 21st January
PARADISE SMELL **DESPERATE STRAITS** Admission 50p — Audition Night	**ADAM & THE ANTS** **RICHARD III** **PLASTIX**
Thursday 19th January	Sunday 22nd January
ANGELS **SPANKER** **THE LASERS**	**JAMMING** **SESSION** Members Free, Guests 50p
Friday 20th January	Tuesday 24th January
CRISIS **THE PURGE • FURS** **THE PLAGUE**	**SCHMO** **ADDIX**

JANUARY

M O N D A Y

3

1980 AMOS MILBURN, blues pianist, died in Houston, aged 52. The first great post-war R&B pianist, he wrote and recorded the truly seminal 'Chicken Shack Boogie' (1946) one of the first black records to sell a million copies. Now even better known for his string of alcoholic laments — 'Bad Bad Whisky' and 'One Scotch, One Bourbon, One Beer'.

▶ **1976 MAL EVANS,** former Beatles roadie, died in Los Angeles. After he'd been acting rather strangely with a gun, his girlfriend called the police who, in the confusion, shot Evans.

1969 JIMI HENDRIX played the Lulu show on BBC TV. Hendrix played a few bars of his latest hit, stopped twanging and announced a tribute to Cream who'd just decided to break up, going straight into 'Sunshine Of Your Love'. As the show was broadcast live, the technicians were not amused. Lulu's reaction has not been recorded for posterity.

1966 THE PSYCHEDELIC SHOP opened on Haight St., San Francisco, the start of the merchandising of acid dreams. Across town, the first Acid Test was being held at the Fillmore. As LSD was still legal, the police stayed away from this particular butterfly ball.

▶ **1946 JOHN PAUL JONES** (Led Zeppelin) born, Sidcup, England.

1945 STEPHEN STILLS born, Dallas.

1941 VAN DYKE PARKS born, Alabama.

1926 GEORGE MARTIN, the Beatles' producer, born, London.

T U E S D A Y

4

1977 THE SEX PISTOLS went to Heathrow Airport to catch a flight to Amsterdam, closely followed by the Fleet Street Press who discovered just what they wanted — scenes of minor outrage. An airline hostess was reported as saying: 'These are the most revolting people I've ever seen. They called us filthy names and insulted everyone in sight. One of them was sick in a corridor.' Banner coverage in the next morning's papers ensured ten more Disgusteds of Dagenham and a thousand more bolshie young recruits to the punk bandwagon.

▶ **1971 PERFORMANCE,** Mick Jagger's acting debut, premiered in London two years after it was made.

1964 CYRIL DAVIES, kindly uncle of British R&B, died of leukemia. With Alexis Korner he'd formed Blues Incorporated and gone on to lead the Cyril Davies All Stars, helping create the London R&B club circuit which spawned The Stones, The Pretty Things, The Yardbirds and a hundred other R&B also-rans.

1954 ELVIS PRESLEY recorded two acetates — 'Casual Love' and 'I'll Never Stand In Your Way' — at the Sun studios. The myth is that the oedipal Elvis cut these as a birthday present for his mother. In fact, not only was his mother's birthday months off but the Presleys were too poor to own a record player. Elvis was, of course, hoping to be noticed by Sun's owner, Sam Philips. His wish was granted. Philips' secretary, Marion Keisker, put his songs on tape, promising Sam would call. For once, this infamous line was no excuse.

1936 BILLBOARD published the first pop record chart. Joe Venuti was the world's first number one with a bullet.

W E D N E S D A Y

5

1968 THE BEATLES' 'Magical Mystery Tour' shown in colour for the first time, on BBC2 TV.

▶ **1951 PETER 'BIFF' BYFORD** (Saxon, singer) born, Scissett, Yorks.

1945 JIMMY PAGE born, Heston, Middlesex.

1940 FM RADIO — first public demonstraton.

1923 SAM PHILLIPS born, Florence, Alabama. Founder of Memphis' Sun records. While specialising in recording black bluesmen (a very brave act for a white Southerner in the early fifties), Philips told anyone who'd listen 'If I could find a white man who had the Negro sound and the Negro feel, I could make a billion dollars'. In 1954, his dream came true when Elvis Presley cut 'That's Alright Mama', rock'n'roll's Declaration Of Independence.

T H U R S D A Y

6

1977 THE SEX PISTOLS were dropped by EMI records, following the uproar that still lingered from the Pistols' naughty words to Bill Grundy on a TV show the previous December. Rumours at the time — almost certainly started by Pistols' manager, Malcolm McLaren — claimed that EMI had been forced to dump the Pistols by their foreign investors who'd threatened to pull their money out of EMI's very expensive body scanner project. Ironically, even without the Pistols, EMI's body scanner went the way of all flesh.

1964 ROLLING STONES' first bill-topping tour started at Harrow Granada. Amongst the support acts were The Ronettes and Marty Wilde.

►**1947 SANDY DENNY** born, Wimbledon, London.

1946 SYD BARRETT born, Cambridge.

1929 WILBERT HARRISON (of 'Kansas City' and 'Let's Work Together' fame) born.

1963
'The Next Time/Bachelor Boy'
Cliff Richard

F R I D A Y

7

►**1980 HUGH CORNWELL**, of the Stranglers, was found guilty of possessing heroin, cocaine and cannabis. Sentenced to eight weeks and fined £300, he later wrote a book about his experiences in prison, 'Inside Information' (1980).

1973 SLADE appeared at the London Palladium as part of a pop show celebrating Britain's entry into the EEC. They were there at the personal invitation of Edward Heath, British Prime Minister and big fan of Wolverhampton's worst spellers.

1954 MUDDY WATERS recorded 'I'm Your Hoochie Coochie Man', Chess Studios, Chicago.

1948 KENNY LOGGINS born, Everett, Washington.

1944 MIKE McGEAR (brother of Paul McCartney and Scaffold singer) born, Liverpool.

1962
'Blue Hawaii'
Elvis Presley

S A T U R D A Y

8

1947 DAVID BOWIE (David Robert Jones) born, Brixton, London.

1946 ROBBIE KRIEGER (Doors, guitar) born, Los Angeles.

1943 JERRY GARCIA (Grateful Dead, guitar) born.

1941 LITTLE ANTHONY (Gourdine) born, Brooklyn.

1937 SHIRLEY BASSEY born, Cardiff.

►**1935 ELVIS PRESLEY** born, Tupelo, Mississippi. His twentieth birthday present was the release of his third single, 'Milkcow Blues Boogie'.

1966
'Rubber Soul'
Beatles

S U N D A Y

9

►**1981 SPECIALS** Jerry Dammers and Terry Hall appeared in a Cambridge court charged with using threatening words and behaviour at a show in the city the previous autumn. Both were fined £400 and ordered to pay £133 costs.

1973 LOU REED relinquished his confirmed bachelor status to marry Betty, 'a cocktail waitress' in New York City.

►**1944 SCOTT WALKER** (Engel) born, Hamilton, Ohio. Arriving in Britain in 1965, Walker — as one third of the (unrelated) Walker Brothers — became the high-priest of teenage angst. Their records were glossy pop bombast, an equal mixture of adolescent melodrama and Tin Pan Alley calculation. After two years of screaming girls, Scott left and recorded a succession of lush, depressed solo albums. As his career began to wane he opted for the easy money of a TV show where he'd sing any old junk they asked him to and smile widely at the succession of family entertainer hacks they'd wheel on. Sensibly, he abandoned this course in the early seventies and went into seclusion, emerging only for a short-lived Walker Brothers reunion in 1975 which produced two albums of harsh, frightened music which prefigured Bowie's 'Heroes' by two years. The longer he stayed hidden, the more romantic his reputation grew. His late sixties interpretations of the songs of Jacques Brel were acclaimed as the high point of pop's flirtations with neurotic nihilism; Scott became ever more the patron saint of tortured genius. Like all recluses, he's unencumbered with the paradoxes of a dialogue with his public. Hidden away, he can be explained neatly, simply and beatifically.

1971
'Grandad'
Clive Dunn

JANUARY

MONDAY

10

1976 HOWLIN' WOLF (bluesman) died, Chicago.
1956 ELVIS PRESLEY recorded 'Heartbreak Hotel', his first single for RCA and the record that introduced the world to rock'n'roll, at the RCA Nashville studios.

► **1948 ATLANTIC RECORDS** announced its formation with Ahmet Ertegun as vice-president and Herb Abramson as president. Its beginnings — with records by Melrose Colbert and The Tiny Grimes Quintet — were inauspicious but Atlantic went on to become the most successful fifties independent label, forging an uptown R&B style that was as strong on wit as it was on innovative arrangements. The Coasters, The Drifters, Ruth Brown, Ray Charles and Joe Turner all made their greatest music at Atlantic — very classy black pop that sold as well in the suburbs as it did in the ghetto. In the sixties, Atlantic almost single-handedly invented soul, building on the basis created by the gospel piano of Ray Charles and creating passionate brassy frames for the artistry of Aretha Franklin, Wilson Pickett, Ben E. King and Solomon Burke. When it sold out to Warner Brothers in the late sixties, Atlantic became just another large, wealthy record company but the history of Atlantic from 1950 to 1968 is the history of black America's capture of the high ground of pop music.

1947 MARTIN TURNER (Wishbone Ash) born.
1945 ROD STEWART born, Highgate, London.
1945 DONNY HATHAWAY born, Chicago.
1943 JIM CROCE born, South Philadelphia.
► **1935 RONNIE HAWKINS** born, Huntsville, Arkansas.
1927 JOHNNY RAY born.

TUESDAY

11

► **1977 KEITH RICHARDS** went on trial at Aylesbury charged with possession of LSD and cocaine the police had found in his Bentley when he crashed it on The Stones' British tour of the previous summer. The small market town took on an air of the circus as all available hotel rooms were commandeered by Fleet Street hacks and music press sycophants. Asked precisely what being a lead guitarist entailed, Keith replied 'It means I make a lot of noise.' The light relief over, Keith was found guilty on the cocaine charge but acquitted on the LSD. Keith didn't go to jail. And the circus left town.

1963 THE WHISKY-A-GO-GO, the first American discotheque, opened in Los Angeles.

1956 THE COASTERS' first recording sesson, Hollywood Recorders, produced 'Down In Mexico, and 'Turtle Dovin''. Bobby Nunn provided lascivious bass tremors while Carl Gardner let loose his light, lead tenor.

1924 SLIM HARPO (James Mocre) born, West Baton Rouge. A truly idiosyncratic bluesman, Harpo had a fractured Lousiana style that transferred beautifully to the caustic rhythms of The Rolling Stones who recorded Harpo's 'Hip Shake' and 'King Bee'.

WEDNESDAY

12

1981 THE SEX PISTOLS' 'Never Mind The Bollocks...' album was among 800 records given to the White House by the Recording Association of America. Whether it was intended as a farewell gift to Carter or a warm welcome to Reagan is unclear.

1963 THE BEATLES' 'Please Please Me', the first commandment of Beatlemania, was released.

► **1963 BOB DYLAN,** returning from an Italian holiday with his girlfriend, Suze Rotolo (that's her on the cover of 'Freewheelin'), stopped off in London to record a radio play for the BBC, 'Madhouse On Castle St,', singing 'Blowin' In The Wind' and the unrecorded 'Swan On The River'.

1947 ARLO GUTHRIE born, Coney Island.
1945 MAGGIE BELL born, Glasgow.
1941 LONG JOHN BALDRY born, London.

#1 UK 45

1958
'Great Balls Of Fire'
Jerry Lee Lewis

#1 UK 45

1969
'Lily The Pink'
Scaffold

#1 UK LP

1970
'Abbey Road'
Beatles

THURSDAY

13

1979 DONNY HATHAWAY, black singer and arranger, best known for his work with Roberta Flack, committed suicide, jumping from the roof of New York's Essex House hotel.
1973 ERIC CLAPTON returned to live appearances with a show at The Rainbow after spending two years cleaning up his heroin habit.
1969 ELVIS PRESLEY recorded in Memphis for the first time since he'd left Sun records for the big lights and shiny Cadillacs of RCA in 1955. The sessions, which lasted till January 23, followed hot on the heels of his comeback TV show, produced the hit single 'Suspicious Minds' and the bulk of 'From Elvis In Memphis', his most mature album.
1964 THE BEATLES' 'I Want To Hold Your Hand', the second commandment of Beatlemania, was released in America, becoming their first transatlantic chart topper.
1961 SUGGS (Madness) born, Hastings, Sussex.

FRIDAY

14

1978 THE SEX PISTOLS played their final show at Winterland, San Francisco, the last date on their only American tour. After half an hour, Johnny Rotten put the audience out of their misery, turning down requests for an encore with the question 'Have you ever had the feeling you've been cheated?'
1973 PAUL GADD, the future Gary Glitter, buried one of his previous stage personae, Paul Raven, dumping a coffin full of Raven records into the Thames.
1967 JIMI HENDRIX's first single, 'Hey Joe', charted.
1967 THE FIRST HUMAN BE-IN spread out over Golden Gate Park's polo field. A harbinger of a million free festivals.
▶**1966 DAVID BOWIE** released his first record under that name, 'Can't Help Thinking About Me'.

SATURDAY

15

▶**1971 GEORGE HARRISON's** 'My Sweet Lord' released. After years in the courts, the publishers of 'The Chiffons' 'He's So Fine' (1963) proved that 'My Sweet Lord' was a direct lift of their song.
1967 THE ROLLING STONES appeared on the Ed Sullivan show to promote their new single, 'Let's Spend The Night Together'. Sullivan insisted they change the words to 'Let's spend some time together'. The outrageous rebels complied.
1941 CAPTAIN BEEFHEART (Don Van Vleit) born, Glendale, California.

SUNDAY

16

1981 STEVIE WONDER headlined a concert in Washington D.C., designed to put pressure on the US Government to make Martin Luther King's birthday (January 15) a national holiday.
1980 PAUL McCARTNEY was put into a Tokyo prison when the local police discovered half a pound of marijuana in his baggage. The tour was cancelled but after ten days in jail, McCartney was released with a hefty finger-wagging.
1973 CLARA WARD died, Los Angeles. Clara (Gertrude) Ward led the Philadelphia based Ward Singers, an all female gospel group whose four part harmonies formed the bedrock of Philadelphia soul. Without Clara Ward, there would have been no O'Jays, no Teddy Pendergrass whose 'Love T.K.O.' is gospel moved from the church to the bedroom.
1967 PINK FLOYD played at the Institute of Contemporary Arts, discussing their performance with the audience when they'd finished.
1957 THE CAVERN CLUB, Liverpool, opened as a music venue, starting with trad jazz. Later, a group called The Beatles played there a few times.
1942 BARBARA LYNN born, Beaumont, Texas. An exquisite Southern woman soul singer, she both played guitar on the sessions and wrote her own material — marvellous, private songs, like 'You'll Lose A Good Thing' and 'You're Losing Me' which treated men as almost-equals, fickle creatures easily tempted away by bright and shiny young things.

JANUARY

MONDAY

17

1970 BILLY STEWART died with three of his band when their car plunged off a bridge over the River Neuse, North Carolina. Stewart was an extraordinary soul singer, much given to trilling like a canary — a style later ressurected by Dexy's Kevin Rowland. Luxuriating in a big fat voice, Stewart could transform the idiotic 'Sitting In The Park' into a sweet, lovely song and 'Summertime' into a violent clash of ecstatic Southern passions.

1948 MICK TAYLOR (with the Rolling Stones 1969-74) born, Welwyn Garden City.

1944 FRANCOISE HARDY born, Paris. French pop singer who introduced the word 'chanteuse' to the English language and was more notable for her chic, scrawny looks than her chic, scrawny voice.

1943 CHRIS MONTEZ born, Los Angeles.

TUESDAY

18

1981 WENDY O'WILLIAMS, muscular singer with the Plasmatics, was arrested in Milwaukee, charged with 'simulating masturbation with a sledgehammer in front of an audience'. As the police decided to arrest Miss O'Williams during the Plasmatics show, a free-for-all naturally developed, during which the singer was pinned to the floor by Milwaukee's finest. A cut above her eye required twelve stitches.

1980 PINK FLOYD's 'The Wall' went to the top of the American album charts, staying there till April when it was finally displaced by Bob Seger's 'Against The Wind'.

1980 BOB DYLAN, after try-outs in San Francisco, started his first national tour since his conversion to born-again Christianity. For the first time in his long career, Dylan parted company with music critics.

1973 THE ROLLING STONES played a benefit show at the Los Angeles Forum, for the victims of the previous year's earthquake in Nicaragua. (Jagger's wife of the time, Bianca, is of course Nicaraguan.) Despite the fact that they had some difficulty shifting the hundred dollar seats — aimed at wealthy music business figures — The Stones raised about half a milion dollars.

1941 DAVID RUFFIN born, Meridian, Mississippi.

1941 BOBBY GOLDSBORO born, Marianna, Florida.

1918 ELMORE JAMES born, Durant, Mississippi.

WEDNESDAY

19

1966 RADIO CAROLINE, the first British pirate radio ship, ran aground with future Radio One DJ, Tony Blackburn on board.

1949 ROBERT PALMER born, Batley, Yorkshire. A singer better known for an uncanny ability to be seen in the correct, fashionable company than for his thin, almost constipated voice. In the sixties he sang with the R&B band, the Alan Brown Set. In the late sixties, with the jazz-rock Dada which transformed itself fashionably into the loud and bluesy Vinegar Joe (which had Palmer sharing vocals with future insipid ballad singer, Elkie Brooks). His solo career then took him to New Orleans where he recorded with critical favourites Little Feat, cutting polite, pretty versions of their savage local gumbo. At the end of the decade, he — along with everyone else — discovered disco and rhythm machines. (And he has absolutely horrid taste in trousers.)

1946 DOLLY PARTON born, Sevierville, Tennessee.

1943 JANIS JOPLIN born, Port Arthur, Texas.

1939 PHIL EVERLY born, Brownie, Kentucky. With his older brother Don, Phil was half of the Everly Brothers, the Holy Twins of the fifties. With their genetically ordained harmonies, they sang of love, lost and found, hurt and joy....but mostly lost and hurt. They were the Southern boys left alone at home without a date on Friday night. 'Bye Bye Love', 'Cathy's Clown', 'All I Have To Do Is Dream', delicate, lonely, exquisite songs. Don got deeply hooked on pills, had a breakdown in the early sixties, leaving Phil to tour alone. After sporadic re-unions, they finally dissolved their epic partnership in 1973.

T H U R S D A Y

20

▶ **1965 ALAN FREED** died of uremia and a broken heart, Palm Springs, Florida. From the early fifties to the early sixties, Alan Freed was *the* rock'n'roll DJ. Neatly characterised in the film 'American Hot Wax', he was a strange, often perplexing figure. A middle-aged bachelor with a hint of a father fixation, nearly always half drunk, a cigarette never far from his lips or pork sausage fingers, his fortunes exactly paralleled those of the music he championed. Becoming a DJ in his hometown of Akron, Ohio, he moved up to the graveyard shift on WJW Cleveland, an easy-listening, suburban station. Impressed by how many white kids were buying black R&B records he began to slot the music into his show, now renamed the Moondog Rock'n'Roll Party. (He coined the word rock'n'roll — from Wild Bill Moore's 1947 R&B hit 'We're Gonna Rock, We're Gonna Roll' — as a smooth way round the racial connotations of R&B.) So successful was the programme that when, in 1952, he booked a live R&B show, the Moondog Ball, into a ten thousand seat hall, it drew a hopeful audience of twenty five thousand, equal parts black and white. Panicked by the prospect of such wholesale racial mixing, the city authorities banned the show, entering history as the first organisation to claim that rock'n'roll was more than just music, it was a threat to public safety. Along with the music itself, Freed rode a giant wave of success, coasting to the prime spot on WINS New York and the starring role in a host of quite dreadful rock'n'roll movies. While others tried to whiten out rock'n'roll, Freed stuck to his principles, always playing the black originals rather than the limpid white covers. When the payola investigations began, Freed refused to sign a statement that he'd never accepted money for playing records, pointing out that it wasn't illegal and, anyway, he only ever took money as a thank-you *after* he'd played the record. He was summarily thrown off WINS, his perverse sense of ethics having destroyed his career.

1964 MEET THE BEATLES, the third commandment of Beatlemania was released.

1963 ELVIS PRESLEY surpassed even his own talent for lazy, thoughtless pap at a session in Paramount Studios, Hollywood, cutting not only 'No Room To Rhumba In A Sports Car' but also 'You Can't Say No In Acapulco'.

F R I D A Y

21

1966 THE TRIPS FESTIVAL was held in San Francisco, following close on the heels of the Human Be-In and the Fillmore Acid Test.
1966 GEORGE HARRISON married former model Patti Boyd at Epsom Registry Office.
▶ **1942 EDWIN STARR** born, Nashville.

S A T U R D A Y

22

▶ **1972 DAVID BOWIE** admitted he was gay, or maybe bisexual, when interviewed by *Melody Maker*'s Michael Watts. Almost overnight, council estates were full of former skinheads dying their hair pink and claiming they swung both ways.
1967 THE ROLLING STONES refused to appear on the revolving stage at the end of 'Sunday Night At The London Palladium' TV show, a tired warhorse of showbiz clichés.
1959 BUDDY HOLLY recorded for the last time. Alone in his New York aprtment, he taped demos, including 'Peggy Sue Got Married' and a delicate 'Slippin' And Slidin''.
1931 SAM COOKE born, Chicago.

S U N D A Y

23

▶ **1978 TERRY KATH**, guitarist and singer with Chicago, died. Playing with a gun at a friend's house, he tried to prove it wasn't loaded by pointing it at his head and pulling the trigger.
1972 BIG MAYBELLE (Smith) died, 48, Cleveland, Ohio. A 260 pound heroin addict, Maybelle was a sensitive R&B singer, who — between dime bags — cut some rich, sweet tunes in the mid-fifties, notably 'Candy' and 'Mean To Me'.

JANUARY

MONDAY

24

1979 THE CLASH finally had a single released in America, 'I Fought The Law', taken from the British 'Cost Of Living' EP, a mere two years after they were signed to Columbia USA.

1970 JAMES 'SHEP' SHEPHERD died in New York. Composer and singer of the Heartbeats' 'A Thousand Miles Away' and Shep and the Limelights' 'Daddy's Home' (the classic of doo wop revived by Cliff Richard in 1981), Shepherd was found beaten to death in his car on the hard shoulder of the Long Island Expressway.

1941 NEIL DIAMOND born, Brooklyn.

1941 MICHAEL CHAPMAN born, Leeds.

1936 DOUG KERSHAW born, Tiel Ridge, Louisiana.

TUESDAY

25

1973 DAVID BOWIE, indulging his well-publicised fear of flying, boarded the QE2 at Southampton to begin a hundred-date world tour. **1971 GRACE SLICK AND PAUL KANTNER** were blessed with a child. Having planned to call her God, they backed out at the last moment, opting for the slightly less promethean China.

1964 PHIL SPECTOR was a panellist on the British TV pop show, 'Juke Box Jury'. Keeping his dark glasses company were Adam Faith and Jean Metcalfe, doyen of BBC radio's British forces request show.

1958 GARY BRIAN TIBBS (Vibrators, Roxy Music, Adam and the Ants) born, Northwood, Middlesex.

1958 LESLEY WOODS (Au Pairs) born, Hockley, Essex.

1958 ELVIS PRESLEY'S 'Jailhouse Rock' became the first single to enter the British charts at number one.

1956 ANDY COX (The Beat) born.

▶ **1943 ANITA PALLENBERG** born.

WEDNESDAY

26

1980 FRANK SINATRA played in front of the largest audience ever to assemble for one performer. 175,000 people at the Maracana Stadium, Rio de Janiero, Brazil.

1978 EMI RECORDS refused to press copies of Buzzcocks' 'Oh Shit'.

1977 PATTI SMITH fell offstage during a show in Florida, injuring her neck and spine so severely that she spent the next few months strapped straight by a brace.

▶ **1976 GARY GLITTER** announced his retirement which, in true showbiz tradition, lasted less than five years.

1956 BUDDY HOLLY recorded for Decca in Bradley's Barn, Nashville, cutting four tracks including the R&B standard 'Midnight Shift' and his first single, 'Blue Days — Black Nights', written by KDAV Lubbock DJ, Ben Hall, and released in April in the States and July in Britain.

1948 CORKY LAING born, Montreal.

▶ **1934 HUEY 'PIANO' SMITH** born, New Orleans. Number three New Orleans R&B pianist to Fats Domino and Professor Longhair and much more fun than either. As leader, songwriter and piano player of the Clowns, Huey Smith cut a succession of records which sound like three minute excerpts from the same endless, drunken party. 'High Blood Pressure', 'Little Liza Jane', 'Well, I'll Be John Brown', the original 'Rockin' Pneumonia And The Boogie Woogie Flu' and its ludicrous, inevitable follow-up 'Tu-ber-cu-lucus And Sinus Blues'. Huey Smith grew up as a blues musician but his music was the epitome of things teenage. His piano wobbled around like a drunk walking home. The horn section, led by the rich deep throat of Lee Allen's tenor sax, honked and squawked in and out of the songs, as if it were pausing for shots of bourbon between the choruses. Bobby Marchan sang lead on the best sides but the real delight of the vocals were the backing singers, chorusing with heavenly, inane answering phrases. What more profound statement can there be than the chorus of 'Don't You Just Know It?' 'Ah-ah-ah-ah, hey-hey-ho, doo-bah-doo-bah, doo-bah-doo-bah, ah-ah-ah-ah, heeeey-heeeey-ho'. Music to cheer the hearts of condemned men.

THURSDAY

27

1980 CAPRICORN RECORDS, the music behind the ascendancy of Jimmy Carter, filed for bankruptcy in Macon, Georgie. The creation of former Otis Redding manager, Phil Walden, Capricorn was a one artist/one style label, totally dependent on The Allman Brothers and their physical and spiritual descendents. Walden reached the peak of his power as a behind-the-scenes broker for Carter's peanutocracy but, as the public deserted Carter and the Allmans with almost indecent haste, so Walden's star plummeted.

1972 MAHALIA JACKSON the gospel name every one knows, died, 61, heart failure. Born in New Orleans, she was the first gospel singer who made you feel she knew *just* what she was turning her back on when she stood up for Jesus. If 'We Shall Overcome' was her unfortunate epitaph, 'Move On Up A Little Higher' had a drama that the vegetarian peace rally anthem will never match.

1951 BRIAN DOWNEY (Thin Lizzy) born.

1945 NICK MASON (Pink Floyd) born, Birmingham.

1944 KEVIN COYNE born, Derby.

▶ **1930 BOBBY BLAND** born, Rosemark, Tennessee. Like B.B. King — with whom he started out as one of the Memphis Beale Streeters — Bobby 'Blue' Bland always sounds more hurt than despairing. A blues singer of delicacy, he had a score of hits in the late fifties and early sixties — 'Further Up The Road', 'Turn On Your Lovelight', 'Call On Me' — but was unable to weather the transition to the world of Wilson Pickett's loud and aggressive 'Midnight Hour'.

FRIDAY

28

1978 SHAM 69 began their second national tour with a show at the London School of Economics. Some of the band's more partisan — or perhaps merely racist — fans decided to riot in a minor way. As the débris was being cleared away, the students blamed Sham 69 who, of course, blamed the students.

1965 ELVIS PRESLEY made his national TV debut on the Dorsey Brothers' 'Stage Show'.

SATURDAY

29

1978 DAVID COVERDALE announced the formation of Whitesnake.

1971 ALLEN KLEIN renowned hustler and former manager of both The Rolling Stones and the Beatles, was found guilty on ten charges of 'unlawfully failing to make and file return of Federal income taxes'.

SUNDAY

30

1980 PROFESSOR LONGHAIR (Roy Byrd) died, 61, New Orleans. The almost forgotten king of New Orleans R&B piano, Longhair had a lop-sided shuffle style so relaxed it sounded like he was trying to lose his drummer. The most ecentric fruit of the New Orleans marching funeral, Longhair had a succession of local hits — 'She Ain't Got No Hair', 'Ball The Wall', the rhapsodic 'Tipitina' — but only 'Mardi Gras', re-issued every year for the local festival, ever gave him an audience beyond the ghetto of local musicians and blues archivists.

1976 JESSE FULLER (composer of 'San Francisco Blues') died.

1969 THE BEATLES played together live for the last time — on the roof of their Apple HQ in London's Saville Row. The lunchtime concert was filmed for the 'Let It Be' movie and produced the 'Get Back' single at the end of which John Lennon can be heard to ask if he and the group have passed the audition.

1957 BILLY LEE RILEY cleared up the mystery of what little green men did on their days off when he recorded 'Flying Saucers Rock'n'Roll' at Sun in Memphis with Jerry Lee Lewis on pumping Pentacostal piano.

1947 STEVE MARRIOTT born, Bow, London.

1943 MARTY BALIN (Martyn Jerel Buchwald) born, Cincinnati, Ohio.

1928 RUTH BROWN born Portsmouth, Virginia.

M O N D A Y

31

1976 BUSTER BROWN, writer and singer of R&B hit 'Fannie Mae', died.

1970 SLIM HARPO died of a heart attack, 56, Port Allen.

1965 P.J. PROBY split his trousers from knee to crotch at the Ritz cinema, Luton. Two nights before, the seams had parted on a Croydon stage. The moralists of British cinema chains deemed this unsuitable entertainment for their halls of culture and banned Proby. Born James Marcus Smith in Texas, Proby learned his trade recording demos for Elvis, finally becoming a gross, overblown true star in mid-sixties Britain when his velvet suits and ponytail set many a teenage girl's heart a-flutter. His split trousers put a sudden stop to all that; his career never recovered. Sinking into sporadic alcoholism, he eventually disappeared without trace. Nik Cohn, author of the splendidly neurotic *'Pop From The Beginning'*, considered Proby a pop genius. He might well have been right.

► **1956 JOHN LYDON** (Rotten) born.

1951 PHIL COLLINS born.

1951 PHIL MANZANERA born.

1946 TERRY KATH BORN, Chicago.

1979
'Hit Me With Your Rhythm Stick'
Ian Dury

F E B R U A R Y
T U E S D A Y

1

► **1968 LISA MARIE PRESLEY,** the only heir to Elvis born, Memphis.

1967 PINK FLOYD turned professional.

1949 RCA RECORDS issued the world's very first 45rpm single, *the* technological breakthrough behind the emergence of rock'n'roll. Lighter, cheaper, less breakable than the 78, the 45 was perfect for both jukeboxes and the independent record companies — who couldn't handle the amount of breakages shipping 78s entailed. Initially, RCA saw albums of five or six 45s containing a whole classical symphony as competition to Columbia's recently launched twelve inch microgroove long players. By 1950 even RCA was beginning to have its doubts. When an executive claimed that their system meant a change-over time of a mere seven seconds, the new RCA classical chief, George Marek, replied: 'It's like this. You're in bed with your best friend's wife, and every five minues, the door opens. It isn't open long, only seven seconds...'

1937 DON EVERLY born, Brownie, Kentucky.

1969
'Albatross'
Fleetwood Mac

W E D N E S D A Y

2

► **1979 SID VICIOUS** died, NYC. Brought up on the hippie Katmandu trail, Sid — born John Beverly — stood no chance of slotting neatly into a world where most children go to the local primary school. After a teenage fixation on David Bowie — then at his Ziggy zenith — Sid became close friends with John Lydon (Rotten) at college. When Rotten became The Sex Pistols' singer, Sid hung on his coat tails, inventing the pogo, chain-whipping a journalist, fuelling the Sex Pistols mythology of violence. When Pistols bassist Glen Matlock was thrown out for 'liking the Beatles', Sid was the obvious replacement. The tenor of the times was such that the fact he couldn't play seemed utterly irrelevant. When the band dissolved into an acrimonious shambles at the end of their first US tour, Sid — already a junkie — lost the one centre to his life. Left to his own devices, he sunk into a life bounded by syringes and his own small-scale fame. Ever with him on this journey into the city of night was his junkie American girlfriend, Nancy Spungen. Shortly after they moved to New York, Nancy was found stabbed in their Chelsea Hotel apartment. Sid was charged with the murder but always protested his innocence. Out on bail, he attended a party celebrating his release given by his junkie mother. His tolerance for heroin washed away by Ryker's Island prison, one small taste was enough to kill him. He died before he reached hospital, becoming both a silly, clown-like casualty and Punk's Only True Martyr to those who organise marches to commemorate his death.

1963 THE BEATLES strated a tour supporting Helen Shapiro at the Bradford Gaumont.

► **1937 ROBERTA FLACK** born, Asheville, North Carolina.

1967
'Monkees'

THURSDAY

3

1982 ALEX HARVEY died of a heart attack in Belgium. The Pagliacci of British rock'n'roll.
1967 JOE MEEK died. Producer of The Tornadoes' 'Telstar' and North London's answer to Phil Spector, Meek was one of the bright stars of British pop before the Beatles. An auteur in the days of incompetent engineers, he created eery pop dreams with the barest of equipment — often recording the drums in the bathroom. Eclipsed by the success of pop *groups*, he sank into despair which caused him to shoot his landlady and then turn the shotgun on himself.
1959 BUDDY HOLLY died, 22. The last great fifties rock'n'roll star. Mild, bespectacled, deferential Southern manners bred deep into him, he was the bridge between the crazy Saturday night of rockabilly and the R&B based pop of The Beatles — who recorded his 'Words Of Love'. His influence vastly exceeded his span of fame; his first hit, 'That'll Be The Day', was less than eighteen months before his death on the mid-West section of The Winter Dance Party tour. Wanting to get his laundry done before the next show at Moorhead, North Dakota, Holly hired a light plane. Shortly after take-off from Mason City, Iowa, the craft dipped into a snow-covered field eight miles north west of the airport. With him died **THE BIG BOPPER** (Jape Richardson) who hit with the rumbustious 'Chantilly Lace' and **RICHIE VALENS**, the 18 year old singer of 'La Bamba' and 'C'mon, Let's Go'. The event was later turned into treacly melodrama by Don McLean who christened it 'The day the music died'.

FRIDAY

4

1975 LOUIS JORDAN died, pneumonia, 57, Los Angeles. Born in Brinkley, Arkansas, Jordan was the Jerry Lewis of R&B, a clown prince whose humour hid an enormous amount of intelligence and thought. Jordan fronted the Tympani Five, an outfit of varying size but never five strong, and recorded a stream of novelty songs in the late 40s/early 50s — 'Choo Choo Ch'Boogie', 'Ain't Nobody Here But Us Chickens', 'Caldonia' — which had a rhythmic snap which looked back to the thirties big bands and forward to Chuck Berry: their spiky, witty lyrics owed more to the brittle lyricism of Cole Porter than the crawling king snakes of Delta blues. Jordan was as near as you could get to poppy rock'n'roll without inventing Eddie Cochran.
1969 THE BEATLES appointed Eastman and Eastman, New York lawyers and family of McCartney's bride-to-be, as 'general consul to Apple', the day *after* an Apple press release which read 'The Beatles have asked Mr Allen Klein of New York to look into their affairs and he has agreed to do so.' The legal disagreements which the Beatles used as an excuse to disintegrate had begun.
1948 ALICE COOPER (Vincent Furnier) born, Detroit.
1894 ADOLPHE SAX, inventor of the saxophone, died in poverty. There were no saxophones at his funeral.

SATURDAY

5

1972 DAVID SEVILLE died. Creator and orchestrator of the Chipmunks — his own voice speeded up four different ways — Seville flattered his Liberty Records bosses by naming the Chipmunks after three of the company's top men: Theodore (Keep, chief recording engineer); Simon (Si Waronker, president and general manager); Alvin (Al Bennett, vice chairman and general manager).
1945 BOB MARLEY born, St Annes, JA.
1935 ALEX HARVEY born, Glasgow.

SUNDAY

6

1967 THE BEATLES renewed their recording contract with EMI for a further nine years after worldwide sales of 180m records in three years.
1965 RIGHTEOUS BROTHERS' 'You've Lost That Lovin' Feelin' ' topped the charts both sides of the Atlantic. It was the zenith of the career of its producer, 'tycoon of teen' and professional neurotic, Phil Spector.
1960 JESSE BELVIN died in a car crash. Lead singer on Penguins' 'Earth Angel' a three minute doo wop passion play.

FEBRUARY
MONDAY

7

1965 GEORGE HARRISON had his tonsils out.
1964 BEATLES' landing at Kennedy airport, NYC, the fourth commandment of Beatlemania. The massive crush of teenage girls — at least partly paid for by their record company — ensured every American had heard of the Beatles by the following morning.
► **1934 KING CURTIS** born, Forth Worth, Texas.
1934 EARL KING (Solomon Johnson) born, New Orleans. R&B guitarist and singer, he wrote 'Let The Good Times Roll', later made famous by Jimi Hendrix as 'Come On'.
1933 WARREN SMITH born, Louise, Mississippi. A Sun rockabilly star, he recorded 'Ubangi Stomp' — the only direct line from Africa to 706 Union Avenue, Memphis — and 'Red Cadillac And A Black Moustache', the ultimate example of rock'n'roll's commodity fetishism.

#1 UK 45
1981
'Woman'
John Lennon

#1 UK LP
'Double Fantasy'
John Lennon

TUESDAY

8

1980 DAVID BOWIE was divorced from Angie. He got custody of their child, Zowie; she picked up a cheque for £30,000.
1972 BEATLES' fan club closed down.
1973 MAX YASGUR died. The farmer whose land gave birth to the Woodstock Generation succumbed to a heart attack in a Florida hospital.
1960 PAYOLA HEARINGS began in front of a Congress committee. What started out as an inquiry of rigged TV game shows was broadened to include payola — taking money for playing records on the radio, then not illegal — at the urging of ASCAP, the songwriters organisation most threatened by the upsurge of rock'n'roll — the vast majority of rock'n'roll songs were handled by ASCAP's rival, BMI. After looking into the affairs of some 'small-fry DJs', the committee took on American Bandstand host, Dick Clark, and lost. Despite the fact that no less an authority than the *New York Times* estimated that Clark had given free exposure to acts on labels on which he had an interest which would have cost him twenty five million dollars at the going advertising rate, Clark was able to win over the committee with some very dubious statistics about the relevant records' 'Popularity Scores'. Payola was finally made illegal in September of that year with an FCC amendment banning the taking of money or gifts for airplay.
► **1944 JIM CAPALDI** born.

#1 UK 45
1968
'Blackberry Way'
Move

WEDNESDAY

9

1981 BILL HALEY died, 55. Haley was a long-time country singer who switched to covering black R&B hits in the early fifties, changing his band's name from the Saddlemen to the Comets. Already middle-aged and portly by the time he cut 'Rock Around The Clock', his famous kiss curl made him look Winnie the Pooh gone beat. But, somehow, he caught the mood of the times. Haley himself — who had the riotous character of a bread roll — was confused and tried hard to present himself as a benign uncle figure. His anodyne style of rock'n'roll, which depended on emasculating tough black originals, faded quickly but 'Rock Around The Clock' itself assumed a totemic significance. A hit on five separate occasions, it became a touchstone of nostalgia for all those who'd forsaken their stiletto heels or BSA 500s for the vacuum cleaner or the Ford production line. Haley hawked the same act round the world for the rest of his life and finally, after a year of eccentric behaviour he succumbed to a heart attack at his home in Harlingen, Texas.
1972 PAUL McCARTNEY played unannounced at Nottingham University, his first live appearance since the Beatles farewell in San Francisco five years previously.
1964 THE BEATLES made their American TV debut on the Ed Sullivan show — the fifth commandment of Beatlemania.
1939 BARRY MANN born, Brooklyn. A Brill Building songwriter, Mann racked up 17 UK and US hits, ten written with his wife Cynthia Weill. In his catalogue are the Crystals' 'Uptown', the Animals 'We've Gotta Get Out Of This Place' and the Righteous Brothers' 'You've Lost That Lovin' Feeling'. In 1961, he had a hit himself with 'Who Put The Bomp', simultaneously revealing the origin of the bip-de-bip.

#1 US 45
1959
'Staggerlee'
Lloyd Price

T H U R S D A Y

10

1974 PHIL SPECTOR was injured in a mysterious car crash. Badly burned, he underwent intensive plastic surgery, radically altering his appearance and turning him into even more of a recluse than he already was. There are also rumours of a car crash on his return from the hospital.

► **1964 DONOVAN** (Terrence Leitch) born, Glasgow.
1943 RAL DONNER, the great Presley copyist — 'You Don't Know What You've Got (Till You Lose It)' — born, Chicago.
1939 ROBERTA FLACK born, Washington DC.

F R I D A Y

11

► **1979 STIFF LITTLE FINGERS** released their debut album, 'Inflammable Material', the first independently distributed punk album to make the British charts.

1978 MAGAZINE's debut single, 'Shot By Both Sides', entered the UK chart.
1967 MOTHERS OF INVENTION debut album, 'Freak Out', entered the US charts.
1965 RINGO STARR married Maureen Cox at Caxton Hall, London. Brian Epstein was the best man.
1963 THE BEATLES recorded their debut album, 'Please Please Me' at EMI's Abbey Rd. studios in London, cutting ten tracks in thirteen hours.
► **1941 SERGIO MENDES** born, Niteroi, Brazil.
1940 BOBBY 'BORIS' PICKETT born, Massachusetts.
1939 GERRY GOFFIN half of the Goffin-King writing team born, Queens, NYC. With his wife, Carole King, he was responsible for thirty US and UK hits, amongst them the Shirelles 'Will You Still Love Me Tomorrow', the Drifters' 'Up On The Roof' and Little Eva's 'Locomotion'.
1935 GENE VINCENT (Eugene Vincent Craddock) born, Munden Point, Norfolk, Virginia.
1981 FRANK SINATRA got his entertaining licence back from the Las Vegas authorities. After suggestions that he was tied up with the Mafia, he's had his licence revoked 18 years earlier and hadn't been able to sing at a Las Vegas nightclub since.

S A T U R D A Y

12

1967 KEITH RICHARDS' country house in West Wittering, Redlands, was raided by the West Sussex police. Keith and Mick Jagger were charged on drugs offences, marking the start of the judicial farce which culminated that summer with The Times running a leader criticising the jail sentences eventually handed down to Jagger and Richard.

1950 STEVE HACKETT born.
1935 RAY MANZAREK (Doors) born.
1935 GENE McDANIELS, gospel-trained pop singer of 'Chip Chip' and 'Tower Of Strength', born, Kansas City.
► **1972 MICHAEL JACKSON's** first solo single, 'Got To Be There' entered the UK chart.

S U N D A Y

13

1981 ISLAND RECORDS introduced the 'One Plus One' format for their cassette releases. As one side of the tape was entirely blank, obviously encouraging home-taping, the record industry lap dog, the BPI, accused·Island of breaking ranks in the fight against 'illegal' home-taping.

1980 PHILIP LYNOTT of Thin Lizzy married Caroline Crowther, the mother of his child and the daughter of British TV comic actor, Leslie Crowther.
1980 JOHN LYDON's house was raided by the London police who gained entry by breaking the front door down with an axe. Lydon greeted them by waving a ceremonial sword in their direction. He was later charged with possession of a miniature tear gas container.
► **1945 PETER TORK** (Monkees) born, Washington, D.C.
1945 KING FLOYD, composer and singer of soul hit 'Groove Me', born, New Orleans.
1919 TENNESSE ERNIE FORD, DJ turned singer of '16 Tons', born, Bristol, Tennessee.

FEBRUARY
MONDAY

14

1981 GEN X, broke up a mere two months after emerging from a long period of hibernation with two new members. Gen X singer and clothes horse, Billy Idol, flitted off to New York to start a a solo career .

1972 GREASE opened as a stage show in New York, at the Martin Eden theatre.

1970 DAVID BOWIE was voted 'Greatest Hope' in a poll of Disc readers.

1947 TIM BUCKLEY born, Washington D.C.

1937 MAGIC SAM (Sam Maghett), the last great original Chicago bluesman, born, Grenada, Mississippi.

#1 US 45
1970
'Thank You Falettinme Be Mice Elf Agin'
Sly Stone

TUESDAY

15

1981 MICHAEL BLOOMFIELD was found dead in his car in San Francisco. The first white American guitar hero, Bloomfield grew up with the blues, learned to play them with Paul Butterfield and helped teach Bob Dylan how to crank it out loud when he played on the sessions for 'Like A Rolling Stone' and 'Blonde On Blonde'. A guitarist of no little panache, he was never able to handle the fame that his guitar herodom brought. Although he retreated from the spotlight, the mould of fear was set and he died at thirty seven, a suspected victim of a heroin overdose.

1974 THE BOTTOM LINE, New York City's premier showcase venue, opened.

▶ **1968 LITTLE WALTER** died in a Chicago knife-fight. *The* blues harmonica player, Walter had a range of tone and emotional reach which took him far beyond the crude stylings of other blues harpists. Both as member of the classic Muddy Waters band and on his own, he played with a sweet fierceness which many have tried — and failed — to match. His 'Juke' (1952) was the first true rock'n'roll instrumental, so loud and harsh it seems to be spoiling for a fight, breathing out a passion that dissolves pain and pleasure right into each other in a catharsis of screeching, howling NOISE.

1965 NAT KING COLE, the first man on 'Route 66' and the first black pop singer to gain widespread white middle-class respect, died of lung cancer in Santa Monica.

1944 MICK AVORY (Kinks) born, Hampton Court.

1941 BRIAN HOLLAND born, Detroit. As one third of Motown's Holland-Dozier-Holland writing partnership, Holland had over thirty hits.

#1 UK LP
1981
'Face Value'
Phil Collins

WEDNESDAY

16

1979 ELVIS COSTELLO and the Attractions played the country Palomino Club in North Hollywood, with the added whine of John McFee on steel guitar. For the first time since he went public, Costello displayed the depth of his affection for country music, playing a set which included Jim Reeves' 'He'll Have To Go', 'If I Could Put Them All Together (I'd Have You)' and 'Psycho', later issued as the flip of 'Sweet Dreams'.

1957 6.5 SPECIAL was first broadcast, on BBCTV — from six to seven on a Saturday evening. The first TV show masterminded by the Eric von Stroheim of pop, Jack Good, it featured some music but was, in fact, an uneasy mix of sport, comedy and variety with a little pop music thrown in to attract the young audience.

▶ **1935 SONNY BONO** born, Detroit. The archetypal Angeleno hustler. After learning the music business ropes as session man and gofer with Phil Spector, he achieved pop stardom wrapped in a fur jerkin, while she favoured the Red Indian look, they sang the asinine 'I Got You Babe', an instant success with dewy-eyed romantics the world over. They were massive for about two weeks in the mid-sixties. Much later, Cher dumped Sonny in favour of Greg Allman, then sensibly heaved him out in favour of TV stardom and the cover of *People* magazine.

1923 BESSIE SMITH, the 'Empress of the Blues', made her first visit to the studio, cutting 'Downhearted Blues' and 'Gulf Coast Blues', released that June.

#1 UK 45
1963
'Please Please Me'
Beatles

THURSDAY

17

1970 JONI MITCHELL announced her retirement onstage at the Albert Hall. The retirement was unusually brief even by showbiz standards — it never happened.

1969 BOB DYLAN AND JOHNNY CASH recorded together at the Columbia studios, Nashville. Only their duet on 'Girl From The North Country' has been officially released.

1967 THE BEATLES' 'Penny Lane' released, their first single not to top the UK charts since 'Please Please Me' in 1963.

1941 GENE PITNEY born, Hartford, Connecticut. With a voice like a three octave hernia, he strained his way to a handful of hits in the mid-sixties. His 'Twenty Four Hours From Tulsa' made Roy Orbison sound happy. And Scott Walker restrained.

►**1939 JOHN LEYTON** born, Essex.

FRIDAY

18

1978 SNIFFIN' GLUE, the Hansard of punk, ceased publication in the very same week that saw punk gain a new hold on the British charts with debuts for both Blondie ('Denis') and Buzzcocks ('What Do I Get?'). Sniffin' Glue was the Evostik dream of Mark P — formerly Mark Perry, a South London bank clerk — created in a haze of euphoria induced by his own peculiar Damascus road, the Ramones' first London show. Like Paul, Mark P was an instant, violent and intemperate convert who handed down a dogmatic gospel in each of the fanzine's handful of mimeographed issues, drawing a rigid line across the world, separating the approved from the despised. 'Fucking great' and 'fucking shit' were the invariable adjectives on the two sides of this critical chasm. Conscious of his own literary limits and fed up with the scores of Xeroxed imitations of his admittedly ground-breaking fanzine, Mark P followed his own advice to 'start your own group', folded the magazine before it lost its mythical edge of the opposition and concentrated on his 'musical' venture, Alternative TV, who owed more to Zappa than they did to the Ramones. His co-editor, Danny Baker, became one of TV's token cheery Cockney chappies.

1968 DAVE GILMOUR joined the Pink Floyd, sharing the guitar work with Syd Barrett, whose disintegrating personality occasioned Gilmour's drafting into the group.

1965 THE WHO's first single, 'Can't Explain', charted.

SATURDAY

19

1980 BON SCOTT, AC/DC singer, died, 33. A notorious boozer, he was left to sleep off a particularly determined binge in a car, where he died, choking on his own vomit.

1972 PAUL McCARTNEY released 'Give Ireland Back To The Irish', a presumably heart-felt but inane reaction to the shooting of thirteen Northern Irish citizens by the British Army on 'Bloody Sunday'. BBC radio banned it, justifying their action with the 'non-political' clause in their charter.

1972 LEE MORGAN, jazz trumpeter died, 33, NYC. During a break between sets at Slug's saloon, he had a row with his wife. Before he went back to work, she left the club, picked up a gun, returned and shot him.

1948 TONY IOMMI (Black Sabbath) born.

►**1940 WILLIAM 'SMOKEY' ROBINSON** born, Detroit. Lauded by Dylan as 'America's greatest living poet', Smokey Robinson has always been a songwriter out of his time, less concerned with coining slogans than in perfecting deceptively simple couplets. If he'd been born white, he'd have a string of hit shows running on Broadway. Although he was always Tamla's greatest songwriter, he's remained an elusive figure, reachable only through his songs

SUNDAY

20

1978 MEATLOAF's 'Bat Out Of Hell' was released in the UK, staying in the charts right up till the release of his 1981 follow-up 'Deadringer'.

1969 CANDY, the film which featured Ringo's first performance as a 'straight actor', had its world premier.

1945 ALAN HULL (Lindisfarne) born, Newcastle.

1941 BUFFY ST. MARIE born, Maine.

FEBRUARY
MONDAY

21

1980 JACOB MILLER, reggae singer, died in a car crash in Kingston, JA.

1976 FLORENCE BALLARD, an original Supreme, died of a heart attack in a Detroit hospital. With the Supremes till 1967, she'd drenched herself in luxury — one pink, one golden Cadillac. Never on royalties, always on a weekly wage, she'd sunk unto poverty, dying on welfare while Diana Ross was still living in the style to which Florence Ballard had once been accustomed.

1975 DAVID BOWIE released the 'Young Americans' single, the first fruit of his flirtation with contemporary sweet soul.

1970 SIMON AND GARFUNKEL's 'Bridge Over Troubled Water' entered the UK album chart at number one, staying in the top ten for 126 weeks, 38 of them at the top.

1964 THE ROLLING STONES released 'Not Fade Away', their third single and the first to reach the top ten.

1943 DAVID GEFFEN, one-time boss of Elektra-Asylum and the man who lured John Lennon out of retirement shortly before his death at the end of 1980, born, NYC.

► **1933 NINA SIMONE** born, North Carolina.

1927 GUY MITCHELL, the man who taught us all about 'Singing The Blues', born, Detroit.

1911 CLARENCE GARLOW, rhythm and blues artist, born, Welsh, Louisiana.

1981
'Double Fantasy'
John Lennon

TUESDAY

22

1980 MALCOM McLAREN, former manager of the Sex Pistols, fired Adam from the Ants. Adam had paid Malcom a few hundred pounds to take the Ants in hand, help find them a direction, an image, a marketing strategy. McLaren helped them to the Burundi beat — which they used on 'Car Trouble' — then decided to shove Adam out into the cold, using the group as the basis of Bow Wow Wow who — with schoolgirl singer, Annabella — went on to become critical darlings and commercial dogs.

► **1978 SID VICIOUS & NANCY SPUNGEN** were charged with possession of dangerous drugs.

1969 DAVID BOWIE supported Tyrannosaurus Rex at the Free Trade Hall, Manchester, presenting his one man mime show about the trials and tribulations of a young religious boy in Communist Tibet. (Honest)

1968 GENESIS' first single, 'The Silent Sun', was released.

1965 HELP, the Beatles' second movie, was started in the Bahamas where filming continued till March 12.

1961 RANKING ROGER (The Beat) born.

1980
'Crazy Little Thing Called Love'
Queen

WEDNESDAY

► **23**

1979 THE ANGELIC UPSTARTS, the *reductio ad absurdum* of punk's promises who'd been known to include kicking a pig's head around as part of their stage show, left Polydor records, who seemed to have abandoned hope of reclaiming even their modest investment.

1978 WHITESNAKE, the HM band formed by former Deep Purple singer, David Coverdale, played their first show, at the Sky Bird Club, Nottingham.

1967 PRINCE BUSTER's 'Al Capone' was the first JA record to enter the UK chart. (Millie, although Jamaican, had recorded 1964's 'My Boy Lollipop' in London — with Rod Stewart playing harmonica.)

1963 THE BEATLES made their first British national TV appearance — on ITV's 'Thank Your Lucky Stars'.

► **1958 DAVID SYLVIAN** (Japan) was born David Batt, Beckenham, Kent.

1946 RUSTY YOUNG (Poco steel player) born, Long Beach, California.

1944 JOHNNY WINTER born, Beaumont, Texas. White bluesman with enough disabilities to impress the 'if he's a cripple, he must be a genius' school of blues fans — albino, one-time junkie, grievously underweight, legally blind...and Texan.

1974
'Devil Gate Drive'
Suzi Quatro

T H U R S D A Y

24

1980 BOOMTOWN RAT Pete Briquette married Akron singer, Jane Aire.

1979 ROCK'N'ROLL SWINDLE, the soundtrack to the Sex Pistols' feature film, was rush-released to forestall possible competition from French imports. A double album, it was both hailed as a cynical masterpiece and derided as the last nail in the coffin of the punk dream. Both viewpoints were, of course, correct. If it contained little in the heroic mould — nobody could possibly idolise Ten Pole Tudor's torturing of 'Who Killed Bambi' — it was vastly more interesting than the turgid HM drone of the Pistols' only true album, 'Never Mind The Bollocks'. Its release marks a convenient cut-off point for the born again punk true believers whose Eden was a Roxy Club they never entered. Hereafter, according to their gospel, all was commercialism. Without the benefits of a carbon dating procedure, they were about two years late with their timing.

1965 P.J. PROBY was banned by BBCTV following the trouser splitting incident on his tour of the previous month. The screen never saw the like of his velvet bow and Little Lord Fauntleroy suit again.

1944 NICKY HOPKINS born, South London.

1942 PAUL JONES, (Paul Pond) born, Portsmouth.

1962
'Rock A Hula Baby'/'Can't Help Falling In Love With You'
Elvis Presley

F R I D A Y

25

1977 ANITA PALLENBERG, Keith Richard's common law wife, was detained at Toronto Airport when customs officials found in her possession a small lump of hashish and traces of heroin on a burnt spoon. The scene was set for Keith's bust three days later.

1957 BUDDY HOLLY recorded 'That'll Be The Day' at Norman Petty's studio in Clovis, New Mexico. Released under the Crickets' name, it gave him his first hit record.

▶ **1945 ELKIE BROOKS** born, Manchester.

1943 GEORGE HARRISON born, Liverpool.

1958
'Get A Job'
Silhouettes

S A T U R D A Y

26

1979 THE SEX PISTOLS' court case revealed that, out of the Pistols' total receipts of £800,000, only £30,000 was left.

1977 BUKKA WHITE, bluesman died 67.

1953 BIG MACEO (Maceo Merriweather) writer of 'Worried Life Blues' died in Chicago of a heart complaint.

1947 SANDIE SHAW (Goodrich) born, Dagenham, Essex.

1945 BOB HITE born, Torrance, California.

▶ **1932 JOHNNY CASH** born, Dyess, Arkansas. (His real name was J.R. Cash. Johnny was a Christian name of convenience given to him in the army.)

▶ **1928 FATS DOMINO** born, New Orleans. If, as locals claim, the rhythmic base for rock'n'roll came out of the Crescent City, then Fats and his rolling thunder piano were right there at the birth of the music. A large domestic-looking man, he made an even less likely rock'n'roll star than Bill Haley but, despite his lack of flash, he was *the* black success of the fifties. 65 hits on the Billboard hot hundred and fifteen on the R&B charts before that. A simple but great piano player — his rumbling runs on 'Before I Grow Too Old' could break your heart — and a man of obvious integrity. Still playing all his hits with a care that show hasn't forgotten why he cut them in the first place. He's rock'n'roll's Mr Nice Guy from his flat-topped head to his stubby, diamond ringed fingers.

1966
'These Boots Are Made For Walking'
Nancy Sinatra

S U N D A Y

27

▶ **1976 SLIK,** the teenybop group which included future Ultravox singer, Midge Ure, debuted at the Glasgow Apollo — two weeks *after* their debut single, 'Forever And Ever' topped the UK chart.

1971 PAUL McCARTNEY's first solo single, 'Another Day' entered the UK chart.

1967 PINK FLOYD recorded their first single, 'Arnold Layne' at the Sound Techniques studio in Chelsea, London.

1965 P.J. PROBY, despite the trouser-splitting had a hit with 'I Apologise', a version of the 1951 Billy Eckstein hit.

1959 BILLY FURY's first single, 'Maybe Tomorrow' charted.

1951 STEVE HARLEY (Steve Nice) born, South London.

1978
'Blondes Have More Fun'
Rod Stewart

MONDAY

28

► **1978 THE DAMNED,** the most anarchic of punk groups, broke up. (Their retirement didn't last long at all. After a mini-reunion under the banner of the Doomed, they were trading again under the Damned name by the end of the year.)

► **1977 GLEN MATLOCK,** the Sex Pistols' bassist and tune writer, was sacked by the band because, according to manager McLaren, 'he liked the Beatles'. His replacement was Sid Vicious. 'His best credential' was, in McLaren's words, the chain-whipping he'd given journalist Nick Kent at the 100 Club the previous summer.

1977 KEITH RICHARDS' thirty second floor suite at Toronto's Harbour Castle Hotel was raided by the Mounties. Arriving at five-thirty in the afternoon — while Keith was still asleep — they turned up nearly an ounce of heroin and a small amount of cocaine. Inevitably, given the quantity of the drug found, the Mounties charged him with trafficking.

1977 RAY CHARLES was attacked onstage by a man who rushed on and tried to strangle him with a rope.

1974 BOBBY BLOOM, singer and writer of 'Montego Bay', 28, shot himself in Los Angeles.

1968 FRANKIE LYMON died, NYC. As lead singer with the Teenagers, he had a world-wide hit with 'Why Do Fools Fall In Love?' in 1956 when he was just thirteen. After his voice had broken he was never able to regain the impetus of his earlier career and quickly sunk into that favourite hobby of Harlemites, junkiedom. After years of false starts and false cures, he joined the US army who let him fly up from Augusta, Georgia for a recording session in New York. The following day, he was found dead from a heroin overdose in his grandmother's bathroom.

1957 THE 5 ROYALES, led by Lowman Pauling's acerbic guitar, went into the King Studios in Cincinnati where they recorded 'Think', a two time R&B hit. For them and for James Brown.

► **1942 BRIAN JONES** born, Cheltenham, Gloucester.

1942 JOE SOUTH born, Altanta, Georgia.

1966 THE CAVERN CLUB, the cradle of the Beatles and Merseybeat, closed with debts of £10,000.

1939 JOHN FAHEY, white blues guitarist born, Takoma Park, Maryland.

MARCH
TUESDAY

1

► **1980 PATTI SMITH** married Fred 'Sonic' Smith, former guitarist with early seventies 'revolutionary' rock'n'roll group, MC5, in Detroit.

1974 QUEEN began their first major UK tour in Blackpool.

► **1969 JIM MORRISON,** Doors singer, gave a vivid demonstration of the band's much-touted 'sexual politics' by exposing himself onstage at the Dinner Key auditorium, Miami. Charged some weeks later with lewd and lascivious behaviour, he came to trial the following year and was sentenced to six months hard labour, plus a five hundred dollar fine on the charge of indecent exposure and sixty days of hard labour on the secondary charge of profanity. Before his appeal could come before a court, he was dead.

1945 ROGER DALTREY born, Hammersmith, London.

1944 MIKE D'ABO (Manfred Mann singer who replaced Paul Jones) born.

WEDNESDAY

2

1974 TELEVISION, the New York art punk group, played their first show at the Townhouse Theatre, 46th St. In this earliest version of the group were Richard Lloyd, Tom Verlaine and Richard Hell, who quickly split off to form his own group, the Voidoids and invent the ripped & torn t-shirt, one of the basics of punk evening wear.

1968 SYD BARRETT left the Pink Floyd just a few weeks after Dave Gilmour had joined as second guitarist.

1950 KAREN CARPENTER born, New Haven, Connecticut.

► **1949 RORY GALLAGHER** born, Ballyshannon, Northern Ireland.

1943 LOU REED (Louis Firbank) born, New York.

T H U R S D A Y

3

1980 SOTHEBY'S, the London auction house, put on offer a variety of rock memorabilia. A paper napkin signed by Elvis Presley at the Riviera Hotel, Las Vegas, fetched £500 and four US dollar bills signed by the Beatles went under the hammer at £220.

1972 GARY GLITTER released his debut single under the name that brought him untold success as the Bacofoil turkey, 'Rock And Roll Part Two'. It had nothing to do with rock and roll but everything to do with the nursery rhyme stomp.

1971 THE BEATLES had a five year ban imposed on them by South African radio lifted.

► **1967 THE JEFF BECK BAND,** featuring Rod Stewart as singer, Ron Wood on bass and Aynsley Dunbar on drums, made a 'disastrous' debut at the Finsbury Park Astoria.

1966 BUFFALO SPRINGFIELD, the Los Angeles folk rock band which included in its line-up both Neil Young and Steve Stills, was formed. The name, according to guitarist Richie Furay, came from the side of a steam roller they saw flattening the street outside their Fountain Avenue flat.

1928 DAVE DUDLEY, writer of the truckers and pills anthem, 'Six Days On The Road', born.

1927 LITTLE JUNIOR PARKER born Arkansas.

 #1 UK 45
1966
'The Sun Ain't Gonna Shine Anymore'
Walker Brothers

F R I D A Y

4

► **1979 MIKE PATTO,** singer with Time Box, Spooky Tooth and Boxer, died of lymphatic cancer.

1977 THE ROLLING STONES played the first of two nights at the tiny El Mocambo club, Toronto. Under the shadow Keith's arrest four days before on a charge of heroin dealing, the Stones recorded both nights for the 'Love You Live' double album issued later the same year.

1971 THE ROLLING STONES announced that they intended to become tax exiles in the South of France.

1948 CHRIS SQUIRE (Yes) born, London.

1944 MARY WILSON, (Supremes) born, Mississippi.

1944 BOBBY WOMACK born, Cleveland, Ohio.

 #1 UK 45
1973
'Cum On Feel The Noize'
Slade

S A T U R D A Y

5

► **1965 DAVID BOWIE's** second single, 'I Pity The Fool' was released under the name the Mannish Boys.

1963 PATSY CLINE, the country singer with a voice of almost Home Counties Women's Institute purity, died in a Dyersburg, Tennessee plane crash with fellow country stars, **Cowboy Copas** and **Hawkshaw Hawkins**. Ironically, they were on their way to Nashville to appear in a benefit show for the widow of DJ Cactus Jack Call who'd been killed in a car crash. Born Virginia Hensley in Winchester, Virginia, Cline had been a performer since the age of eight but it was only in the last five years of her life that she found fame with dignified country soap operas such as 'She's Got You' and 'I Fall To Pieces'.

1960 ELVIS PRESLEY was released from his two year's service in the US army.

1939 TOMMY TUCKER (Robert Higgenbotham), the R&B singer who urged the world to put on its 'High Heel Sneakers', born, Springfield, Ohio.

1929 J.B. LENOIR, blues singer, born, Monticello, Miss.

#1 US 45
1966
'The Ballad Of The Green Berets'
Sgt. Barry Sadler

S U N D A Y

6

► **1970 CHARLES MANSON,** in jail for murder, released an album, 'Lie', to help pay his legal costs.

1968 SANDIE SHAW married fashion designer, Jeff Banks.

1947 KIKI DEE (Pauline Matthews) born, Bradford.

1944 MICKY JUPP born, Worthing, Sussex.

1936 SYLVIA ROBINSON (nee Vanderpool) born, New York. The most dynamic black woman in the American music business. In the fifties, she teamed up with session guitarist, Micky Baker, for a series of hits under the name Micky and Sylvia, the biggest of which was 'Love Is Strange', a UK hit for the Everly Brothers. After the partnership split, she founded All Platinum records, where she hit with her own 'Pillow Talk', Shirley and Co's 'Shame Shame Shame' and Brother To Brother's 'In The Bottle'. In the mid-seventies Sylvia started up Sugarhill, the label which has brought to the world the best rappers from Harlem and the Bronx.

 #1 UK 45
1960
'Running Bear'
Johnny Preston

M A R C H
M O N D A Y

7

1980 THE CRAMPS' debut album, 'Songs The Lord Taught Us', was released.

1976 ELTON JOHN was immortalised in wax at Madame Tussaud's, London.

1973 JOHN HAMMOND, the Columbia records executive who claims credit for discovering Bessie Smith, Billie Holiday and Bob Dylan, had his third heart attack at a showcase performance for his latest discovery, Bruce Springsteen.

1966 THE SHADOWS OF KNIGHT's 'Gloria' reached the US top ten.

1963 JACK ANGLIN, country singer, died in a car crash on the way to the funeral of Patsy Cline.

1952 THE NEW MUSICAL EXPRESS published its first edition.

1943 CHRIS WHITE (Zombies and producer) born.

1934 KING CURTIS (Ousley), *the* rock'n'roll sax player, born, Fort Worth, Texas.

T U E S D A Y

8

1974 BAD COMPANY made their UK debut at Newcastle City Hall.

1973 PAUL McCARTNEY was fined £100 for cultivating cannabis on his Scottish farm.

1973 PIGPEN (Rod McKernan), Grateful Dead organist, died of alcohol poisoning at his apartment in Corte Madera, California.

1963 JULIAN LENNON, the only child of the marriage of John and Cynthia Lennon, was born.

1958 GARY NUMAN born.

1948 LITTLE PEGGY MARCH, singer of the squeaky early sixties teen dream, 'I Will Follow Him', born.

1947 RANDY MEISNER (Eagles) born, Nebraska.

1947 BILLBOARD's chart of 'Most Played Juke Box Race Records' — their black chart of the day — contained five different versions of that winter's R&B sensaton, 'Open The Door, Richard' — by Count Basie, Tiger Haynes' Three Flames, Dusty Fletcher, Louis Jordan and Jack McVea. The only other three records on the chart were all by Louis Jordan — 'Ain't Nobody Here But Us Chickens', 'Let The Good Times Roll' and 'Texas And Pacific'.

➤ **1945 MICKEY DOLENZ** (Monkees) born, Los Angeles.

W E D N E S D A Y

9

1977 THE SEX PISTOLS, having been sent packing by EMI with only a £30,000 cheque for their pains, signed to A&M records, on a table in front of Buckingham Palace.

➤ **1972 ALLEN KLEIN** presented UNICEF with a cheque for over a million dollars, the first part of the royalties from 'The Concert For Bangla Desh'. As the intention was that a five dollar royalty would be paid on each album, this appeared to leave a shortfall of almost nine million dollars on the more than two million copies of this double album set which had been sold.

1972 LOS ANGELES MUSIC BUSINESS LIBERALS turned out in droves for a Forum benefit concert to raise campaign funds for George McGovern, the liberal Democratic presidential candidate who was wiped out at the polls by Nixon. Carole King, James Taylor, Barbra Streisand and Quincy Jones played while working as ushers were Carly Simon, Mama Cass, Britt Eckland, Lou Adler, Jack Nicholson, Julie Christie, Jon Voight and Burt Lancaster.

1967 BRIAN JONES entered hospital with a respiratory problem.

➤ **1958 MARTIN DAVID FRY** (ABC) born, Stretford, Manchester.

1949 TREVOR BURTON (Move, Balls) born, Birmingham.

➤ **1945 ROBIN TROWER** born, London.

1942 MARK LINDSAY (Paul Revere and The Raiders) born, Eugene, Oregon.

1933 LLOYD PRICE born, New Orleans, Price's biggest hit was 'Personality' a pop novelty, but before the decline set in, he cut a handful of great R&B sides including the cool drawl 'Lawdy Miss Clawdy' and a thundering celebration of the mythical black hipster 'Staggerlee'.

THURSDAY

10

1962 LARRY PARNES, the showbiz promoter who gave Marty Wilde, Billy Fury and Georgie Fame their stage names, started off his latest package tour, featuring Joe Brown, Susan Maughan, Shane Fenton (the future Alvin Stardust), Rolf Harris, Heinz and Jess Conrad.

1960 RECORD RETAILER, which later became *Music Week*, published the first British album chart. 'The Explosive Freddy Cannon' was the first number one.

► **1940 DEAN TORRANCE** (Jan & Dean) born, Los Angeles.

1929 HUEY MEAUX born, Kaplan, Louisiana. The keeper of the holy flame of Tex Mex music, the meeting point of cowboy yodels and somber accordians. One of the few survivors of the wheeler-dealer world of fifties regional labels, Meaux's style is the pachucho with a cash register back beat.

FRIDAY

11

1977 THE SLITS, then an all-girl punk group, played their first live show, as support to the Clash at London's Harlesden Roxy.

1967 DICK JAMES, the Beatles' music publisher, announced that there had been a total of 446 different versions of 'Yesterday' recorded.

SATURDAY

12

1953 RUFUS THOMAS, 'the oldest teenager in the music business', signed to Sun and went into the studio the very same day to cut his R&B hit 'Bear Cat', an answer record to Big Mama Thornton's 'Hound Dog'.

► **1939 NEIL SEDAKA** born, Brooklyn.

1933 MIKE STOLLER born, Belle Harbour, Long Island. The musical half of the Leiber/Stoller songwriting partnership, the First White Teenagers of rock'n'roll. Both white Eastern Jewish kids in love with the blues, they met up in Los Angeles at the turn of the fifties and began to write for the burgeoning R&B market, crafting 'Hound Dog' for Mama Thornton two years before Presley went near a studio. Musically-skilled, literate and witty, they brought a new sophistication to R&B, first on the West Coast and then as independent producers in New York. Theirs is a vast catalogue of some of the best uptown R&B and rock'n'roll. As the first independent producers, they not only wrote the songs but shaped them in the studio and, in the case of the Coasters at least, invented the group. Irritated by the increasingly trivial (but still wonderful) nature of their work, they left the pop mainstream to write for their own age group. So far their only real success in this vein has been Peggy Lee's 'Is That All There Is?' but for fifteen years, they were the white soul of R&B, as near as you could get to being white bluesmen without actually inhabiting the body of Elvis Presley.

SUNDAY

13

1974 JOHN LENNON AND HARRY NILSSON were thrown out of the Troubadour in Los Angeles after they'd created a disturbance during the Smothers Brothers act.

1971 THE BEATLES suffered the indignity of having a receiver appointed to oversee their financial affairs.

1969 PAUL McCARTNEY married Linda Eastman at London's Marylebone Registry Office. Across town, the police were raiding George Harrison's home where they discovered 120 marijuana joints for which they arrested George and his wife, Patti.

► **1955 CHARLIE PARKER,** jazz sax player and main spirit of bebop, died, NYC. Although the death certificate states 'lobar pneumonia', Dr. Freymann, a physician who examined the corpse gave four possible causes of death — stomach ulcers, pneumonia, heart attack and advanced cirrhosis, estimating Parker's age as fifty to sixty. He was actually thirty three. And still they write 'Bird Lives' on alley walls.

► **1948 JAMES TAYLOR** born, Boston.

1926 THE SAVOY BALLROOM opened at 596 Lenox Avenue, Harlem. The Lindy Hop, Jiving, Truckin', the Suzy Q, they all began life at the Savoy.

M A R C H

M O N D A Y

14

1972 **LINDA JONES** died, NYC. The deepest of deep soul singers, she recreated Jerry Butler's 'For Your Precious Love' as a prayer of apocalyptic passion and breathed the soul of Dinah Washington into the slow-burning furnace of her 'Hypnotised' album. A diabetic, she collapsed after a show at Harlem's Apollo and, although rushed to hospital, fell into a coma from which she never recovered.
1971 **THE ROLLING STONES** played two shows at London's Roundhouse as a 'farewell' to British fans before going into tax exile in France.
1947 **PETER SKELLERN** born.
1933 **QUINCEY JONES** born.
1931 **PHIL PHILIPS** (Philip John Baptiste) singer of the basso profundo cajun hit of 1959, 'Sea Of Love', born, Lake Charles, Louisiana.

1981
'Jealous Guy'
Roxy Music

T•U E S D A Y

15

1980 **RUDE BOY**, the Clash movie, opened at the Prince Charles Theatre, London.
1968 **THE BEATLES** released the Fats Domino-influenced, 'Lady Madonna'. Later, producer Richard Perry, working on the 'Fats Is Back' album, tried to persuade Domino to cover the song and repay the compliment. Fats didn't want to know, said he didn't understand the lyrics. Perry persisted. Fats remembered he had a daughter called Donna, he'd sing it to her. And they cut the song.
► 1947 **RY COODER** born, Los Angeles.
1945 **BILLBOARD** published the first album chart. 'The King Cole Trio', featuring Nat King Cole, was its first number one.
1944 **SLY STONE** (Sylvester Stewart) born, Dallas. A man alone. DJ turned record company man turned singer turned musical revolutionary. 'Dance To The Music' took the riotous colours of psychedelia into the black ghettos and formed — with James Brown's martial funk — the rhythmic base of all black American music through to Earth, Wind & Fire. Still Sly stood apart, recording the most negative record ever made, 'There's A Riot Goin' On', taking too many drugs and gradually slipping into the limbo of the once-famous.
► 1941 **MIKE LOVE** (Beach Boys) born, Los Angeles.
1940 **PHIL LESH** (Grateful Dead) born, Berkeley, California.
1912 **LIGHTNIN' HOPKINS**, blues singer, born, Leon County, Texas.

1969
'Dizzy'
Tommy Roe

W E D N E S D A Y

16

► 1979 **ELVIS COSTELLO** was involved in a bar room brawl in the Holiday Inn, Columbus, Ohio. Stories vary in detail, but broadly, while enjoying a relaxing drink with Stephen Stills and Bonnie Bramlett who'd been playing in town that night, Costello made some unfavourable remarks about America and its musicians. Bramlett took umbrage and slapped Costello round the head. Later, Bramlett leaked the story to the press, stressing that Costello had made racist remarks. Faced with an outcry, Costello was forced to hold a New York press conference where he apologised with ill grace, unable to believe that Americans had taken his off-hand remarks seriously.
1977 **THE SEX PISTOLS** were dropped by A&M records a week after signing. A&M claimed that the Pistols had wrecked their offices and harrassed their secretaries. The Pistols picked up their £40,000 severance pay and moved on to Virgin.
1976 **ARTHUR GUNTER**, R&B singer and writer of one of Presley's earliest singles, 'Baby Let's Play House', died.
1975 **T-BONE WALKER**, the first and greatest electric R&B guitarist died, 65, Los Angeles.
► 1968 **TAMMI TERRELL** (Montgomery) died. Best-known for 'That's All You Need To Get By', a duet with Marvin Gaye, she collapsed into his arms onstage, dying later from a brain tumour. Her death was so unexpected it's always been rumoured that the tumour was a result of a particularly savage beating.
1964 **THE BEATLES'** 'Can't Buy Me Love' set the record for advance orders in the USA — 2,100,000. Undoubtedly, the seventh commandment of Beatlemania.

1968
'Dock Of The Bay'
Otis Redding

THURSDAY

17

1979 BILL TINSLEY of WATN, Watertown, New York, started the longest ever non-DJ continuous radio broadcast. He was on air till March 31, a total of 336 hours.

1979 ZENON DE FLEUR (Hierowski), guitarist with London R&B band, the Bishops, died of injuries received in a car crash on March 9.

1972 HORSLIPS, the Irish band, turned professional, their way of celebrating St. Patrick's Day.

► **1962 CLAIRE PATRICIA GROGAN** (Altered Images) born.

1962 BLUES INCORPORATED, the R&B band formed by Alexis Korner and Cyril Davies and featuring Charlie Watts on drums, opened their own club, 'The Ealing Club'...'Turn left, (from the tube station) cross at Zebra, and go down steps between ABC Teashop and Jewellers' read their first ad.

1951 SCOTT GORHAM (Thin Lizzy) born.

1950 WDIA MEMPHIS became the first black operated radio station in the Southern United States.

1944 JOHN SEBASTIAN born, New York.

FRIDAY

18

1977 THE CLASH's first single, 'White Riot', was released. A London apocalypse in under two minutes.

1973 WINGS played a benefit show at London's Hard Rock Cafe for Release, the drug counselling charity.

1972 RINGO STARR filmed Marc Bolan at the height of his fame, a sold-out concert at Wembley. By the time the film, 'Born To Boogie' was completed, Bolan's star had already begun to wane but it stands as a remarkable document to the potential for mass hysteria in otherwise normal middle-class teenage girls.

► **1970 IMMEDIATE RECORDS**, founded by Stones' manager, Andrew Loog Oldham, and 'Happy To Be Part Of The Industry Of Human Happiness', went into liquidation.

1970 COUNTRY JOE McDONALD was fined 350 dollars for shouting 'Fuck' (the finale of 'The Fish Cheer') at a Massachusetts concert. He was convicted on the basis of a statute from 1783.

1965 THE ROLLING STONES were caught in the act of pissing against a filling station wall after a show at the Romford ABC. They were eventually fined £5 each. Much later, Keith explained that they were only caught because of Bill Wyman's Zeppelin of a bladder. Once he'd opened up, he was about as easy to stop as Niagara Falls.

► **1941 WILSON PICKETT**, the baaaadest of baaaad soul singers, born, Prattville, Alabama.

IMMEDIATE →

at better record shops every...

SATURDAY

19

1982 RANDY RHOADS, a member of Ozzy Osbourne's band, was killed in a plane crash. Joy-riding in a light aircraft before a Florida concert, the plane clipped the band's tour bus and crashed into a house.

1980 ELVIS PRESLEY's secret autopsy was subpoenaed by the Shelby County court in the process of investigating the gross over- subscribing of drugs by Presley's doctor, Dr. George Nichopoulos.

► **1976 PAUL KOSSOFF**, former Free guitarist, died of a heart attack on a flight from Los Angeles to New York.

1974 HARRY WOMACK, brother of Bobby and co-writer of 'It's All Over Now', was stabbed to death in his brother's Hollywood apartment.

► **1959 TERRY HALL** (Specials, Fun Boy Three) born, Coventry.

1937 CLARENCE 'FROGMAN' HENRY born, Algiers, New Orleans. Singer of 'But I Do', rock's finest reptilian croaker.

SUNDAY

20

1970 DAVID BOWIE married the American girl he'd met at a King Crimson press reception, Mary Angela Barnett, at Bromley Registry Office.

1969 JOHN LENNON married Yoko Ono, Gibraltar.

1960 ELVIS PRESLEY's first recording session after leaving the army. Working in RCA's Nashville studios, he cut six tracks over the next two days, including the impossibly sexy 'Mess Of Blues'.

1937 JERRY REED, born, Atlanta, Georgia.

MARCH

MONDAY

21

1980 THE JAM's 'Going Underground' entered the UK singles chart at number one, the first single to do so since Gary Glitter's 'I Love You Love' in November 1973.

► **1976 DAVID BOWIE** was charged with possession of eight ounces of marijuana found in his room at the Flagship Americana Hotel, Rochester, New York. He and his three companions were all released on bail of two thousand dollars each which Bowie paid.

1970 THE BEATLES' 'Let It Be' entered the Billboard Hot Hundred at number six, the highest-ever new entry.

► **1969 JOHN LENNON AND YOKO ONO** began their bed-in for peace at the Amsterdam Hilton.

1952 ALAN FREED hosted the Moondog Coronation Ball in Cleveland, Ohio, the first sign that black R&B had a large, young white following. Freed promoted the show from his WJW radio programme, selling 18,000 advance tickets for a hall that held only 10,000, all irresistably drawn by a bill that included blues smoocher, Charles Brown, the Moonglows, the Orioles and Billy Ward and the Dominoes with their heavenly tenor, Clyde McPhatter, future Drifter and solo star. Chaos reigned at the show, with at least as many locked out as let in. The Cleveland Press reported: 'Police reinforcements were forced to disperse a crushing mob of 25,000.'

TUESDAY

22

► **1956 CARL PERKINS**, rushing from a Memphis recording session to New York TV appearances, was involved in a Delaware car crash. His brother was badly hurt but, although Carl received only minor physical injuries, his career which was then at its zenith with the rockabilly war chant 'Blue Suede Shoes' — hit a slump from which it never recovered. A twenty four year old Tennessean, Perkins was the insurance held by Sun Records' Sam Phillips when he was forced to let Elvis Presley go to the big money and gold lamé suits of RCA. With Elvis gone, Phillips gave all his artists a free hand to record the bluesy material which had previously been the sole preserve of the Memphis Tornado. Perkins, an almost totally intuitive musician, figured the style out just about overnight. Even more than Presley, Perkins was — in Greil Marcus' illuminating phrase — the rockabilly moment. Presley's understanding of the black music he adapted and turned to his own needs was profound and subtle; growing up on Memphis' black ghetto street, R&B was as much his culture as were the hillbilly and gospel tunes he heard at home. Perkins, on the other hand, was an outsider who sensed the core of liberation in R&B and grasped it with both hands. His 'blackest' track 'Put Your Cat Clothes On', is music that mixes joy and desperation till you can't tell one from the other. It's full of the feeling that, if you don't cut it now, there's no second chance; the moment is of too much importance to consider any reflection. The epitome of the Southern dream that maybe Saturday night could go on forever, Perkins finally ran up against the walls *his* Southern dreams had built round him. In 1956, it seemed he could be even bigger than Elvis — 'Blue Suede Shoes'/'Honey Don't', his third single topped all three Billboard charts, pop, R&B and country. (Only two other singles, Presley's 'Don't Be Cruel' and Jerry Lee Lewis' 'Whole Lotta Shakin'' have ever achieved this distinction.) In 1958, depressed by his brother's death, he drifted into an alcoholism which inevitably left him a stunted figure, forever trapped in 'might have beens'. But, for two years, he was *it*, Huckleberry Finn with a Gretsch Countryman and some great poetry about clothes.

WEDNESDAY

23

► **1979 LINTON KWESI JOHNSON**, the poet of the reggae culture, released his second album, 'Forces Of Victory'.

1964 JOHN LENNON, as winner of the Foyle's literary prize for his publishing debut 'In His Own Write', was presented with the award at a celebratory London luncheon. Clearly awed, his entire acceptance speech was 'Thank you very much. You've got a lucky face.'

#1 UK 45
1964
'Little Children'
Billy J. Kramer And The Dakotas

#1 UK 45
1975
'Bye Bye Baby'
Bay City Rollers

#1 UK 45
1968
'Legend Of Xanadu'
Dave Dee, Dozy, Beaky, Mick And Tich

THURSDAY
24

1978 BRITISH RECORD COMPANIES were given the power to seize bootleg and pirate records and tapes by the high court.
1973 LOU REED was bitten on the bum by a fan at a concert in Buffalo who jumped past the guards, shouted ''Leather!'' and attacked the prince of darkness.
1964 THE NEW MUSICAL EXPRESS, for the first time, had an all British top ten on its singles' chart.
1. 'Anyone Who Had A Heart' — Cilla Black
2. 'Bits And Pieces' — Dave Clark Five.
3. 'Diane' — The Bachelors.
4. 'I Think Of You' — The Merseybeats.
5. 'Needles And Pins' — The Searchers.
6. 'Not Fade Away' — The Rolling Stones.
7. 'Little Children' — Billy J. Kramer and The Dakotas.
8. 'I'm The One' — Gerry and The Pacemakers.
9. 'Candy Man' — Brian Poole and The Tremeloes.
10. 'Boys Cry' — Eden Kane.
And not a Beatle single amongst them.
1958 ELVIS PRESLEY was inducted into the US army in Memphis.

FRIDAY
25

1980 THE POLICE played a show in Bombay, India, the first rock band to appear there since Hawkwind ten years before.
1980 PINK FLOYD's 'Dark Side Of The Moon' became the most successful album ever on the *Billboard* charts when it achieved 303 weeks, just passing Carole King's 'Tapestry'.
1976 DUSTER BENNETT, oneman British blues band, died in a car crash.
1967 JEFFERSON AIRPLANE's 'Surrealistic Pillow' and The Doors' debut album entered the US charts.
1961 ELVIS PRESLEY recorded his show on the U.S.S. Arizona, anchored off Honolulu, his last live concert till the end of the decade.
1947 ELTON JOHN (Reg Dwight) born, Pinner, Middlesex.
1942 ARETHA FRANKLIN born, Memphis.

SATURDAY
26

1973 NOEL COWARD died.
1972 MOTT THE HOOPLE called it a day. Horrified, David Bowie offered them a helping hand and 'All The Young Dudes', single-handedly reviving their career.
1970 PETER YARROW of Peter, Paul and Mary admitted 'taking immoral liberties' with a fourteen year old girl in Washington D.C.
1968 LITTLE WILLIE JOHN (William J. Woods) died of pneumonia in Washington's Walla Walla prison seven years after starting his sentence for killing a man in a street brawl. Only twenty four when he went to jail, he was an R&B singer of true, measured passion. A teenage star of the fifties, he recorded the original and sharpest version of 'Fever' and a host of fierce, edgy ballads and rockers, all of them — including the nearly psychotic 'Leave My Kitten Alone' — songs of love.
1944 DIANA ROSS born, Detroit.

SUNDAY
27

1979 TOYAH played her first gig, at Dingwalls Dance Hall, London.
1974 GUY PELLAERT's 'Rock Dreams' was published. Beautiful, witty, sharp visions of rock'n'roll stars and their vanities with a wonderful evocative text by Nik Cohn.
1972 ELVIS PRESLEY recorded 'Burning Love' at his first studio session with his seventies stage band.
1966 P.J. PROBY — a year *after* the fuss of the splitting trousers — was order offstage in Hereford and described as 'disgusting and obscene'.
1964 THE BEATLES had the top six singles in the Australian chart.
1952 SUN RECORDS of Memphis, the first home of Elvis Presley, released their first single, 'Drivin' Slow' by Johnny London.

MARCH

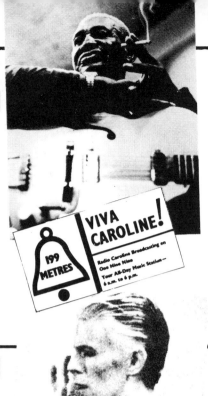

MONDAY

28 **1974 ARTHUR 'BIG BOY' CRUDUP** died, 69, at the North Hampton-Accomac Memorial Hospital, Nassawadox, Virginia. A Mississippi bluesman, Crudup wrote 'That's All Right Mama', the song which Presley revived for his first single. Although Presley sent Crudup a plaque in 1956 as a thank-you for the song, the old bluesman never received royalties from Presley's publishers for either 'Mama' or 'My Baby Left Me' which Presley also recorded. Shortly before his death, it looked as though the publishers would stop withholding the payments when they agreed to a sixty thousand dollar settlement. Then they changed their minds, having decided a court action would cost them less and condemned Crudup to a death in utter poverty.

► **1964 RADIO CAROLINE**, the first British off-shore pirate radio ship went on air. Named after John Kennedy's daughter and founded by professional Irishman and low rent seer, Ronan O'Rahilly, Caroline drew an instant mass teenage audience with its solid, nourishing diet of pop music, a true rarity on the BBC, Britain's only official radio network.

VIVA CAROLINE!
199 METRES
Radio Caroline Broadcasting on
One Nine Nine
Your All-Day Music Station —
6 a.m. to 6 p.m.

TUESDAY

29 **1980 RON SELLE**, a songwriter, sued the Bee Gees, claiming they'd lifted 'How Deep Is Your Love?' from him.

► **1978 DAVID BOWIE's** first tour for two years and his first since his radical change of style with 'Low' opened in San Diego.

1943 VANGELIS (Papathanasiou) born, Valos, Greece.

1871 THE ROYAL ALBERT HALL was opened by Queen Victoria in honour of her dear, departed husband.

WEDNESDAY

30 **1980 BOB DYLAN** received the Grammy for Best Male Rock Vocalist in the year he made his worst-ever album, the turgid narrowly proselytising 'Saved', gospel that made you want to sign up right below Faust. Accepting the award Dylan felt obliged to rub the point home: "The first person I want to thank is the Lord."

1978 CLASH members Paul Simonon and Nicky Headon were arrested on charges of criminal damage. More precisely, they were nabbed for murdering a few racing pigeons belonging to a neighbour of the Clash's Camden Town rehearsal studio. The lads had been enjoying an afternoon's innocent fun, taking pot shots at the birds with air guns when the police came out of the sky in a helicopter, thinking they were about to apprehend dangerous terrorists rather than stupid little boys.

1974 THE RAMONES played their first show, at The Performance Studio, E23rd. St., NYC. Their future singer and stage lamp post, Joey, was hidden away at the back on drums.

1976 THE SEX PISTOLS appeared for the first time at the 100 Club, the home base for their early reputation.

1956 HMV RECORDS announced the release of 'Heartbreak Hotel' by 'The King Of Western Bop', Elvis Presley, his first British single. It cost five shillings and seven pence (28p) including tax.

1956 JOHNNY CASH recorded his first national hit, 'I Walk The Line', for Sun Records, Memphis. Not quite hard enough to be rockabilly, not quite resigned enough to be country, it hit the charts in September four months after it was released.

1948 JIM DANDY (Black Oak Arkansas) born, Black Oak, Arkansas.

1945 ERIC CLAPTON born, Ripley, Surrey.

► **1942 GRAHAM EDGE** (Moody Blues) born, Rochester, Staffordshire.

1933 WILLIE NELSON born, Texas.

► **1914 SONNY BOY WILLIAMSON** (John Lee Williamson, Sonny Boy number one) born, Jackson, Tennessee. Loud and harsh blues harmonica player and one of the first Southerners to move the sound of the blues into the city with electric instruments. He's best known for his recording of Humbert Humbert's theme tune, the drooling 'Good Morning, Little Schoolgirl'.

THURSDAY

31

1980 EMI RECORDS reported a year's trading loss of £2,800,000.

1978 GENESIS' 'Then There Were Three' released.

1969 GEORGE HARRISON AND PATTI BOYD were fined £250 each on drugs charges arising from a raid earlier in the month, seemingly timed to coincide with Paul McCartney's wedding.

► **1967** JIMI HENDRIX set fire to his guitar for the first time, onstage at London's Finsbury Park Astoria.

1964 BILLBOARD's singles chart belonged to the Beatles.
1. 'Can't Buy Me Love'
2. 'Twist And Shout'
3. 'She Loves You'
4. 'I Want To Hold Your Hand'
5. 'Please Please Me'
(The Beatles also held down the singles at numbers 14, 44, 49, 69, 78, 84 and 88.)

1927 BUTTERBEANS & SUSIE recorded the very early assertion of women's rights, 'I Want A Hot Dog For My Roll'.

APRIL

FRIDAY

1

1976 THE SEX PISTOLS supported the 101'ers at London's Nashville Rooms. Singer of the R&B oriented 101'ers, Joe Strummer was so impressed by the demonic freshness of the Pistols, he very soon left his band to form the Clash with Mick Jones and Paul Simonon.

1972 THE MAR Y SOL FESTIVAL started at Vega Baja, Puerto Rico. When it finished two days later, it left four dead, including a sixteen year old boy who was slashed to death in his sleep by a cocaine dealer.

1969 THE BEACH BOYS announced they were suing their record company, Capitol, for $2,041,446.64.

1961 MARK WHITE (ABC) born.

1976 THE ROLLING STONES' first British tour for three years drew one million postal applications and a useful £30,000 of revenue for the Post Office.

► **1946** RONNIE LANE born, East London.

1946 ARTHUR CONLEY born, Atlanta, Georgia.

1939 RUDOLPH ISLEY born, Cincinatti, Ohio.

1928 HMV introduced the first autochange record player, price £128.

1915 WILLIE DIXON, blues singer, writer and bass player, born, Vicksburg, Mississippi.

SATURDAY

2

1943 LARRY CORYELL born, Galveston, Texas.

1941 LEON RUSSELL (Russell Bridges) born, Lawton, Oklahoma.

► **1938** MARVIN GAYE born, Washington D.C.

SUNDAY

3

1979 KATE BUSH made her live debut at the Liverpool Empire.

1970 BRINSLEY SCHWARZ were eventual victims of the hype used to boost their career. A plane load of journalists were flown from London to New York where the Brinsleys were to support Van Morrison at the Fillmore East. Hopelessly delayed, the flight arrived just in time for the writers to be rushed to the show by a police motorcade. The journalists were not amused: the band received scant attention and certainly not the press coverage their managers, Famepushers Inc., had aimed for. The estimated cost was £120,000.

1960 ELVIS PRESLEY, over the next two days, recorded the bulk of 'Elvis Is Back', his first album after leaving the army and the last he made while still in touch with the loud and nasty R&B that got him singing in the first place.

► **1941** JAN BERRY (Jan & Dean) born, Los Angeles.

1939 JEFF BARRY born. Writer of tiny, dramatic epics of adolescent dreams with his wife Ellie Greenwich — 'Da Doo Ron Ron', 'Leader Of The Pack' and the over-reaching pride of 'River Deep, Mountain High'.

1973
'Twelfth Of Never'
Donny Osmond

1968
'Lady Madonna,'
Beatles

1977
'Knowing Me, Knowing You'
Abba

1961
'Blue Moon'
Marcels

A P R I L
M O N D A Y

4 **1981 BUCKS FIZZ** won the Eurovision Song Contest with 'Making Your Mind Up', the first British act to win since the Brotherhood of Man's 'Save Your Kisses For Me' in 1976. The Norwegian entry, 'Aldril Livet' by Finn Kalvick, incidentally, completed a perverse double for Norway by scoring absolutely no votes, a remarkable performance only achieved once before — by Norway's 1978 entry, Jan Teigen's 'All Kinds Of Everything'.

1952 DAVE HILL (Slade) born, Fleetcastle, Devon.

1950 KURT WEILL, composer of music for Brecht, died. As the man who brought the bump and grind of whorehouse jazz to the rarefied European world of Brecht's 'Threepenny Opera' and 'Mahogony', Weill has achieved even greater fame since his death, scoring at least four pop hits with Anglicised versions of his early work — Bobby Darin's 'Mack The Knife', The Doors' 'Alabama Song' and Bowie's two variants on Weill, 'Alabama Song' and 'Baal'. Quite how Weill, that cunning old German, would have taken this fame is uncertain. As he spent the end of his life in Hollywood — while Brecht fled to the workers' paradise of East Germany — there's no doubt the money would have come in handy. Whether he would have picked up the Grammy in person, though, is a topic for debate.

1948 PICK WITHERS (Dire Straits) born.

1948 BERRY OAKLEY (Allman Brothers) born, Florida.

1941 MAJOR LANCE, singer of the deliciously indecisive 'Um Um Um Um Um Um' born, Chicago.

▶ **1915 MUDDY WATERS** (McKinley Morganfield), the blues' greatest statesman born, Rolling Fork, Mississippi.

T U E S D A Y

5 **1981 BOB HITE**, singer with Canned Heat and blues archivist, died of a heart attack, 38, in Venice, California.

1961 BOB DYLAN played his first show that paid decent money — twenty dollars for singing to the New York University Folk Music Society in Greenwich Village.

1951 EVERETT MORTON (The Beat) born.

1950 AGNETHA ULVAEUS (Abba) born, Jonkopping, Sweden.

1944 CRISPIAN ST. PETERS (Peter Smith) born, Swanley, Kent. Singer who had a top three hit with 'You Were On My Mind' in 1966, followed it up with the irresistably idiotic 'Pied Piper' and disapeared forever.

1942 ALLAN CLARKE (Hollies) born, Salford.

▶ **1941 ERIC BURDON** born, Newcastle.

1941 DAVE SWARBRICK, English folk violinist, born.

1941 DAVID LA FLAME (It's A Beautiful Day) born.

1928 TONY WILLIAMS, the Platters' lead tenor, born.

W E D N E S D A Y

6 **1971 THE ROLLING STONES** signed a distribution deal for their own Rolling Stones label with Atlantic Records.

1968 CLIFF RICHARD came second in the Eurovision Song Contest with 'Congratulations'.

1968 PINK FLOYD announced officially that Syd Barrett had left them for the land of legend and an extraordinarily sporadic solo career.

1963 ABC PARAMOUNT RECORDS announced that they'd signed Fats Domino who'd been with Imperial since the start of his recording career in 1949.

1944 MICHELLE GILLIAM (Mamas and Papas) born, Long Beach, California.

▶ **1937 MERLE HAGGARD** born, Oildale, California, of Okie parents who'd made the 'Grapes Of Wrath' pilgramage to the Promised Land. Most country singers make up some kind of roughneck past for themselves. Merle Haggard's the real thing. For fifteen years, his heavy, lazy eyes saw little but prison doors open and close. After a three stretch in San Quentin, he finally opted for the straight life and wrote up his life in songs, some of country music's sharpest, most poetic statements — 'Mama Tried', 'Lonesome Fugitive', 'The Bottle Let Me Down' — singing them with a grit that showed it all still hurt.

#1 UK 45
1964
'Can't Buy Me Love'
Beatles

#1 US 45
1971
'Just My Imagination'
Temptations

#1 UK 45
1963
'How Do You Do It?'
Gerry and the Pacemakers

T H U R S D A Y

7

1981 KIT LAMBERT, the Who's first manager, died from head injuries sustained in a fall at his mother's house.

► **1969 JOHN LENNON** released his first solo single, 'Give Peace A Chance', recorded in a Toronto hotel bedroom.

1967 TOM DONAHUE, a San Francisco DJ and hustler — he promoted the Beatles' Cow Palace concert — started to programme 'progressive' music on KPMX, an FM stereo San Francisco station in bad shape. It was, in his words, 'a format that embraces the best of today's rock and roll, folk, traditional and city blues, raga, electronic music, and some jazz and classical selections. I believe that music should not be treated as a group of objects to be sorted out like eggs with each category kept rigidly apart from the others...'

1956 COLUMBIA RECORDS announced that all future pop releases would be on 45 only, the 78 format being restricted to 'hillbilly' records.

1951 JANIS IAN born.

1938 SPENCER DRYDEN (Jefferson Airplane) born.

1915 BILLIE HOLIDAY (Eleanora Fagan), blues and jazz singer, born, Baltimore. Her biography starts 'Mom and Pop were just a couple of kids when they got married. He was eighteen, she was sixteen, and I was three.'

F R I D A Y

8

1978 THE DAMNED reformed to play their first farewell, a show at London's Rainbow Theatre.

1977 THE CLASH released their debut album. A London apocalypse in just over half an hour. Urban fly-overs suddenly became extremely chic.

1965 THE SOUND OF MUSIC film soundtrack entered the UK album chart, staying there for 362 weeks.

1973 NEIL YOUNG's first film, 'Journey Through The Past', was premiered at the US Film Festival in Dallas.

1947 STEVE HOWE born, London.

1942 ROGER CHAPMAN (Family and Chapman-Whitney's Streetwalkers) born, Leicester.

S A T U R D A Y

9

1976 PHIL OCHS, folk singer friend of Bob Dylan, hung himself at his sister's house, 36. A few years earlier, he'd released an album entitled 'Phil Ochs' Greatest Hits', a savage irony as he never moved beyond the cult audience that Dylan escaped when he reached out for a mass audience with 'Another Side Of Bob Dylan'. Ochs' sense of humour had obviously deserted him.

► **1969 KING CRIMSON** played their first real live show, at London's Speakeasy club, haunt of the almost famous.

1965 THE ROLLING STONES' dress sense was, reported the *Daily Express*, attacked by Welsh headmaster, E.M. Roberts. Particularly critical of the 'corduroy' trousers, he said it was a 'disservice to the young if adults interpreted freedom as a complete disregard of the rules...'

1944 GENE PARSONS (Byrds) born.

1943 TERRY KNIGHT (Grand Funk Railroad) born, Michigan.

1932 CARL PERKINS born, Lake County, Tennessee.

S U N D A Y

10

1975 RONNIE QUINTON, Ritchie Blackmore's personal roadie in Deep Purple, died in a head-on car crash near Malibu Beach.

1970 JIM MORRISON, irritated by the power being turned off at a Boston concert, asked the audience if "anyone would like to see my genitals".

1962 STU SUTCLIFFE, once a member of the Beatles, died suddenly at 21 of a brain haemorrhage.

1958 CHUCK WILLIS collapsed with a stomach ulcer and later died in an Altanta hospital. Just before his death, he hit with '(I Don't Want To) Hang Up My Rock And Roll Shoes'. Just after, with 'What Am I Living For?'.

► **1947 BUNNY WAILER** (Neville O'Reilly Livingstone) born, Kingston, JA.

► **1938 GLEN CAMPBELL** born, Delight, Arkansas.

1921 SHEB WOOLEY, singer of 'The Purple People Eater', born.

A P R I L

MONDAY

11

1963 THE BEATLES' 'From Me To You', their first chart-topping record, was released.

1961 BOB DYLAN played his first important show, supporting Detroit bluesman John Lee Hooker at New York's Gerde's Folk City, then the major venue for aspiring folkies. Dylan only played five songs — 'House Of The Rising Sun', 'A Song To Woody', a black blues and a couple of Woody Guthrie songs — but the crowd seemed to quite like him anyway.

► **1956 NEVILLE STAPLES** (Specials, Fun Boy Three) born, Christiana, Jamaica.

TUESDAY

12

1979 JACK BRUCE started that year's comeback. On this particular occasion, he was working with an R&B band, No Mystery.

1966 JAN BERRY, half of Jan & Dean, crashed his Corvette, splitting open his skull. It took four years of surgery before he could speak properly again.

1963 BOB DYLAN made his first major concert appearance, at the New York Town Hall.

► **1950 DAVID CASSIDY** born, NYC.

1944 JOHN KAYE born, East Germany. Escaping under gunfire in 1958, he fled to the Promised Land where he formed the world's first heavy metal band, Steppenwolf.

► **1940 HERBIE HANCOCK**, jazz keyboard player and the classiest of the jazz funksters, born, Chicago.

WEDNESDAY

13

1973 ROGER DALTREY released his first solo album, 'Daltrey' produced by Adam Faith, once a teenbeat heart-throb himself and now Leo Sayer's manager.

1967 A ROLLING STONES' concert in Warsaw erupted into a riot. When 7000 were locked outside the Stones' first appearance behind the Iron Curtain, the police waded in with tear gas and batons in an attempt to dispel the 2000 youths still hanging around outside the hall, Warsaw's Palace of Culture.

1956 ALAN FREED's 'Moondog's Rock'n'Roll Party' transferred to Radio Luxembourg.

► **1946 AL GREEN** born, Forrest City, Arkansas. Like just about all black American singers, he started singing in the church, in a gospel group with his brothers. He had a small hit in the sixties with 'Back Up Train' but it wasn't till the turn of the decade that he found his unique, gossamer fine style and his very own Svengali, Memphis producer, Willie Mitchell. Around Green's light nasal voice and falsetto whoops, Mitchell wrapped a rhythm track so steady and solid you could use it to build on. Starting with a cover of the Temptations 'I Can't Get Next To You', he ran up a string of hits in the seventies — 'Tired Of Being Alone', 'Call Me', 'Let's Stay Together', 'Love And Happiness', 'I'm Still In Love With You', 'Take Me To The River', all of them sung directly to an absent, imaginary other, probably the secret of his immense appeal to women record buyers. If the formula — for that's what it was — scarcely varied from record to record, it didn't matter. Like Chuck Berry, he was a stylist who'd found a frame in which he could place a whole range of — mostly pleading — emotions. Criticism of the frame misses the point; the picture it surrounds is what's important. For half a dozen years, he was the biggest name in black American music, singing to an audience running right across the racial divide. But, after being scalded by a jilted lover in the mid-seventies, he retreated into himself, heading back to his beloved church, becoming the Reverend Al Green, refusing to sing secular material. Inevitably, his gospel work is his usual style, the Lord's name being substituted for the woman's. And, of course, it's so sexy even atheists find it bordering on the sacrilegeous. But, if the angels in Heaven don't sing like Al Green, I'm going to the other place.

1946 ROY LONEY (ex-Flamin' Groovies) born, San Francisco.

1944 JACK CASADY (Jefferson Airplane) born, Washington D.C.

1934 HORACE KAY (Tams) born.

T H U R S D A Y

14

1980 GARY NUMAN released a video of one of his concerts. The first commercially available pop video cassette in the UK.

1976 ERIC FAULKNER, a Bay City Roller, fell victim to the pressures of teeny bop stardom, taking an overdose of pills at his manager's house. He was revived in an Edinburgh hospital.

1967 DAVID BOWIE released 'The Laughing Gnome', a hideous product of his obsession with Anthony Newley. It died the death, of course, when first released but the record company embarrassed Bowie dreadfully by re-issuing it in 1973 when it got to number four on the British charts.

1945 RITCHIE BLACKMORE born, Weston-Super-Mare, Somerset.

1940 LORETTA LYNN born, Butchers' Hollow, Van Lear, Kentucky. The year is actually an estimate. She herself said "When I was born, Franklin Delano Roosevelt was the president for several years. That's the closest I'm gonna come to telling my age..."

1973
'Houses Of The Holy'
Led Zeppelin

F R I D A Y

15

1970 GEORGE GOLDNER died, 52. A New York fifties music business hustler, Goldner ran a succession of store-front labels — End, Gone, Rama, Gee — which presented a host of wonderful, addictive, often hopelessly amateurish street corner doo wop groups. Little Anthony and the Imperials, the Chantels, whose 'Maybe' was one of doo wop's greatest prayers. The Flamingos and their stately 'I Only Have Eyes For You'. In the sixties, he teamed up with Leiber & Stoller to form Red Bird, home of the Shangri-Las' adolescent hallucinations. Bill Millar, authoritative British music writer, summed Goldner up perfectly when he said: "He was not entirely punctilious about royalty payments. But he cut some nice records, and he did more for integration than the Supreme Court."

► **1944 DAVE EDMUNDS** born, Cardiff.
► **1939 MARTY WILDE** (Reginald Smith) born, London.
1898 BESSIE SMITH, classic blues singer born Chattanooga, Tennessee. (The date is from the *Chicago Defender*. Other sources give 1895.)

1965
'Freewheelin''
Bob Dylan

S A T U R D A Y

16

1972 ELO played their first live show, at the Greyhound, Croydon.

1971 THE ROLLING STONES released 'Brown Sugar', the first of their records to appear on their own Rolling Stones label.

1969 THE MC5 were dropped by their record company Elektra after the Detroit band placed an ad in their local paper saying 'Fuck Hudsons', a rather intemperate response to a Detroit record store which refused to stock MC5 albums.

1939 DUSTY SPRINGFIELD (Mary O'Brien) born.

1966
'Somebody Help Me'
Spencer Davis Group

S U N D A Y

17

1974 VINNIE TAYLOR, member of Sha Na Na died, probably from a surfeit of heroin.

1970 PAUL McCARTNEY released his first non-Beatles record, his solo album, 'McCartney', cleverly timed to coincide with the Beatles' own 'Get Back'.

► **1960 EDDIE COCHRAN** died in a car crash on his way back to London after a show in Bristol. Just 22, Cochran was the sweet side of nasty rock'n'roll. Young, good-looking, with a great songwriting girlfriend in Sharon Sheeley, always worried that mom and pop would get home before he'd finished partying with the kids. A handful of his records — 'C'mon Everybody', 'Pink Pegged Slacks', 'Sittin' On The Balcony' and especially 'Summertime Blues' — still work the charm when people gather to dream of innocence.

1959 STEPHEN SINGLETON (ABC) born.

1953 THE NEW MUSICAL EXPRESS had the first British chart-topper six months after they'd started running the first UK charts — Lita Roza's 'How Much Is That Doggie In The Window?'

► **1946 BILL KREUTZMANN** (Grateful Dead) born.
► **1941 BILLY FURY** (Ronald Wycherly) born, Liverpool.

1971
'Joy To The World'
Three Dog Night

A P R I L

M O N D A Y

18

1981 YES finally split, it was announced. Alan White and Chris Squire, it was reported, intended to link up with Jimmy Page and Robert Plant.

1979 RAINBOW recruited Don Airey as keyboard player.

1964 THE ROLLING STONES topped the bill at the Mad Mod Ball.

1953 WILLIE MAE THORNTON's 'Hound Dog' hit the number one spot in eleven out of twelve cities on the R&B hot charts in *Cashbox* which described it as a 'Once in a lifetime' event.

1941 MIKE VICKERS (Manfred Mann) born.

T U E S D A Y

19

1978 PATTI SMITH's 'Because The Night', her only real hit, was released.

1944 MARK VOLMAN (Turtles, Flo & Eddie) born, Los Angeles.

1942 ALAN PRICE born, Fairfield, County Durham. The music man behind the original Animals, putting gravelly organ swirls behind the black & white Geordie minstrel fantasies of Eric Burdon, making the histrionics of 'We've Gotta Get Out Of This Place' almost believable. Alone, he introduced the world to the songs of Randy Newman — 'Simon Smith And His Amazing Dancing Bear', 'Tickle Me' — worked with Georgie Fame and underpinned the sprawling narrative of Lindsay Anderson's most ambitious movie, 'O! Lucky Man', with some sardonic songs and a diffident, Greek chorus-like performance. But somehow he's never been able to escape the taint of becoming a professional Geordie. All earthy realism, plain talk and haway the lads.

1928 ALEXIS KORNER born, Paris, of Austrian/ Turkish/Greek parentage. In many ways, the European equivalent of Atlantic Records' founders, the Ertegun Brothers — a metropolitan, cosmopolitan sophisticate in love with the blues. As at home helping the Stones sort themselves out as he is making a few quid out of his rumbling vocal tones, doing a voice-over for a soap powder ad.

W E D N E S D A Y

20

1981 JOHN PHILLIPS, founder of the Mamas and Papas, was sent to jail for drug dealing offences to which he'd plead guilty. Although sentenced to eight years, all but thirty days of his time was suspended. He was placed on five years' probation on condition that he did two hundred and fifty hours of community service during the following year and attended a drug abuse programme.

1976 THE ROLLING STONES released 'Black And Blue', their first album since Mick Taylor left the group.

1968 DEEP PURPLE played their first live show, in Tastrup, Denmark.

1968 APPLE RECORDS, the Beatles' label, advertised for songwriters and musicians, asking them to send their tapes to Apple's Saville Row headquarters.

1956 NAT KING COLE was attacked by a white mob onstage in that most racist of all town, Birmingham, Alabama. Nastily beaten up, he was playing with — of all people — the British Ted Heath Orchestra.

1955 ALAN FREED promoted his first rock'n'roll show at the Brooklyn Paramount. Unusually for the time, there was no colour bar.

1939 JOHNNY TILLOTSON, singer of 'Poetry In Motion', born, Jacksonville, Florida.

1939 BILLIE HOLIDAY recorded 'Strange Fruit', a painful, lyrical song about a racist Southern lynching. She'd taken the words from a poem by Lewis Allan and, after carrying it around for months, had it set to music by pianist Sonny White. Issued later that year, it was a big hit in the white liberal community while its flip, 'Fine And Mellow', was a smash on Harlem juke boxes.

1935 'YOUR LUCKY STRIKE HIT PARADE', the first 'chart' of any kind, started on US radio. Introduced by Warren Hill, it featured the biggest fifteen hit songs of the week and lasted till April 29, 1959 after switching over to TV on July 10, 1950. The very first number one was 'Soon'.

1959
'It Doesn't Matter Anymore'
Buddy Holly

1969
'Israelites'
Desmond Dekker

1957
'All Shook Up'
Elvis Presley

T H U R S D A Y

21

1978 SANDY DENNY died. A robust but delicate folk singer — 'Who Knows Where The Time Goes' which she wrote while with Fairport Convention must be one of the sweetest songs ever — who'd been enmeshed in 'personal problems' for many years, she fell down her stairs and died of a brain haemorrhage four days later.

1971 DON DRUMMOND died. *The* ska trombonist, the man behind the lazy, easy horn sounds on all the Skatalites records and the fire-breather of 'Man In The Street'. He died in Jamaica's Bellevue mental asylum where he'd been locked up after murdering his common-law wife.

1969 JANIS JOPLIN and her Kozmic Blues Band played London's Albert Hall.

1963 THE BEATLES went to see the Stones play at the Crawdaddy Club, Richmond.

1945 MODERN RECORDS was formed, Billboard announced. One of the new wave of R&B based independent labels, Modern was started by the three brothers Bihari, blues lovers from Oklahoma. Over the years, it expanded to become one of the gutsiest R&B labels, putting out records under its own imprint and those of its subsidiary labels, RPM, Kent, Crown and Flair. If B.B. King was its main man, Young Jessie's 'Hit Git And Split' was probably its best single track. John Lee Hooker, Elmore James, Little Willie Littlefield and Etta James all did some of their best work for the Biharis' Modern.

1939 ERNIE MARESCA, writer of Dion's greatest moment 'The Wanderer', born.

F R I D A Y

22

1979 KEITH RICHARDS played the charity concert for the blind ordered by a Toronto judge as penance for his heroin conviction. Two capacity shows at Toronto's 5000 seat Oshawa Hall.

1977 THE JAM released their first single, 'In The City'.

1969 JOHN LENNON changed his name officially to John Ono Lennon.

1964 THE RECORD MIRROR R&B poll showed:
1. Rolling Stones
2. Manfred Mann
3. Yardbirds

1956 THE COASTERS signed to Atlantic records.

1956 SCREAMIN' JAY HAWKINS, the coolest ghoul of all, recorded the voodoo screech 'I Put A Spell On You' for Okeh. Most authorities claim it was cut at the tail end of a lengthy drunken binge.

▶**1950 PETER FRAMPTON** born, Beckenham, Kent.

S A T U R D A Y

23

1978 SID VICIOUS filmed his performance of 'My Way' used in the 'Great Rock'n'Roll Swindle' film.

1977 ANDREW CZECZOWSKI ceased to manage the Roxy, the London club which he'd started as the first all-punk venue — a mere four months after it'd opened.

1971 THE ROLLING STONES released 'Sticky Fingers', their first album on their own Rolling Stones label.

1967 PINK FLOYD's 'Arnold Layne', despite a ban by BBC radio, became the first 'underground' record to reach the UK top twenty.

1939 RAY PETERSON, singer of one of the creepiest death discs, 'Tell Laura I Love Her', born, Denton, Texas.

▶**1936 ROY ORBISON** born, Wink, Texas.

S U N D A Y

24

1976 THE SEX PISTOLS received their first major press coverage, a double page feature in *Sounds*.

1975 PETER HAM, singer with Badfinger, became depressed at the band's inability to follow up their one hit, 'Come And Get It' and hung himself

1968 THE CONFEDERATION OF BRITISH INDUSTRY complained that Radio One was affecting the output of factory workers.

1959 THE DRIFTERS released 'There Goes My Baby', the first R&B or rock'n'roll record to feature a string section.

1942 BARBRA STREISAND born, Brooklyn.

APRIL

MONDAY

25

1981 DENNY LAINE left Wings. Paul McCartney was reported as saying, "We simply shan't be Wings anymore".

1980 HUGH CORNWELL, a Strangler, was released from London's Pentonville prison where he'd served a six weeks sentence for possessing heroin. He told the press: "It's the most depressing, demoralising, inhuman place I have ever spent any time in."

1978 ALTERNATIVE TV, the band formed by punk fanzine *Sniffin Glue* editor and founder, Mark P, played the last ever new wave show at London's 100 Club.

1977 ELVIS PRESLEY made his last recording, at the Civic Center, Saginaw, Michigan, cutting three tracks which were issued — heavily overdubbed — on the 'Moody Blue' album.

1974 PAM MORRISON, widow of Doors' singer, Jim Morrison, died of a drugs overdose.

1970 OTIS SPANN, blues pianist, died.

1933 JERRY LEIBER, one half of rock'n'roll's greatest writing partnership, Leiber & Stoller, born, Baltimore.

➤ **1945 BJORN ULVAEUS** (Abba) born, Gothenburg, Sweden.

1923 ALBERT KING, blues guitarist writer of 'Born Under A Bad Sign', born, Indianola, Mississippi.

➤ **1918 ELLA FITZGERALD** born.

1970
'ABC'
Jackson Five

TUESDAY

26

1980 THE BEAT released 'Mirror In The Bathroom', Britain's first digitally recorded single.

1969 PAUL McCARTNEY denied rumours of his death. That year's hula hoop, the 'Paul Is Dead' campaign claimed that Paul had died long ago but the Beatles had hushed it up. The prime piece of evidence, so supporters of the theory claimed, was Paul's appearance on the cover of 'Abbey Rd.' — apparently white suits and bare feet signify death in some, generally unspecified, Eastern culture.

1964 THE ROLLING STONES played the *New Musical Express* pollwinners concert and released their debut album, 'The Rolling Stones'.

1945 GARY WRIGHT born, Englewood, New Jersey.

➤ **1942 BOBBY RYDELL** born, Philadelphia.

1946 RONNY DAYTON, of the hot rod group Ronny and the Daytonas, born, Tulsa, Oklahoma.

1938 DUANE EDDY born, Conning, New York.

1938 MAURICE WILLIAMS born, Lancaster, South Carolina. Singer — with his backing group, the Zodiacs — of rock's most exulted, most desperate plea, 'Stay'. One minute thirty seven seconds of intuitive genius in full-flight.

1980
'Call Me'
Blondie

WEDNESDAY

27

1981 RINGO STARR married Barbara Bach at London's Marylebone Registry Office.

1976 DAVID BOWIE was held up for several hours on his special train by Russian-Polish border guards who searched his possessions and found Nazi memorabilia and books. He was reported at the time as saying that Britain would benefit from a fascist leader and offered himself as a candidate for Prime Minister... eventually: "I don't intend to jump straight from pop to politics."

1972 PHIL KING, front man of Blue Oyster Cult, was shot three times through the head with a .38 Magnum in the course of an argument over gambling, New York.

1969 JOHN LENNON's erotic lithographs, seized in a January raid on a London art gallery, were declared 'unlikely to deprave or corrupt'. They were handed back.

1968 TRAFFIC's 'Dear Mr. Fantasy' entered the US album chart.

1957 SKIFFLE dominated the UK charts, with four skiffle singles in the top twenty, including Lonnie Donegan's 'Cumberland Gap' at number one.

➤ **1959 SHEENA EASTON** born.

1947 ANN PEEBLES born, East St. Louis. Stable-mate of Al Green and backed up by the same thick, sweet Willie Mitchell productions. She sang as that classic figure of soul, the woman scorned, but threatening revenge. 'I Can't Stand The Rain', 'I'm Gonna Tear Your Playhouse Down', heady brews of clear-eyed passion.

1963
'I Will Follow Him'
Little Peggy March

THURSDAY

28

1981 GARY NUMAN made his 'final live appearance', at Wembley.

1979 MARTIN BRAMAH left the Fall, the British avant garde punk group.

1976 THE ROLLING STONES started their European tour — their first in three years — at the Festhalle, Frankfurt, West Germany.

1975 TOM DONAHUE, the 'inventor' of 'progressive'/free-form radio programming, died.

1968 HAIR had its Broadway opening at the Biltmore Theater.

1963 ANDREW LOOG OLDHAM saw the Rolling Stones play for the first time, at the Crawdaddy Club, Richmond. A free-lance publicist who'd worked with the Beatles early on, Oldham went down there with his boss, Eric Easton. One set and he had no doubts about his future. As George Melly, the most perceptive commentator on early British pop culture, put it, 'He looked at Jagger as Sylvester looks at Tweety Pie.'

FRIDAY

29

1977 THE ADVERTS, one of the earliest punk groups, released their first single, 'One Chord Wonders'.

1972 JOHN LINDSAY, Mayor of New York City, asked the federal authorities to cease deportation proceedings against John Lennon and Yoko Ono.

1967 THE 14 HOUR TECHNICOLOUR DREAM at London's Alexandra Palace, the emergence of London's 'underground' into the public eye. On the bill were Pink Floyd, Soft Machine, the Pretty Things, the Crazy World of Arthur Brown, Tomorrow, John's Children, Savoy Brown, the Graham Bond Organisation, Champion Jack Dupree and the Flies.

1963 ANDREW OLDHAM AND ERIC EASTON signed a management contract with the Rolling Stones within a day of seeing them for the first time.

1948 MICHAEL KAROLI (Can) born.

1947 TOMMY JAMES born, Dayton, Ohio.

1928 CARL GARDNER, Coasters' lead singer, born.

SATURDAY

30

1978 ROCK AGAINST RACISM, the British organisation formed in the furore following some casually racist remarks made onstage by Eric Clapton, held a rally in London's Victoria Park. Over a hundred thousand people turned up to watch a host of black and white bands. The Clash topped the bill.

1966 RICHARD FARINA, friend of Bob Dylan and songwriter, died when he crashed his motorbike straight after the party held to celebrate the publication of his only book 'Been Down So Long, It Looks Like Up To Me.'

1965 BOB DYLAN started his last pre-electric British tour in

➤ **1943 BOBBY VEE** (Robert Veline) born, Fargo, North Dakota.

1877 CHARLES CROS, French poet and scientist (1842-1888) left sealed papers at the French Academy of Sciences describing the theory of manufacturing a phonograph

MAY

SUNDAY

1

1980 THE FACE published its first issue.

1979 SATURDAY NIGHT FEVER, the double album soundtrack of the film, had sold 25 million copies it was announced.

1966 THE BEATLES played their last show in Britain, the *New Musical Express* poll winners concert.

1967 ELVIS PRESLEY married Priscilla Beaulieu in Las Vegas.

1945 MIMI FARINA (nee Baez) born.

➤ **1955 RITA COOLIDGE** born, Nashville.

1942 THE AMERICAN WAR PRODUCTION BOARD commandeered all facilities for the production of jukeboxes, turning them over to the manufacture of war materials.

➤ **1939 JUDY COLLINS** born, Seattle, Washington.

1930 LITTLE WALTER (Marion Walter Jacobs) blues harmonica player, born, Marksville, Louisiana.

M A Y

M O N D A Y

2

1980 PINK FLOYD's 'Another Brick In The Wall' was banned by the South African authorities. Black school children had adopted it as a protest against their second-rate education system and the authorities therefore considered it "prejudicial to the safety of the state".

1979 THE WHO played their first show since the death of Keith Moon at London's Rainbow with Kenny Jones as drummer and Rabbitt Bundrick on keyboards.

1967 THE BEACH BOYS, it was announced, had abandoned 'Smile', the grand design of Brian Wilson which he could never manage to finish. Rumours abounded that he'd stopped work on it after a house next door to the studio had burned down — he'd considered this directly caused by a track they'd cut, 'Fire'. The reality seems to have been a little more prosaic. Work on 'Smile' petered out rather than being shelved — and burnt, according to some — in a flash of mystic inspiration.

▶ **1957 ELVIS PRESLEY** recorded 'Jailhouse Rock', his greatest movie performance, at MGM, Culver City, California.

1946 LESLEY GORE, singer of 'It's My Party', born, Tenafly, New Jersey.

1935 LINK WRAY born.

1904 BING CROSBY born, Tacoma, Washington.

T U E S D A Y

3

1973 BRINSLEY SCHWARZ, DUCKS DELUXE AND BEES MAKE HONEY, doyens of the London pub rock circuit, played a benefit at Camden Town Hall for Ian Dury's first band, Kilburn and the High Roads who needed the money to fix up their broken down Transit van.

1972 LES HARVEY, brother of Alex and guitarist with Stone the Crows, died from an electric shock onstage at the Top Rank, Swansea.

1971 GRAND FUNK RAILROAD, after a year of refusing to talk to journalists, held a press conference. Out of the 150 writers invited, only six turned up. Manager Terry Knight described it as "the grossest case of non-recognition in the history of the business".

1969 JIMI HENDRIX was arrested at Toronto airport on charges of possessing narcotics and bailed out on a $10,000 surety.

1963 ANDREW OLDHAM AND ERIC EASTON formalised their management contract with the Rolling Stones.

1959 DAVID BALL (Soft Cell) born, Salford.

▶ **1955 STEVE JONES,** former Sex Pistol, born.

▶ **1950 MARY HOPKIN** born, Pontardawe, Glamorgan.

1937 FRANKIE VALLI (Francis Castelluccio) born, Newark, New Jersey.

▶ **1936 JAMES BROWN** born, Augusta, Georgia.

W E D N E S D A Y

4

1979 ELVIS COSTELLO's 'Accidents Will Happen' was released.

1968 MARY HOPKIN appeared on the British TV show, 'Opportunity Knocks', bringing her to the attention of Paul McCartney who went on to produce her first single, the enormously successful adaptation of an old Russian folk tune, 'Those Were The Days'.

1964 THE MOODY BLUES were formed. "There was so much competition (amongst groups in Birmingham)", said Ray Thomas, "that the only way to get any gigs was to put together a local supergroup — so that's what we did." Within nine months they had a world-wide hit with their cover of the American soul singer Bessie Banks' 'Go Now'.

▶ **1956 GENE VINCENT's** first recording session, at Owen Bradley's Nashville Studios. He cut 'Race With The Devil' and both sides of his first single, 'Woman Love'/'Be Bop A Lula' (originally the flip side).

1949 ZAL CLEMINSON (Sensational Alex Harvey Band) bo[rn]

1932 TAMMY WYNETTE born, Itawambe County, Mississippi. (Some sources give May 5, Red Bay, Alabama.)

1886 THE 'GRAPHOPHONE' (the earliest record player) patent was granted to Chichester Bell and Charles Sumner Tainter.

1981
'Morning Train (9 to 5)'
Sheena Easton

1956
'Heartbreak Hotel'
Elvis Presley

1974
'Waterloo'
Abba

T H U R S D A Y

5

1972 REVEREND GARY DAVIS, sacred blues singer, died of a heart attack, 72, New Jersey. The Rolling Stones covered his 'Prodigal Son' for their 'Beggars' Banquet' album, originally claiming the composer credit themselves.
1968 BUFFALO SPRINGFIELD played their final show before breaking up.
1967 THE KINKS released 'Waterloo Sunset', probably the only decent piece of work ever to come out of the whole Swinging London schtick.
1962 CLIFF RICHARD was awarded a gold disc for 'The Young Ones'.
► **1959 IAN McCULLOCH** (Echo and the Bunnymen) born, Liverpool.
1948 BILL WARD (Black Sabbath) born.
1938 JOHNNIE TAYLOR, singer of 'Who's Making Love', born, Crawfordsville, Arkansas.
1937 JOHN LEE 'SONNY BOY' WILLIAMSON, blues harmonica player and singer, played at his first recording session — in the Aurora studios, Illinois — cutting three blues, 'Good Morning, Little Schoolgirl', 'Bluebird Blues' and 'Sugar Mama Blues', all of them much covered by other artists.

1973
'Aladdin Sane'
David Bowie

F R I D A Y

6

1979 DAVID CARTER of Radio London made the longest ever local radio broadcast in the UK, forty eight and a half hours, running through to May 8.
1978 THE VIBRATORS, punk's original bandwagon jumpers, played a show in Preston at which a member of the audience was killed.
1976 MUDDY WATERS played in a circus tent in Canberra, Australia. The elephants, he reported, moved to the music.
1967 THE GRATEFUL DEAD's debut album entered the US charts.
► **1920 PEGGY LEE** (Norma Dolores Egstrom) born, Jamestown, North Dakota.

1972
'Prophets, Seers And Sages'
Tyrannosaurus Rex

S A T U R D A Y

7

1978 BOB DYLAN's forthcoming appearance at Earl's Court, his first British shows since the Isle of Wight festival in 1969, drew an unprecedented amount of ticket applications. 90,000 tickets were sold in the first eight hours.
1960 JOE MEEK, British early sixties producer extraordinaire, had his first hit. The Flee-Reckers enter the UK chart at 26 with the Meek production 'Green Jeans'.
1956 JOHNNY BURNETTE and his Rock'n'Roll Trio cut their first single, the rockabilly invocation 'Tear It Up', for Coral Records.
► **1950 JANIS IAN** born, New York.
► **1948 PETE WINGFIELD**, writer, producer, songwriter and musician, born.
1939 JIMMY RUFFIN born, Springfield, Missouri.
1939 JOHNNY MAESTRO (Mastrangelo) born, Brooklyn. Singer with doo wop group, the Crests, who had a US top five with '16 Candles' in 1958.

1966
'Pretty Flamingo'
Manfred Mann

S U N D A Y

8

1974 GRAHAM BOND, organist and leading light of British sixties R&B, jumped beneath a train at Finsbury Park tube station. It took the police two days to identify the body.
1947 MARC BOLAN (Feld) born, Hackney, London.
1943 PAUL SAMWELL-SMITH (Yardbirds) born.
1943 JOHNNY BRAGG, sentenced to three life sentences, went to the Tennessee State Penitentiary where he formed the Prisonaires, a vocal group who were allowed to record for Sun records of Memphis. They had a minor R&B hit with 'Walking In The Rain', a big international pop hit for Nabob of Sob, Johnny Ray. On his release, Bragg joined the Marigolds and cut some records still greatly prized for their pace and indecipherability amongst the Northern Soul fraternity.
1941 JOHN FRED, singer with his backing group, the Playboys, born, Baton Rouge, Louisiana.
► **1940 RICK NELSON** (Eric Hilliard) born, Teaneck, New Jersey.

1976
'Fernando'
Abba

M A Y

M O N D A Y

9

1981 ADAM AND THE ANTS 'Stand And Deliver' entered the UK singles chart at number one, the first record to do so since the Jam's 'Going Underground' over a year before.

1971 FREE split up immediately after a tour of Australia and the Far East.

1971 T. REX started a national tour of Great Britain with the maximum ticket price pegged to 60p.

1963 PAUL McCARTNEY met Jane Asher for the first time, at a Royal Albert Hall concert.

1962 DAVE GAHAN (Depeche Mode) born, London.

1937 SONNY CURTIS, of the Crickets and writer of 'I Fought The Law', born, Meadow, Texas.

1937 DAVID PRATER, the Dave half of Sam & Dave, soul's Double Dynamite, born, Ocilla, Georgia.

➤ **1914 HANK SNOW**, country singer, writer of 'I'm Moving On', born.

1964
'Don't Throw Your Love Away'
Searchers

T U E S D A Y

10

1978 CLASH members, Paul Simonon and Nicky Headon, appeared in court on criminal damages charges arising from their pigeon shooting escapade earlier in the year.

➤ **1969 FRANK SINATRA's** 'My Way' entered the UK singles chart, staying there for 127 weeks.

1967 THE ROLLING STONES took advantage of the British judiciary's offering them a season ticket for drugs offences appearances. Mick Jagger and Keith Richards were in court for a hearing arising from the police raid on Keith's country home, Redlands, in February. Both were allowed out on bail of £100 each and sent for trial at West Sussex Quarter Sessions. Meanwhile, back in the jungle, the London police raided Brian Jones flat and found drugs. Allowed out on bail of £250, Jones appeared at Marylebone Magistrates Court the following day.

1963 THE ROLLING STONES went into London's Olympic studios where they recorded both sides of their first single, 'Come On'/'I Want To Be Loved' and two tracks still unissued, Bo Diddley's 'Pretty Thing' and the Clovers' 'Love Potion No. 9'.

1957 SID VICIOUS (John Beverly) born.

1954 BILL HALEY released 'Rock Around The Clock', described on the label as a 'foxtrot'.

1946 GRAHAM GOULDMAN (10 CC) born.

1946 DAVE MASON born, Worcester.

1935 LARRY WILLIAMS born, New Orleans.

➤ **1921 BERT WEEDON**, the man whose how-to book launched a million guitar players, born, East Ham, London.

#1 UK 45
1963
'From Me To You'
Beatles

W E D N E S D A Y

11

1981 BOB MARLEY died, 36, Cedars of Lebanon Hospital, Miami. A great reggae singer whose status as a prophet will decline as fast as his reputation as a sweet singer (fully the equal of the Impressions' Jerry Butler whom he so admired) will rise. Merchandised as a ghetto rebel, he was never really suited to the role. He had far too much of the vagueness of the poet ever to make more than a dilettante musical politician. Rather, he was a gentle, careful singer who cut his very best track not too long before his death — 'Redemption Song', the almost painfully moving experience of a man facing up to his fears of death and triumphing over them. It's such a powerful recording that it sounded like that even if you didn't know Marley was very ill. When he had a toe amputated a couple of years earlier, it was announced that it was the result of a football accident. In fact, it was the first sign of the cancer he spent the last months of his life trying to chase away, staying at Dr. Essels controversial cancer clinic right up to forty hours before his death.

1976 THE SEX PISTOLS started their residency at London's 100 Club.

➤ **1973 WINGS** started their first national tour of Britain with a show in Bristol.

1956 ELVIS PRESLEY's 'Heartbreak Hotel' entered the UK singles chart at number 15, his first British hit.

1941 ERIC BURDON born, Walker-On-Tyne.

1938 CARLA BLEY born, Oakland, California.

#1 US 45
1959
'The Happy Organ'
Dave (Baby) Cortez

THURSDAY

12

1977 **THE SEX PISTOLS** signed to Virgin records, after being thrown out by first EMI and then A&M. Their manager, Malcolm McLaren later glorified the exploits in his ten rules for successful swindling.

► **1976** **KEITH RELF**, Yardbirds singer and founder of Renaissance, died at his house when the guitar he was playing suddenly became live.

1972 **THE ROLLING STONES** released 'Exile On Main St.'

1971 **MICK JAGGER** married Bianca Perez Morena de Macais, at St. Tropez town hall. The Faces played at the reception later that day.

1967 **PINK FLOYD** performed at London's Queen Elizabeth Hall, the world's first quadrophonic concert.

1964 **RADIO ATLANTA**, a pirate radio ship, first broadcast, joining forces with Radio Caroline in July to form Caroline South and North — the latter anchored off the Isle of Man.

1954 **THE EVENING NEWS** published an article by 'a family doctor' which read, in part, 'Teddy boys...are all of unsound mind in the sense that they are all suffering from a form of psychosis. Apart from the birch or rope, depending on the gravity of their crimes, what they need is rehabilitation in a psychopathic institution...Not only have these rampageous youngsters developed a degree of paranoia with an inferiority complex, but they are also inferior apart from their disease...It is the desire to do evil, not lack of comprehension which forces them into crime.'

1951 **JACKIE BRENSTON's** 'Rocket 88', considered to be the first rock'n'roll record, topped the US R&B charts.

► **1948** **STEVIE WINWOOD** born, Birmingham.

1946 **IAN McLAGEN** born, London.

1944 **JAMES PURIFY** born, Pensacola, Florida.

1942 **IAN DURY** born, London.

1928 **BURT BACHARACH**, songwriter, arranger, producer, born, Kansas City, Missouri.

1968 **THE ROLLING STONES** made a surprise appearance at the *NME* pollwinners concert, their first British show for two years.

FRIDAY

13

1977 **THE JAM** released their debut album.

1975 **BOB WILLS**, The King Of Western Swing', died.

1967 **THE BEE GEES** 'New York Mining Disaster 1941' entered the UK charts, their first hit single.

1967 **THE CREAM's** debut album, 'Fresh Cream', entered the US charts.

► **1950** **PETER GABRIEL** born.

1950 **STEVIE WONDER** (Stephen Judkins) born, Saginaw, Michigan.

1949 **OVEREND WATTS** born, Birmingham.

► **1943** **MARY WELLS** born, Detroit.

1941 **RICHIE VALENS** (Richard Valenzuela) born, Pacoima, California.

SATURDAY

14

1943 **JACK BRUCE** born, Bishopsbriggs, Lanarkshire.

1940 **TROY SHONDELL** (Gary Shelton), one hit wonder with 'This Time', born, Indiana.

1936 **BOBBY DARIN** (Walden Robert Cassotto) born, Philadelphia.

SUNDAY

15

1981 **PUBLIC IMAGE LTD.** played a show at New York's Ritz Club, hiding behind a video screen for the entire set. Unsurprisingly, the audience kicked up a little fuss, forcing John Lydon's rock'n'roll band to flee the hall.

1970 **RADIO NORTHSEA INTERNATIONAL** was bombed by frogmen hired by Radio Veronica, a rival pirate radio ship.

1953 **MIKE OLDFIELD** born, Reading.

► **1948** **ENO** (Brian Peter George St. John Le Baptiste de la Salle Eno) born.

1937 **TRINI LOPEZ** born, Dallas, Texas.

#1 UK LP
1967
'More Of The Monkees'

#1 US 45
1967
'The Happening'
Supremes

#1 UK 45
1961
'Surrender'
Elvis Presley
'Runaway'
Del Shannon

#1 UK 45
1965
'King Of The Road'
Roger Miller

M A Y

M O N D A Y

16

1977 PATTI SMITH made her first British appearance, at London's Roundhouse. As it was the very first opportunity for Londoners to see an American 'new wave' act, every one of the tiny coterie of punks were there and the event took on almost religious significance. Which must have got to Patti Smith — the first show was hasty and harried but by the following day she'd adjusted well enough to her new-found star status (something she'd yet to experience in America) to fulfil at least some of the expectations laid on her.

1974 BRIAN MAY of Queen was flown back to London after collapsing with hepatitis in New York.

1969 PETE TOWNSHEND went to jail for the night. While he was playing at the Fillmore East, a plainclothes cop jumped onstage and grabbed for the mike so he could tell the audience the supermarket next door was on fire. Thinking he was just (?!?) a member of the audience, Townshend kicked him off the stage.

➤ **1955 HAZEL O'CONNOR** born, Coventry.

1944 BILLY COBHAM born, Panama.

T U E S D A Y

17

1980 IAN CURTIS, singer and writer of the Manchester band, Joy Division, hung himself shortly after finishing work on their second album, 'Closer', and just before they had their one big hit, 'Love Will Tear Us Apart'. A depressive character, Curtis was immediately eulogised as the martyr he plainly wasn't. Of all the drivel that appeared, the sickest must have been the claim in *Sounds* that this man "died for you", denying him even the simple peace of the dead.

1980 PETER CRISS announced he was leaving Kiss.

1980 YES recruited two new members from the latter day pop group, Buggles — Trevor Horne and Geoff Downes — as replacements for Jon Anderson and Rick Wakeman.

1978 LOU REED began recording his shows at New York's Bottom Line — which went through to May 21. The result was 'Live: Take No Prisoners', the double album upon one track of which Reed wonders whether American rock writer, Robert Christgau, is a "toe fucker".

1973 GM RECORDS was launched by Rod Stewart's manager, Billy Gaff, with a reception at London's Ritz.

1971 'GODSPELL' opened at the Cherry Lane Theater, NYC.

1967 'DON'T LOOK BACK', the Pennebaker documentary of Bob Dylan's 1965 UK tour, premiered in San Francisco at the Presidio Theater.

1952 CHESS, the Chicago blues label, launchd its subsidiary, Checker, soon to be the home of Bo Diddley.

1950 BILL BRUFORD born.

1944 JESSE WINCHESTER born, Louisiana.

➤ **1942 TAJ MAHAL** (Henry Saint-Claire Fredricks Williams) born, New York.

W E D N E S D A Y

18

1969 THE EDWIN HAWKINS SINGERS' 'Oh Happy Day' was released in Britain, becoming the only black gospel record to reach the UK top five. A California youth gospel choir, the Edwin Hawkins Singers had cut an album of eight songs for $750 in 1967 to raise funds. Only 600 copies were sold at the time but, in February 1969, a copy was given to KSAN San Francisco DJ, Abe Keshishian, who started to give it heavy play, especially on 'Oh Happy Day'. As various record companies started bidding for the rights, Buddah won out with a $55,000 advance and $25,000 'bonus'. Jumped on by the rock, the pop and the R&B stations, it sold a million within two weeks of release, peaking at number two in the charts on both sides of the Atlantic.

1963 THE BEATLES started their first national tour, at the Slough Adelphi, supported by Roy Orbison and Gerry and the Pacemakers.

➤ **1958 TOYAH WILCOX** born.

1954 WRECKLESS ERIC (Goulden) born, Newhaven, Sussex.

1949 RICK WAKEMAN born, Perivale, Middlesex.

1911 JOE TURNER, the blues shouter who cut the first version of 'Shake, Rattle & Roll', born, Kansas City, Missouri.

THURSDAY

19

1976 KEITH RICHARDS was arrested in his crashed Bentley when the British motorway police discovered 'substances'. He appeared in court on cocaine and LSD charges the next year.

➤ **1969 COLEMAN HAWKINS**, the bluesiest of all jazz tenor sax players, died.

1956 MARTYN WARE (Heaven 17) born.

1960 ALAN FREED, the DJ who coined the phrase 'rock'n'roll' (which he tried, unsuccessfully, to patent), was indicted by the payola investigation for taking $30,650 from six record companies to plug their records.

1958 BOBBY DARIN released 'Splish Splash', Atlantic Records' first eight track recording.

➤ **1951 JOEY RAMONE** (Jeffrey Hyman) born, Forest Hills, New York.

1945 PETE TOWNSHEND born, Chiswick, London.

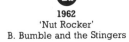

FRIDAY

20

1971 CHICAGO bass player, Pete Cetera, got into a row with three men at a Chicago Cubs baseball game about the length of his hair. They knocked four of his teeth out and put him in hospital where he underwent five hours of surgery.

1967 THE BBC banned the Beatles' 'Day In The Life' on the grounds that it might encourage drug taking.

1961 NICK HEYWARD (Haircut 100) born.

➤ **1954 THE PLATTERS** recorded the original version of their 'Only You' at Radio Recorders, Hollywood. Tony Williams sung lead and the tenor part was handled by Cornell Gunter, then only fourteen.

1946 CHER (Cherilyn Sarkasian La Pier, later Bono, later Allman) born, El Centro, California.

1944 JOE COCKER born, Sheffield, Yorkshire.

SATURDAY

21

1980 JOE STRUMMER was arrested by the German police after he smashed a guitar over a fan's head at a Hamburg concert. The audience were demanding the Clash play 'White Riot'. The Clash were demurring.

1977 THE CLASH were arrested after a show at St. Albans Civic Hall. The police who stopped their van discovered keys and towels from a Newcastle hotel. Strummer and Nicky Headon were allowed to go free on bail of £20 each.

1976 THE ROLLING STONES started their stint at Earl's Court, their first London shows in three years. There were six nights in all — May 21-23 and 25-27. The very lavishness — phallic confetti launcher, flower shaped hydraulic stage — of their show and the difference of their performance did as much as anything to fuel the fires of the embryonic punk movement, giving the punks for the first time a visible 'enemy' to despise, a very necessary thing for building youth movements.

➤ **1968 BRIAN JONES** was arrested on cannabis charges. He appeared at Marlborough Street Magistrates Court and was released on £2000 bail.

1968 PETE TOWNSHEND married Karen Astley, his clothes designer, at Didcot Registry Office.

1965 THE WHO released 'Anyway, Anywhere, Anyhow' and appeared on Ready Steady Go, wearing 'Pop Art' clothes for the first time. (They were designed, of course, by Townshend's future wife.)

➤ **1948 LEO SAYER** born, Shoreham, Sussex.

1941 RONALD ISLEY born, Cincinnati, Ohio.

SUNDAY

22

1980 ENGELBERT HUMPERDINCK was named the father of a three year old illegitimate child by a court and ordered to pay the mother £2,500 and £50 per week maintenance. The mother, Kathy Jetter, revealed that the relationship had started when Humperdinck had invited her to sit on his lap at a concert four years earlier.

1954 JARRY DAMMERS (Specials) born, Coventry, Warwickshire.

1954 BOB DYLAN celebrated his Bar Mitzvah.

1950 BERNIE TAUPIN born, Sleaford, Lincolnshire.

M A Y

M O N D A Y

23

1973 CLIVE DAVIS was fired as head of Columbia Records, accused of fiddling his expenses. When he returned from being told by Columbia chairman, Arthur Taylor, his office was already stripped bare. Straightaway, he set up Arista Records with backing from Columbia Pictures — which has no connection with Columbia Records.

▶ **1967 JOHN COLTRANE** played his last show. The revolutionary of the saxophone got out of his sick bed to help start a series of Sunday concerts at the Olatunji Center of African Culture in Harlem.

▶ **1963 ELMORE JAMES** died of asthma. Chicago bluesman come up from Mississippi, he built his entire career — as Peter Guralnick has pointed out — on one song, the cascading slide guitar rhythms of Robert Johnson's 'Dust My Broom'. Never has so much power been fashioned from so little.

1934 ROBERT A. MOOG, inventor of the Moog electronic synthesiser, born.

1918 BUMPS BLACKWELL born. Number two to Art Rupe at the Los Angeles based independent, Specialty, Blackwell was sent to clean up the dirty blues of 'Tuttu Frutti' and provided the right chaos for the poetry of rock'n'roll's favourite screaming queen.
Awwopbopaloobopalopbamboom, indeed.

T U E S D A Y

24

1971 BOB DYLAN visited the Wailing Wall in Jerusalem, the holiest of all Jewish monuments, on his thirtieth birthday.

1969 MICK JAGGER AND MARIANNE FAITHFULL's house in Cheyne Walk, London was raided by the police who arrested them for possessing marijuana. They were released on £50 bail each.

▶ **1958 JERRY LEE LEWIS**, the fire-breathing, demon chasing Faust of the rock'n'roll piano, ran into a little trouble on his British tour when the British press became suspicious about the age of his new wife, Myra. "Mah wife is cute. She might look young and be young, but she is growed," he'd told the press a few days earlier. On this day, however, all was revealed. Myra was thirteen, not the fifteen that they'd been led to believe, and Jerry had married her before the divorce from his second wife had been finalised. Prompted for an explanation, he was reported as saying: "Myra and I are legally married. It was mah second marriage that wasn't legal. Ah was a bigamist when ah was sixteen. Ah was fourteen when ah was first married. That lasted a year, then ah met June. One day she said she was goin' have mah baby. Ah was real worried. Her father threatened me, and her brothers were hunting me with hide whips. So ah married her just a week before mah divorce from Dorothy. It was a shot-gun wedding." The British press and public, not satisfied by this perfectly charming explanation, forced Jerry Lee to cancel the tour after three dates. This humiliation effectively marked the end of his career till his rebirth as a country star in the sixties and his re-acceptance in the more tolerant atmosphere of the seventies.

1944 PATTI LABELLE born, Philadelphia.

1941 BOB DYLAN, (Robert Allen Zimmerman) born, Duluth, Minnesota.

W E D N E S D A Y

25

1981 ROY BROWN died of a heart attack, 65, Los Angeles. An R&B pianist and singer, he cut harsh jump blues tracks with a pulse that prefigured rock'n'roll by half a dozen years. His stormiest recording, 1947's 'Good Rockin' Tonight', was covered by Presley at one of his very earliest recording sessions.

1968 THE ROLLING STONES released 'Jumpin' Jack Flash', their first British number one for two years.

1965 SONNY BOY WILLIAMSON II, blues harmonica player, died, Helena, Arkansas.

▶ **1958 PAUL WELLER** born, Woking, Surrey.

▶ **1926 MILES DAVIS** born, Alton, Illinois.

1921 HAL DAVID, Burt Bacharach's lyricist, born, NYC.

1981
'Being With You'
Smokey Robinson

#1 US 45
1969
'Get Back'
Beatles

#1 UK 45
1968
'Young Girl'
Gary Puckett and the Union Gap

THURSDAY

26

1974 BERNADETTE WHELAN, a fourteen year old fan, attended a David Cassidy concert at London's White City. In the crush of fans at the front, she had a heart attack. She died four days later without regaining consciousness, prompting a horrified Greater London Council to place new, very stringent safety restrictions on all pop concerts in the city. Although intended to protect life, they were also used to 'uphold moral standards'. Former GLC Arts Committee Chairman, Bernard Brooke-Partridge, used them to stop the Sex Pistols performing anywhere in the London area.

1963 THE BEATLES played the Liverpool Empire on their first national tour. The heroes' first return.

► **1956 CHUCK BERRY** recorded 'Roll Over Beethoven', his fourth single.

1944 VERDEN ALLEN (Mott The Hoople) born.

1942 LEVON HELM (The Band) born, Marvell, Arkansas.

1938 JACKIE LIEBESIT (Can) born.

1933 JIMMIE RODGERS, 'The Singing Brakeman', the first hillbilly star, died of TB, aged 35, in New York City.

1932 FRANKIE LAINE (LoVecchio) started a dance marathon in Atlantic City, New Jersey which lasted till October 18, a total of 3501 hours, breaking the world record and netting him and his partner, Ruth Smith, five hundred bucks a piece.

1962
'Good Luck Charm'
Elvis Presley

FRIDAY

27

► **1977 THE SEX PISTOLS** released their first single on Virgin Records, 'God Save The Queen'.

1964 A COVENTRY HEADMASTER suspended boys from his school for wearing their hair 'Rolling Stones style', only allowing them back when they'd had it trimmed neatly...like the Beatles.

1964 SCREAMING LORD SUTCH, an eccentric British pop star of sorts, launched his own pirate radio station on a disused British War Department sea fort.

1957 THE CRICKETS released their first single, 'That'll Be The Day', featuring Buddy Holly as singer and rhythm guitarist.

1957 SIOUXSIE SIOUX (Susan Ballion) born, London.

► **1943 CILLA BLACK** (Priscilla Maria Veronica White) born, Liverpool.

1935 RAMSEY LEWIS born, Chicago.

1972
'Oh Girl'
Chi-Lites

SATURDAY

28

1981 MARY LOU WILLIAMS died of cancer, 71. 'The queen of Kansas City pianists in the twenties and thirties'.

1969 MICK JAGGER AND MARIANNE FAITHFULL arrested at their London house for possession of marijuana and released on bail of £50 each.

1959 STEVE STRANGE (Harrington) born. Dilletante supreme. Singer and songwriter (with Visage), club-owner, 'New Romantic' clothes horse, 'scene maker'. A Warholian superstar without a Warhol to dignify his transcience.

1945 JOHN FOGERTY born, Berkeley, California.

1944 GLADYS KNIGHT born, Atlanta, Georgia.

1938 PRINCE BUSTER (Campbell) born, Kingston, JA.

1910 T-BONE WALKER, blues guitarist, born, Linden, Texas.

1966
'When A Man Loves A Woman'
Percy Sledge

SUNDAY

29

1981 BRUCE SPRINGSTEEN played London for the first time since 1975 when a Columbia Records publicity campaign with the tag line 'At last London is ready for Bruce Springsteen' backfired badly, having given him an impossible reputation to live up to.

1977 THE JAM pulled out of a Clash tour when they discovered that, as a band signed to a major label, they were expected to cover some of the expenses of the unsigned bands.

ROGER McGUINN played his first solo show since the demise of the Byrds, at the New York Academy of Music.

► **1949 GARY BROOKER** born, Hackney, London.

1949 FRANCIS ROSSI (Status Quo) born, London.

1965
'Long Live Love'
Sandie Shaw

MONDAY

30

1978 SWANSONG RECORDS announced that Led Zeppelin were in the studio, their first attempt at recording since Robert Plant's son was killed in July 1977.

1959 'OH BOY', the British pop TV show master-minded by Jack Good — the man who'd shout 'Limp, you bugger, limp' at Gene Vincent from the wings — was broadcast for the last time. The 'star studded' cast of the final show included Cliff Richard, Marty Wilde and Billy Fury.

➤ **1955 NICKY HEADON** (The Clash) born, Bromley, Kent.

1867 THE NATION, an American periodical, carried a report on a black Christian church service. "...the benches are pushed back to the wall when the formal meeting is over, and old and young, men and women, all stand in the middle of the floor, and when the 'sperichil' is struck up begin first walking and by and by shuffling around, one after the other, in a ring. The foot is hardly taken from the floor, and the progression is mainly due to a jerking, hitching motion which agitates the entire shouter and soon brings out streams of perspiration. Sometimes they dance silently, sometimes the song itself is also sung by the dancers. But more frequently a band, composed of some of the best singers and of tired shouters, stand at the side of the room to 'base' the others, singing the body of the song and clapping their hands together or on the knees. Song and dance are alike extremely energetic, and often, when the shout lasts into the middle of the night, the monotonous thud, thud of feet prevents sleep within half a mile of the praise house.'

TUESDAY

31

1976 THE WHO played at Charlton Athletic football ground, getting themselves into the Guinness Book Of Records as the loudest band ever. Tasco provided the PA which consisted of eighty 800 watt Crown DC 300A amps and twenty 600 watt Phase Linear 200 amps, a total power output of 76,000 watts, giving a volume level of 120 db at fifty metres.

1975 THE ROLLING STONES announced that year's Tour Of The Americas (North and South) by speeding past the press conference, playing live on the back of a flat-bed truck; this was the first time Ron Wood played with them 'onstage'.

➤ **1947 JOHN BONHAM** (Led Zeppelin) born, Birmingham.

1944 MICK RALPHS (Mott The Hoople, Bad Company) born.

1940 AUGIE MEYER, Tex Mex organist who tasted teeny bop fame with the Sir Douglas Quintet in the mid-sixties, born.

JUNE

WEDNESDAY

1

1973 ROBERT WYATT, rather the worse for wear at a party, fell from a window, breaking his spine. Despite never walking again, his work has reached a new mischevious maturity. Not long after, he confounded all those who'd held up his drumming with the Soft Machine as high art by recording a cover of the Monkees' 'I'm A Believer', even appearing on Top Of The Pops to promote it. More recently, he cut an acapella version of the war-time folk song 'Stalin Wasn't Stallin'', a suitably combative record from a confirmed Communist Party member and as unexpectedly beautiful as the short wave radio broadcasts from Iran of which Mr. Wyatt is a particular fan.

1967 THE BEATLES' 'Sgt. Pepper' was released in Britain.

1964 THE ROLLING STONES landed at JFK airport to start their first American tour.

➤ **1953 THE PRISONAIRES**, all long-term inmates at the Tennessee State Penitentiary, Nashville, were escorted to the Sun studios in Memphis under armed guard. A vocal group, they recorded two tracks, 'Baby Please' and 'Just Walking In The Rain'.

1950 DECCA RECORDS introduced the first British 33⅓ long players.

1948 SONNY BOY WILLIAMSON I (John Lee Williamson), blues harmonica player, was beaten up on leaving the Plantation Club in Chicago. Somehow, he got himself home where he died of a bust skull and internal haemorrhaging

➤ **1947 RON WOOD** born, Hillingdon, Middlesex.

#1 US 45
1980
'Funky Town'
Lipps Inc.

#1 UK 45
1964
'You're My World'
Cilla Black

#1 US 45
1963
'It's My Party'
Leslie Gore

THURSDAY

2

1980 GLEN MATLOCK, the bass player and songwriter thrown out of the Sex Pistols for "liking the Beatles", was disqualified from driving for a year after a conviction for drunken driving.

1972 DION AND THE BELMONTS reformed for one night only, for a 'revival' show at Madison Square Gardens. The evening was recorded and released as a live album.

1969 JOHN LENNON recorded his first solo single, 'Give Peace A Chance', in room 1472 at the Hotel La Reine Elizabeth, Montreal. Joining in with John and Yoko were Tommy Smothers on guitar, Timothy Leary, Derek Taylor — the Apple press officer — a Toronto rabbi and a host of others, including local journalists and a TV camera crew. The record was cut on an eight track machine, hired for five hours at a cost of £3,300...And so are anthems created.

1962 ISLAND RECORDS, the UK based independent, issued its first record in Britain, 'Remember'/'Independent Jamaica' by Lord Creator, with the catalogue number W1 001. Like all early Island releases, it was a reggae single, It wasn't till the late sixties that Island's rock acts began to appear on the Island label rather than that of the distributor, Fontana.

► **1959 TONY HADLEY** (Spandau Ballet) born, North London.

1956 GENE VINCENT released his first single, 'Woman Love' — with 'Be Bop A Lula' on the flip.

► **1941 CHARLIE WATTS** born, Islington, London.

FRIDAY

3

1972 MISSISSIPPI FRED McDOWELL, bluesman, died, 68.

1969 DIANA ROSS's two pet dogs died when they scoffed some rat poison left in her dressing room at a Philadelphia night club. She was described as "emotionally upset".

1965 'THE SOUND OF MUSIC' soundtrack went to number one on the British album charts, racking up a total of 68 weeks there over the next three years.

► **1964 RINGO STARR** collapsed and the Beatles brought in Jimmy Nicol as substitute drummer for their Australian and Dutch tours. Never has Andy Warhol's dictum about 'In the future everyone will be famous for fifteen minutes' seemed truer.

1964 THE ROLLING STONES made their debut on American TV, appearing on the Dean Martin show. Mr. Martin was in fine form: "Their hair's not long. It's just smaller foreheads and higher eyebrows".

1959 LITTLE WILLIE JOHN, R&B singer of the original 'Fever' recorded his wildest track, 'Leave My Kitten Alone' at Beltone Studios, NYC.

► **1950 SUZI QUATRO** born, Detroit.

1946 IAN HUNTER born, Shrewsbury. (This is an official birthdate. Ten years earlier is perhaps a more probable.)

1944 MICHAEL CLARKE (Byrds) born, NYC.

1942 CURTIS MAYFIELD born, Chicago.

1942 JOHN G. PEATMAN started to compile the first real charts for his 'Weekly Survey', an American listing of *song* ratings based on combined TV and radio audiences.

SATURDAY

4

1975 THE ROLLING STONES became the first group to receive Russian recording royalties, the result of a change in the Russian copyright laws.

1973 MURRAY WILSON, father of three of the Beach Boys and their manager for a while, died of a heart attack.

► **1963 THE SEARCHERS** released their first single, 'Sweets For My Sweet' which went to number one on the UK charts.

1945 GORDON WALLER, of Peter & Gordon, born.

1940 CLIFF BENNETT born.

SUNDAY

5

1964 THE ROLLING STONES started their first American tour in San Bernadino — the last but one stop on 'Route 66' — supported by Bobby Vee, the Chiffons, Bobby Goldsboro and Bobby Comstock.

1959 BOB DYLAN graduated from Hibbing High School, adding "to join Little Richard", in his graduation book.

1926 BILL HAYES, singer of 'The Ballad Of Davy Crockett', born.

JUNE

MONDAY

6

1981 MAGAZINE, the group formed by ex-Buzzcock, Howard Devoto, broke up four years after they started, unable to make the transition from a large cult to a true mass audience.

1962 THE BEATLES auditioned for EMI at their Abbey Rd. studios under the careful gaze of George Martin. Although really on the look-out for the 'new Cliff Richard' and extremely dubious about their drummer, Pete Best, Martin was impressed enough to consider making a record with them, finally offering a deal the following month.

► **1960 TONY WILLIAMS** left the Platters to start a solo career.

1956 ELVIS PRESLEY appeared on the Ed Sullivan show. Having decided Presley's gyrating hips were rather suggestive, Sullivan and his sponsors asked Presley if he'd mind if they only showed him from the waist up. Elvis demurred. His manager, Colonel Tom Parker, tried to persuade him. "But what do I need that for, Colonel, I already got a Cadillac." "Boy", said the former fairground hustler, "If you do this show, you'll be so famous, you'll be able to afford TEN cadillacs." Elvis appeared on the Ed Sullivan show, from the waist up only.

1944 EDGAR FROESE (Tangerine Dream) born, West Berlin.

1964
'Chapel Of Love'
Dixie Cups

TUESDAY

7

1979 BBC TELEVISION postponed the screening of a documentary on South London reggae poet, Linton Kwesi Johnson, because they felt its 'political content' might be seen as unfair comment on the imminent general election.

► **1970 THE WHO** played the Metropolitan Opera House, NYC, announcing — falsely as it proved — that this would be the final performance of 'Tommy'.

► **1969 THE WHO's** 'Tommy' entered the US album charts.

1969 THE BOB DYLAN/JOHNNY CASH TV special was shown for the first time, on ABC.

1966 CLAUDETTE ORBISON, Roy's wife and the woman for whom he wrote 'Claudette', the Everly Brothers hit, died in a motorbike crash right in front of his eyes.

1963 THE ROLLING STONES released their first single, 'Come On', and appeared on the 'Thank Your Lucky Stars' pop TV show for the first time.

1946 BILL KREUTZMANN JR. (Grateful Dead) born, Palo Alto, California.

► **1940 TOM JONES** born, Pontypridd, South Wales.

1969 BLIND FAITH, the 'supergroup' formed by Eric Clapton, Ginger Baker, Rick Grech and Stevie Winwood, played their first live show, a free concert in London's Hyde Park which drew an audience of 150,000. It turned out to be their only British show; they broke up shortly after the release of their only studio album and completing their only American tour.

1969
'Dizzy'
Tommy Roe

WEDNESDAY

8

1979 THE SPECIALS started their first national tour, in Canterbury, Kent.

1972 JIMMY RUSHING, urbane blues singer, died.

1969 BRIAN JONES announced he was leaving the Rolling Stones, commenting, "I no longer see eye to eye with the discs we are cutting".

1967 LAVERNE ANDREWS, one of the 1940s close harmony vocal swing group, the Andrews Sisters, died.

► **1965 BOB DYLAN** recorded an hour-long show for British TV which was broadcast in two half-hour sections in June.

► **1962 BOB DYLAN's** girlfriend from his early days in New York, Suze Rotolo, left him, sailing to Italy with her mother.

1962 THE NEW MUSICAL EXPRESS published an album chart for the first time.
1. 'Blue Hawaii' — Elvis Presley.
2. 'West Side Story' (Soundtrack).
3. 'It's Trad, Dad' (Soundtrack).
4. 'South Pacific' (Soundtrack'.
5. 'The Young Ones' — Cliff Richard (Soundtrack).

1947 MICK BOX (Uriah Heep) born, Epping, Essex.

1944 BOZ SCAGGS born, Ohio.

1940 NANCY SINATRA born, Jersey City, New Jersey.

1974
'Diamond Dogs'
David Bowie

T H U R S D A Y

9

1972 DAVID BOWIE released 'Ziggy Stardust', introducing the world-at-large to bisexual chic.
1972 ELVIS PRESLEY played New York City for the first time.
1970 BOB DYLAN was awarded an honorary degree by Princeton University.
► **1960 BING CROSBY** was awarded the first ever platinum disc, for selling two hundred million records. (Current platinum targets are: singles, USA, two million, UK, one million; albums, USA one million, UK, three hundred thousand.)
1941 JON LORD (Deep Purple, Whitesnake) born, Leicester.
1932 JACKIE WILSON born, Detroit.
► **1929 JOHNNY ACE** (John Marshall Alexander) born, Memphis.
1923 LES PAUL (Lester Polfus) electric guitar and recording pioneer (and the man Gibson named the guitar after) born.

1958
'Purple People Eater'
Sueb Wooley

F R I D A Y

10

1977 CLASH members, Joe Strummer and Nicky Headon, were arrested for failing to show up at a court hearing — they were appearing in a different court at the time, unable to switch the date of either appearance — and taken up to Morpeth in the north of England where they spent the weekend in jail. In court on the Monday, Strummer was fined £60 for stealing hotel pillow cases and a towel, Headon was fined £40 for stealing a hotel key.
► **1967 'COUNTRY JOE AND THE FISH'** entered the US album chart.
1966 THE BEATLES released 'Paperback Writer', the flip of which, 'Rain' was their first record to use reverse tapes.
1966 JANIS JOPLIN played her first show with Big Brother & The Holding Company, at the Avalon Ballroom, San Francisco.
1964 THE ROLLING STONES visited the shrine of big city blues, the Chess studios in Chicago, spending two days recording, presided over by legends they'd only ever dreamed of meeting — Chuck Berry, Muddy Waters, Willie Dixon. The Stones cut fifteen tracks, including 'It's All Over Now', 'Down The Road Apiece', the entire 'Five By Five' EP and four still-unreleased songs.
1941 SHIRLEY ALSTON (Owens), lead singer with the Shirelles, born.
1910 HOWLIN' WOLF (Chester Arthur Burnett), bluesman, born on plantation between West Point and Aberdeen, Mississippi.

1967
'Whiter Shade Of Pale'
Procol Harum

S A T U R D A Y

11

1978 THE ROLLING STONES released their 'Some Girls' album, their first studio offering in two years and their first album to feature Ron Wood as an official recording studio member of the band.
1969 DAVID BOWIE released 'Space Oddity', his first taste of fame which reached number five in the UK charts on original issue and number one on re-issue in 1975.
1965 THE ROLLING STONES released 'Got Live If You Want It!', an EP memento of their shows which featured one track, 'We Want The Stones', which was nothing more than a crowd chant. Clever businessmen as ever, the Stones claimed the composer royalty for it under their usual pseudonym of the time, Nanker, Phelge.

1966
'Paint It Black'
Rolling Stones

S U N D A Y

12

1972 THE SOUND BROADCASTING ACT was passed in Britain, providing for the establishment of 21 commercial radio stations, Britain's first experiment of mainland radio advertising.
1965 THE BEATLES' MBEs (Members of the Order of the British Empire) were announced — for 'services to export'. A handful of Colonel Blimps returned *their* medals in protest.
► **1943 REG PRESLEY** (Troggs) born, Andover, Hampshire.
1942 LEN BARRY, singer of the Dovells' sharp as a pistol 'Bristol Stomp', born, Philadelphia.
1932 CHARLIE FEATHERS born, Hollow Springs, Mississippi.

1965
'Back In My Arms Again'
Supremes

J U N E

M O N D A Y

13

1971 CLYDE McPHATTER died of a combination of liver, heart and kidney diseases in a Bronx hospital. If, like the Vatican itself, the heavenly choir has put a block on using castrati, Clyde McPhatter's almost impossibly clean falsetto should provide the perfect substitute. The sweetest of all R&B lead singers, McPhatter was the music's eternal virgin, always untrammelled by the implications of the earthy words he was singing. His original version of 'Such A Night' had an innocence that was so at odds with its lyrics, it's only when you hear Presley's bone-crunching version, you realise it's a very sexy, drooling blues. Clyde made it sound like it was part of the Litany. A church-trained singer, of course, he drifted into the secular world first as lead for Billy Ward's Dominoes (with whom he cut 'The Bells', gospel as the theme music for Judgement Day) then as founder and lead singer of the first (1954) incarnation of the Drifters, cutting the politely aggressive 'Money Honey' and a run of chart hits. After a spell in the army, he returned as a solo star with the new sophistication of the swinging finger clicks of 'A Lover's Question', but, after a few hits, left his long-time home, Atlantic records, for a succession of labels which were unable to give his voice the delicate frame it needed. An unworldly angel fallen amongst businessmen.
1969 MICK TAYLOR attended a photo session in London's Hyde Park, his first duty as the Rolling Stones' replacement for Brian Jones.
1942 JAMES CARR, soul singer of 'You Can't Pour Water On A Drowning Man' (truly one of pop music's greatest conceits), born, Memphis.
1940 BOBBY FREEMAN, singer of 'Do You Wanna Dance', born.

#1 US LP
1980
'Glass House'
Billy Joel

T U E S D A Y

14

1974 DAVID BOWIE opened his most elaborate stage expedition, the Diamond Dogs tour, in Montreal.
1970 DEREK AND THE DOMINOES — Eric Clapton's short-lived but sharpest band — played their debut show, at London's Lyceum, Dave Mason played second guitar but left the band before they started their first tour.
1969 THE BEATLES had their last British number one, with 'The Ballad Of John And Yoko'.

#1 US LP
1974
'Band On The Run'
Wings

W E D N E S D A Y

15

1974 MARC BOLAN announced that T. Rex had sold more than 37 million records around the world.
1968 STEVE MILLER's 'Children Of The Future' entered the US album chart.
1967 PETER GREEN left the John Mayall band to form the original Fleetwood Mac.
1966 THE BEATLES released the original version of their American album, 'Yesterday And Today'. As some kind of bizarre way of getting back at their record label, Capitol, who were issuing the album without the Beatles' full approval, they gave them as cover art a shot of the Fab Four, dressed in white coats and surrounded by hunks of meat and dismembered baby dolls.
1958 'OH BOY' was first broadcast on British TV.
1956 JOHN LENNON AND PAUL McCARTNEY met for the first time, at the Woolton Parish Church fete. Lennon, 16, drunk and playing unaccomplished banjo, was with his band, the Quarrymen. Paul, 14, not drunk, was introduced, impressing Lennon immensely — not only could he actually tune a guitar but he knew the real words to Eddie Cochran's '20 Flight Rock' and Gene Vincent's 'Be Bop A Lula'.
Some time later, Paul was asked to join the Quarrymen. Even later, they changed the band's name to the Beatles.
1950 NODDY HOLDER (Slade) born, Walsall, Staffordshire.
1947 DEMIS ROUSSOS born, Alexandria, Egypt.
1943 JOHNNY HALLIDAY (Jean-Philippe Smet) born, Paris. French rocker who always looked the business and sounded like that's all it was.
1941 HARRY NILSSON born, Brooklyn.
1937 WAYLON JENNINGS born, Littlefield, Texas.

#1 US 45
1963
'Sukiyaki'
Kyu Sakamoto

THURSDAY
16
1979 BBC TELEVISION revived 'Juke Box Jury' for a short, unhappy time.
1978 THE CLASH released 'White Man In Hammersmith Palais', a searingly ambiguous tribute to both reggae in particular and black culture in general.
► **1978 SID VICIOUS** released 'My Way', a searingly ambiguous tribute to stardom and late night drunks' dreams.
1973 GARY GLITTER played London's Raindow Theatre, the crescendo of his 'Glitter Over England' tour.
1970 LONNIE JOHNSON, blues guitarist, died, 81, in a Toronto car crash.
1967 THE MONTEREY POP FESTIVAL opened. Lasting 'til June 18, it had a bill which included Jimi Hendrix (his first US show with the Experience), the Who (showing Americans how to destroy consumer durables), Otis Redding (sucking up to the "love crowd") and Janis Joplin.
1964 THE ROLLING STONES flew back from an American tour to honour a previously-booked date at Oxford's Magdalen College. The fee was £100, the airfares were £1500.
► **1954 GARRY ROBERTS** (Boomtown Rats) born.
1941 LAMONT DOZIER, the middle third of Motown songwriting and production partnership Holland-Dozier-Holland, born, Detroit.

FRIDAY
17
► **1981 PAULINE BLACK** played her last show with former 2 Tone band, the Selecter.
1976 IAN DURY AND THE KILBURNS, the short-lived successor to Kilburn and the High Roads, played their final show, at London's Walthamstow Town Hall, supported by the Stranglers and the 101'ers, Joe Strummer's first professional band.
1966 PETER GREEN joined the John Mayall band, the British academy for aspiring young white bluesmen.
1954 RECORD MIRROR published its first edition.
1944 CHRIS SPEDDING born, Sheffield, Yorkshire. Have guitar, will travel...and get extremely well paid for it. Session guitarist, dressed up as a Womble to promote a record on Top Of The Pops, turned down the offer of a regular job with the Rolling Stones, made the worst-ever punk record (with the Vibrators), once headed a band called Sharks, crossed egos with Jack Bruce, worked with the Battered Ornaments, played guitar on P&O luxury liners, fleshed out some of Bryan Ferry's limper conceits, had a pop floss hit with 'Motorbikin'', can imitate any guitarist you can name better than they could do it themselves, became a member of a New York new wave no hope outfit, wrote the string parts for a Donovan album. Little wonder he's so confused he's never stood still long enough to make a half-way decent record under his own name.

SATURDAY
18
► **1961 BEN E. KING's** 'Stand By Me', Leiber & Stoller's adaptation of an old gospel song, topped the American R&B charts.
1949 COLUMBIA RECORDS (USA) announced that they'd sold 3½m 33 rpm records in the year since they'd introduced the new microgroove long players.
1947 BARRY MANILOW born, Brooklyn.
1942 PAUL McCARTNEY born, Liverpool.

SUNDAY
19
1973 CLARENCE WHITE, Byrds drummer, hit by a car and thrown seventy five feet. in Lancaster, California, died after spending several days unconscious.
1970 HOTLEGS released 'Neanderthal Man'. Three of the band — Kevin Godley, Eric Stewart and Lol Creme — later formed 10 CC.
1967 PAUL McCARTNEY admitted to taking LSD.
► **1964 THE BEATLES** released their fieriest collection, the 'Long Tall Sally' EP.
1956 BILL DOGGETT, at a recording session in NYC's Beltone Studios, cut 'Honky Tonk Parts One And Two', a number two US pop hit.

PARLOPHONE
THE BEATLES
LONG TALL SALLY
mono

J U N E

M O N D A Y

20

1981 GERRY COTT left the Boomtown Rats.
1981 BERNE TORMÉ left Gillan.
1980 MARTIN ATKINS was sacked by Public
Image Ltd.
1977 PAUL COOK, Sex Pistols' drummer, was attacked
outside a West London pub.
1971 DAVID BOWIE was amongst the acts at the
Glastonbury Fayre festival. Some of the performers were
collected on a live triple album on Revelation put together
by Elvis Costello's future manager, Jake Riviera, or as he
then was, Andrew Jakeman.
1960 JOHN TAYLOR (Duran Duran) born, Solihull,
Warwickshire.
► **1958 KELLY JOHNSON** (Girlschool) born, Edmonton,
London.
1953 ALAN LONGMUIR (Bay City Rollers) born, Edinburgh.
► **1942 BRIAN WILSON** born, Hawthorne, California.
1937 ROBERT JOHNSON's last recording session, in the
back of a Dallas office building. The Prometheus of the Delta
blues and the man who wrote the patent on every slide
guitar riff you ever heard, he cut his two most terrifying
songs, 'Hellhound On My Trail' and 'My And The Devil Blues'
'Early this morning when you knocked upon my door,
I said "Hello Satan, I believe it's time to go".
Me and the devil was walking side by side,
I'm going to beat my woman until I get satisfied.'
He was dead by the end of the year. Poisoned by a jealous
girlfriend, according to one. Shot in a fight, to another. Or
perhaps he'd had the evil eye put on him. Or maybe — in
that wonderful phrase used to describe Dylan — he'd not so
much burned the candle at both ends as applied a
blowtorch to the middle till it melted clean away.
1936 BILLY GUY, lead singer on the Coasters' 'Searchin'',
born, Attasca, Texas.
► **1924 CHET ATKINS** , guitarist, born, Luttrell, Tennessee.

T U E S D A Y

21

1981 STEELY DAN's Donald Fagen and Walter
Becker admitted that their fourteen year long
partnership had dissolved.
1980 THE STRANGLERS were accused of
starting a riot at Nice University in the South of France.
Three of them were arrested, two were let off but Jean
Jacques Burnel was let out on £10,000 bail.
1966 REG CALVERT, a pirate radio worker, was shot dead
by someone from a rival station, an event which did little to
prolong the life of Britain's pirate radio ships.
1965 THE CHARLATANS, the most legendary of all San
Francisco bands (i.e. they were so awful everyone wanted to
forget them but couldn't), played their first show, at the Red
Dog Saloon, Virginia City, Nevada.
1948 COLUMBIA RECORDS (USA) showed their new 33⅓
rpm long players to the press for the first time.
1946 BRENDA HOLLOWAY born, Atascadero, California.
► **1944 RAY DAVIES** born, Muswell Hill, London.
1932 LALO SCHIFRIN born, Buenos Aires, Argentina.

W E D N E S D A Y

22

1978 DR. FEELGOOD topped the bill at the fifth
anniversary party of London's Dingwalls Dance
Hall.
1969 JUDY GARLAND, the soap opera heroine
they wouldn't have dared dream up, died from an overdose
of pills.
1967 MICK JAGGER AND KEITH RICHARDS's trial arising
from the raid on Richards' country home, Redlands, earlier
that year opened at Chichester assizes.
1963 LITTLE STEVIE WONDER released 'Fingertips', the
second part of which gave him his first hit record.
1948 TODD RUNDGREN born, Philadelphia.
1947 HOWARD KAYLAN (Turtles) born, New York.
1944 PETER ASHER born, London.
1936 KRIS KRISTOFFERSON born, Brownsville, Texas.
1846 ADOLPHE SAX patented the saxophone, his first
successful musical invention after failures with the saxhorn
(an early bugle) and the saxo-trombo (an upright horn).

#1 UK 45
1959
'Roulette'
Russ Conway

#1 UK LP
1962
'West Side Story'

#1 UK 45
1968
'Jumpin' Jack Flash'
Rolling Stones

#1 UK 45
1973
'Rubber Bullets'
10 CC

T H U R S D A Y

23

1972 SMOKEY ROBINSON AND THE MIRACLES sang their final show together, at Madison Square Gardens, New York City.
1970 RINGO STARR flew to Nashville to start work with the best of the local session men on what was to become his second solo album, the country 'Beaucoups Of Blues'.
1967 JOHN ENTWISTLE married Alison Wise, London, telling the *Daily Express*, ''On our first date, Alison carried my amplifier''.
1964 THE ROLLING STONES flew back to London's Heathrow Airport from their first American tour to be greeted by the classic welcome of the Beat Boom, thousands of screaming teenage girls.
► **1940 ADAM FAITH** (Terence Nelhams) born, London.
1929 JUNE CARTER, country singer, wife of Johnny Cash and mother-in-law of Nick Lowe, born, Maces Springs, Virginia.

#1 UK 45
1974
'Always Yours'
Gary Glitter

F R I D A Y

24

1978 GENESIS toped the bill over Jefferson Starship at the annual Knebworth festival, held in the grounds of a stately home twenty miles north of London.
1977 'LIVE AT THE ROXY', the compilation of the delights of the crib of punk, was released.
► **1965 JOHN LENNON's** second book, 'Spaniards In The Works', was published.
1947 MICH FLEETWOOD born, London.
1945 COLIN BLUNSTONE born, Hatfield, Hertfordshire.
1944 JEFF BECK born, Surrey.
1944 ARTHUR BROWN born, Whitby, Yorkshire.
1944 CHARLIE WHITNEY (Family) born, Skipton, Yorkshire.
1944 CHRIS WOOD (Traffic) born, Birmingham, Warwickshire.

#1 UK LP
1977
'Muppets'

S A T U R D A Y

25

1973 'TUBULAR BELLS' was performed live for the first time, at London's Queen Elizabeth Hall, with then Rolling Stone, Mick Taylor, on guitar.
1967 THE BEATLES recorded 'All You Need Is Love' live on the 'Our World' TV show, carried around the globe by satellite to an estimated 150m viewers.
1966 THE BEACH BOYS played a 'Summer Spectacular' at the Hollywood Bowl, supported by The Lovin' Spoonful, Chad and Jeremy, the Outsiders, Percy Sledge, the Sir Douglas Quintet, the Leaves, Love, Captain Beefheart and the Byrds.
1949 BILLBOARD changed the name of their black charts from 'race' to 'R&B' (rhythm and blues).
1945 CARLY SIMON born, New York.
1935 EDDIE FLOYD, singer of 'Knock On Wood', born, Montgomery, Alabama.
1925 CLIFTON CHENIER, undisputed king of black Louisiana bayou music, Zydecko, born, Opelousas, Louisiana.

#1 UK LP
1968
'Ogden's Nut Gone Flake'
Small Faces

S U N D A Y

26

1981 BOB DYLAN played the first of six nights at London's Earls' Court arena, his first British dates since his conversion to fundamental Christianity.
► **1975 CHER's** divorce from Sonny Bono was finalised.
► **1973 MARSHA HUNT** started her — eventually successful — paternity suit against Mick Jagger.
1970 DAVID BOWIE released 'Memory Of A Free Festival'.
1964 THE ROLLING STONES released 'It's All Over Now', their first single recorded in America and first number one.
1956 GENE VINCENT recorded 'Who Slapped John' at Owen Bradley's studios.
1955 MICK JONES (The Clash) born.
► **1943 GEORGIE FAME** (Clive Powell) born, Leigh, Lancashire.
1910 'COLONEL' TOM PARKER, Elvis Presley's manager, born, West Virginia. (At least, that's what he claims. Goldman's recent book on Elvis appears to have unearthed the revelation that the fervent patriot, Tom Parker, was in fact a Dutch-born illegal immigrant.)

J U N E

M O N D A Y

27

1981 MOTORHEAD's 'No Sleep Till Hammersmith' entered the UK album charts at number one.

1971 THE FILLMORE EAST, NYC, closed down with a final show by the Allman Brothers and J. Geils.

1968 ELVIS PRESLEY started to tape his first ever TV special, for NBC. A comeback in more ways than one, it was his first live show since the turn of the decade and the first time he'd sung with a small, tight R&B group since his first year at RCA. The show itself was a compromise — between his manager who wanted production numbers, tuxedos and Christmas songs, and the producer who wanted rock'n'roll. Elvis settled the issue by singing 'Blue Christmas' in black leather while the lead guitarist shouted out 'Play it dirty, play it dirty' and following it up with the deep gospel of 'Where Could I Go But To The Lord', sung in the tux. (The rock'n'roll sections were taped on June 27 and 29, the production number on June 30.)

1967 MICK JAGGER AND KEITH RICHARDS were sentenced at Chichester court. Jagger was found guilty of possessing pep pills and fined £100 and given a six months jail sentence. Richards was found guilty of allowing his house to be used for smoking marijuana, fined £500 and given a year's sentence. Jagger was sent to Brixton jail while Richards went to Wormwood Scrubbs.

1964 THE ROLLING STONES appeared as the entire panel of BBC TV's 'Juke Box Jury'.

1944 BRUCE JOHNSTON (Beach Boys) born, Chicago.

1925 DOC POMUS born, Brooklyn. The musical half of the Pomus/Shuman song-writing team, constructors of some of the toughest R&B written by whites in the fifties. The Coasters' lip-smacking 'Young Blood', the Drifters' rhapsody in rhythm and blues 'Save The Last Dance For Me' and Presley's grittiest pop, 'Mess Of Blues', 'Little Sister', 'Surrender' and 'His Latest Flame'.

1885 PATENTS were applied for on the 'Graphophone', the earliest record player.

T U E S D A Y

28

1973 RICHARD NADER promoted a British Re-Invasion Show at Madison Square Gardens, presenting sixties stars (or, at least, starlets) Herman's Hermits, Gerry and the Pacemakers, Billy J. Kramer, the Mindbenders and the Searchers.

'CROSBY, STILLS AND NASH' entered the US charts.

W E D N E S D A Y

29

1979 LOWELL GEORGE, the spiritual force of Little Feat, died. Officially, of a heart attack.

1975 TIM BUCKLEY died, the victim of a heroin overdose, Los Angeles. Often dubbed a folk-singer or, even worse, psychedelic folk-singer, Buckley far transcended the limits of that particular catch-all. While it's true you could hear the nasal tones of Bob Dylan in his strange, plaintive voice, you could also hear Frank Sinatra, Howlin' Wolf, Hendricks and Smokey Robinson. As powerful as he was delicate, he sounded as dissipated as Gram Parsons, only he was obviously enjoying it a whole lot more than country's poor little rich boy. His 'Greetings From L.A.' must be the most mature, most graphic album ever made about sex — where others would have blurred the issue by being spiritual, Buckley was unashamedly physical.

1973 IAN GILLAN played his last show as Deep Purple's lead singer — he'd given in his notice the previous October — at the Koseinenkin Hall, Osaka, Japan.

1969 SHORTY LONG, the gravel behind 'Here Comes The Judge', died aged 29 when his boat sank off Sandwich Island, Ontario.

1969 THE JIMI HENDRIX EXPERIENCE played their final show, in front of 40,000 in Denver. The police celebrated the occasion by tear-gassing the audience.

1954 SKETCH (Peter Martin) of Linx, born, Silvertown, London.

1948 IAN PAICE (Whitesnake) born, Hounslow, London.

1945 LITTLE EVA (Eva Narcissus Boyd) born, Bellhaven, North Carolina.

THURSDAY

30

1981 JERRY LEE LEWIS was rushed to hospital with ruptured stomach and assorted ulcers. Later he recalled "lyin' on the bathroom floor actually feelin' the life leavin' my body."

1979 JOHNNY ROTTEN AND JOAN COLLINS, an actress, appeared as panellists on BBC TV's revived 'Juke Box Jury'.

1967 MICK JAGGER AND KEITH RICHARDS were released from jail on bail of £7000 each, pending the outcome of their appeal against drugs convictions.

JULY

FRIDAY

1

1979 ELO announced that they intended to send a hot air balloon round Britain rather than tour that summer.

1972 'HAIR' closed on Broadway after 1729 performances.

1969 SUN RECORDS was sold by its founder and owner, Sam Phillips, to Shelby Singleton's new company, Sun International Corporation, in which Phillips became a minority shareholder.

1967 THE TIMES ran a leader criticising the sentences passed on Keith Richards and Mick Jagger for drugs offences. Head-lined 'Who Breaks A Butterfly On A Wheel?', it concluded 'It should be the particular quality of British justice to ensure that MR. JAGGER is treated exactly the same as anyone else, no better and no worse. There remains a suspicion that MR. JAGGER received a more severe sentence than would have been thought proper for any purely anonymous young man'.

1965 THE FCC ruled that AM radio stations would only be allowed to duplicate fifty percent of their material on their FM affiliates, the ruling which, more than anything else, was responsible for the emergence of FM rock radio.

1956 ELVIS PRESLEY made his TV debut, appearing on the Steve Allen show, singing 'Hound Dog' to a Bassett hound while dressing in top hat and tails.

► **1946 DEBBIE HARRY** born, Miami, Florida.

1939 DELANEY BRAMLETT born, Pontotoc, Mississippi.

SATURDAY

2

1966 'THE FUGS' entered the US album charts.

1956 ELVIS PRESLEY, at his fourth recording session for RCA, cut three tracks at their New York studios — 'Don't Be Cruel', 'Anyway You Want Me' and, in thirty takes, 'Hound Dog'.

1954 PETE BRIQUETTE (Boomtown Rats) born.

1926 LEE ALLEN, lyrical New Orleans R&B tenor sax player, born, Pittsburgh, Kansas.

SUNDAY

3

1981 A FOUR SKINS' show at the Hamborough Tavern in West London's predominantly Asian community of Southall provoked a racial riot, the young locals feeling — not unnaturally — that the band's aggressively Aryan name and skinhead following were a very direct form of racial provocation.

1976 BRIAN WILSON played his first stage show with the Beach Boys for twelve years, Anaheim Stadium.

► **1971 JIM MORRISON** was found dead of heart failure in his Paris bathroom. That's the facts. The legends have it that he overdosed, that he was dragged there from a local nightclub, a local brothel, or simply never died, just disappeared to cool out a little and forgot to come back.

► **1969 BRIAN JONES** died, 25, drowning in the swimming pool of his Sussex country house while the Stones were at Olympic studios, working on their first official recordings without him. Rumours have it that he died when two gangsters sent to put the frighteners on him over some drug debts stuck his head in a bucket of water, prompting an asthma attack. Scared, they dumped him, alive, into the pool.

1950 JONA LEWIE born, Southampton.

1940 FONTELLA BASS born, St. Louis, Missouri.

#1 UK LP
1973
'That'll Be The Day'
(Soundtrack)

#1 UK 45
1972
'Take Me Back 'Ome'
Slade

#1 UK 45
1977
'So You Win Again'
Hot Chocolate

4 Albums.
Police
Talking
Heads.

#1 US LP
1967
'Sgt. Pepper'
Beatles

Ry Cooder.
Peter Gabriel.

JULY

MONDAY

4
1976 THE RAMONES made their UK debut, playing an American Independence Day celebration with the Flamin' Groovies at London's Roundhouse, introducing England to the basic thrash that formed the style of just about every punk group except the original four — The Pistols, The Clash, The Damned and Buzzcocks.
1973 DAVID BOWIE announced his retirement onstage at Earl's Court. Later, it emerged that he only meant that Ziggy Stardust, not his creator, was retiring.
1971 DONALD McPHERSON, lead singer of The Main Ingredient, died of leukemia.
1969 GRAND FUNK RAILROAD played the Atlanta Festival, the show which brought them to national attention — down the bill from Blood Sweat And Tears, Janis Joplin and Creedence Clearwater Revival.
► **1952 A BRITISH RECORD** topped the US singles charts for the first time — Vera Lynn's 'Auf Wiedersehen, Sweetheart'
1948 JEREMY SPENCER, Fleetwood Mac guitarist who left to join the Children of God, born.
1938 BILL WITHERS born, Slab Fork, West Virginia.
1900 LOUIS ARMSTRONG born, New Orleans.

TUESDAY

5
1978 EMI RECORDS stopped the printing of the Rolling Stones' 'Some Girls' sleeve after some of those portrayed on it had complained.
1975 PINK FLOYD played the annual Knebworth Festival, the London music business' drunken day out in the country, supported by Capt. Beefheart and Steve Miller.
► **1969 THE ROLLING STONES** played a free concert in London's Hyde Park in front of the largest audience ever assembled in Britain — 600,000 according to some estimates. Jagger read a piece of Shelley's poetry as a tribute to Brian Jones then let loose the boxes of white butterflies they'd assembled to mark the start of the show. Unfortunately, because of the heat, the butterflies, rather than soaring away, slumped to their death, like a thick white snow over the first few rows. Brian would've understood.
1954 ELVIS PRESLEY invented rock'n'roll, recording 'That's Alright, Mama' after hours of failed attempts at Sun Studios. Sun's Sam C. Phillips had tried to record Presley before — notably with a version of a demo he had, 'Without You', in the Spring of that year — but, although the voice was wonderful, he couldn't get *quite* the feel he wanted. Dean Martin songs, country ballads, pop tunes, they'd tried them all. In desparation, Phillips asked Presley if he knew anything else. The young man in the pink suit immediately suggested a mid-forties blues he remembered, title 'That's Alright, Mama'. The rest is, of course, history.
1950 ANDY ELLISON (John's Children, Jet, Radio Stars) born.
► **1943 ROBBIE ROBERTSON** born, Toronto.
1920 SMILEY LEWIS (Overton Amos Lemons), New Orleans R&B singer and guitarist, born, Union, Louisiana.

WEDNESDAY

6
1976 THE DAMNED played their first proper show, at London's 100 Club.
1973 QUEEN released their first single, 'Keep Yourself Alive'/'Son And Daughter'.
► **1971 LOUIS ARMSTRONG** died of lung and heart disease, 71, New Orleans.
1967 BRIAN JONES was hospitalised, a victim of 'strain'.
1965 JEFFERSON AIRPLANE played their first show, at Martin Balin's San Francisco club, the Matrix.
1964 'A HARD DAY'S NIGHT' had its Royal premiere at the London Pavilion cinema (now an opera house).
1959 JOHN KEMBLE (Spandau Ballet) born, North London.
► **1939 JET HARRIS** (Shadows) born, Kingsbury, London.
1937 GENE CHANDLER (Eugene Dixon) born, Chicago.
1932 DELLA REESE (Dellareese Taliaferro) born, Detroit. Gospel singer who worked with Mahalia Jackson at the age of fourteen and had a million seller with 'Don't You Know' in 1959.
1925 BILL HALEY born, Highland Park, Michigan.

T H U R S D A Y

7
1975 KEITH RICHARDS was charged in Arkansas with possession of an offensive weapon — a knife — and reckless driving. Let out after hordes of teenage girls had besieged the jail, he even had the charge dropped, letting Freddie Sessler stand trial for it.

1968 THE YARDBIRDS broke up. Or rather, everyone except Jimmy Page left, giving him just three weeks to put a new band together for a Swedish tour they were contracted to play. The grup he found for the tour, later renamed themselves Led Zeppelin.

▶ **1952 LYNVAL GOLDING** (Specials, Fun Boy Three) born, St. Catherine, Jamaica.

1940 RINGO STARR (Richard Starkey) born, Liverpool.

1932 JOE ZAWINUL (Weather Report) born, Vienna, Austria.

1927 CHRISTOPHER STONE became the first British radio DJ, broadcasting a record show for the BBC from their Savoy Hall studio.

F R I D A Y

8
1978 JOE STRUMMER AND PAUL SIMONON of The Clash were arrested after some hanky panky at the Glasgow Apollo and fined for being drunk and disorderly.

1972 DAVID BOWIE played a 'Save The Whale' benefit for the Friends of the Earth at London's Royal Festival Hall, bringing on his friend, Lou Reed, for an encore of 'White Light/White Heat', 'I'm Waiting For The Man' and 'Sweet Jane'.

▶ **1969 MARIANNE FAITHFULL** ended up in hospital after taking a drugs overdose in Sydney, Australia. There to work on 'Ned Kelly' with Jagger, her overdose meant she was written out of the film.

1964 PAUL McCARTNEY presented his father with a picture of a racehorse as a sixty second birthday gift. Very nice, thought Macca the Elder, but what do I want a picture of a horse for. "Then Paul must have seen my face because he said 'It's not just a picture, Dad. I've bought you the bloody horse'."

S A T U R D A Y

9
1974 THE CROSBY, STILLS, NASH AND YOUNG reunion tour opened in Seattle. Neil Young travelled separately.

▶ **1955 BILL HALEY's** 'Rock Around The Clock' became the first white rock'n'roll record to top the US charts, staying there for eight weeks.

1946 MITCH MITCHELL (Jimi Hendrix Experience) born, London.

1916 JOE LIGGINS, R&B singer of 'Pink Champagne', born.

S U N D A Y

10
1981 JERRY LEE LEWIS was given a fifty/fifty chance of survival by doctors performing abdominal surgery at the Memphis Methodist Hospital.

▶ **1975 CHER** petitioned Greg Allman for divorce, a mere ten days after their marriage.

1964 THE BEATLES had an extremely hectic day. They released both the single and the album of 'A Hard Day's Night'. They were met by 150,000 people thronging the streets of Liverpool for the local premiere of the film 'A Hard Day's Night'. And George Harrison was slightly hurt when he crashed his Jaguar.

1954 GENE HOLDER (dBs) born, Philadelphia.

1954 ATLANTIC RECORDS had the front cover of *Cashbox* to themselves. Beneath a photo of Jerry Wexler, Ahmet Ertegun and Miriam Anderson (all label executives) was a caption which read: '(they) sit before a gallery of their stars, all of whom won top Rhythm and Blues honours in *The Cashbox* Disk Jockey Poll. Ruth Brown was voted 'The Most Programmed Female Vocalist'. The Clovers were 'The Most Programmed Vocal Group'. The Drifters were named 'The Up and Coming Vocal Group'. And Joe Turner received two honours. His 'Honey Hush' was 'The Most Programmed Record' while he himself was voted 'The Most Programmed Vocalist'. Quite a lineup for one record firm.'

▶ **1941 JELLY ROLL MORTON**, died in Los Angeles.

#1 US 45
1962
'The Stripper'
David Rose and his Orchestra

#1 US 45
1972
'Lean On Me'
Bill Withers

#1 UK 45
1978
'You're The One That I Want'
Olivia Newton John and John Travolta

#1 UK LP
1976
'Night On The Town'
Rod Stewart

JULY

MONDAY

11

1969 THE ROLLING STONES released 'Honky Tonk Women', their first recording since Brian Jones was replaced by Mick Taylor.

1966 DELMORE SCHWARTZ died. A great poet, an even better short story-writer ('In Dreams Begin Responsibilities'), also a former teacher and an obsession of Lou Reed, who's written at least two songs about Schwartz — 'European Son' and 'My House'. "Before he died", Reed said, "he was on a drunken binge with me, he had his arm around me and he said: 'You know, I'm going to die one of these days...', he was one of the unhappiest people I knew, he said: 'You can write and if you sell out and there's a heaven from which you can be haunted, I'll haunt you'."

► **1938 TERRI GAITHWAITE** (Joy Of Cooking) born.

1938 DEE CLARK born.

1931 TAB HUNTER (Arthur Andrew Kelm) born.

1937 GEORGE GERSHWIN, broadway song writer, died in a Maryland hospital during an operation for the removal of a cystic tumour.

#1 UK 45
1981
'Ghost Town'
Specials

TUESDAY

12

► **1970 JANIS JOPLIN** played her first show with her final group, the Full Tilt Boogie band, in Louisville, Kentucky.

► **1969 BLIND FAITH** made their American debut at Madison Square Gardens, NYC.
The band that gave brief but incessant currency to the word 'supergroup'. Formed from the ashes of Cream by Eric Clapton and Cream drummer, Ginger Baker, they took in bassist Rick Grech — from Family — and Stevie Winwood — on one of his many short holidays from Traffic. They made one almost wilfully inconsistent studio album and recorded a live double on this American tour — their only tour *anywhere* — which is a spiralling descent into heavy metal with what tunes there are fighting a hopeless battle to clamber through the murk.

1962 THE ROLLING STONES deputised for Blues Incorporated — who were doing a radio show — at the Marquee, their first real show.

1942 JERRY WILLIAMS JR./SWAMP DOGG born. Not so much Jekyll & Hyde as a living example of Freud's Id and Superego conflict. JWR's a neat, precise, speedy soul singer and producer. The Dogg's a night-rider with a voice like fat thrown on the fire, prying nightmares from a diseased brain, never recording for the same company twice, writing songs about there being a hole in Daddy's arm where he puts his money.

► **1941 ROY HARPER** born, Manchester. A singer and writer who's persistently kept to the fringe of the pop business. He's worked with the Floyd, he's sung on a Led Zeppelin album but mostly he's hidden away, dreaming up a lost but unromantic past where old cricketers don't die...they just leave their crease.

1912 WOODY GUTHRIE born, Okemah, Oklahoma. Not so much a folk-singer as the creator of a mythical America where every cowboy, every factory hand, every miner spoke a plain but poetic tongue where the land truly belonged to all, where gangsters gave away their money to impoverished widows, where 'the people' were the font of all that's good and true. Like all the best myths, it nourished a generation, giving Dylan, Baez and their contemporaries a natural language for their early, fumbling attempts at songwriting.

#1 UK 45
1975
'Tears On My Pillow'
Johnny Nash

WEDNESDAY

13

1981 A BLACK TEENAGER was stabbed to death at London's Rainbow Theatre during a concert by Black Uhuru, a reggae group much given to preaching of peace.

1974 RONNIE WOOD played the first of two nights of solo shows at London's Kilburn State theater. Amongst his band is Keith Richards.

1973 QUEEN released their debut album, 'Queen'.

► **1942 JIM McGUINN** (Byrds) born, Chicago. (He changed his name to Roger in 1968 after converting to the Subud faith.)

#1 UK LP
1974
'Caribou'
Elton John

THURSDAY
14

1980 MALCOLM OWEN, singer with the British punk band, the Ruts, died of a heroin overdose in his bath.

1977 THE SEX PISTOLS appeared on Top Of The Pops for the first time, performing their third single, 'Pretty Vacant'.

1973 THE EVERLY BROTHERS announced that they were breaking up the partnership after sixteen years together and over thirty five million records sold.

1972 VAN MORRISON released one of the great parenthetical statements, 'Jackie Wilson Said (I'm In Heaven When You Smile)'.

1939 VINCE TAYLOR born, London. For a brief flash, England's only true rockabilly. When he sung 'Brand New Cadillac' he was the cheap hood of rock'n'roll dreams. Gaunt, empty eyes, cleaning his nails with a switch-blade, passionately unconcerned. He was instantly forgetten at home but the French — always suckers for leather-clad myths — canonised his sneer, made him a star of sorts on their rock'n'roll circuit, keeping him well supplied with brown ale and Brylcreem.

1962
'I Can't Stop Loving You'
Ray Charles

FRIDAY
15

1958 JOHN LENNON's mother, Julia, died in a Liverpool car accident.

1946 LINDA RONSTADT born, Tucson, Arizona.

1940 TOMMY DEE, author of 'Three Stars', the disc commemorating the deaths of Buddy Holly, the Big Bopper and Richie Valens, born.

1937 GEORGE GERSHWIN was buried in two funerals. One in New York where the body was and one in Hollywood where — Hollywood being Hollywood — the body wasn't.

1957
'Teddy Bear'
Elvis Presley

SATURDAY
16

1981 HARRY CHAPIN, politically active singer and writer, died when his car collided with a truck, on Long Island. It's estimated that his benefit concerts had raised $5m for a variety of causes.

1977 JOHNNY ROTTEN was interviewed by Capital Radio's Tommy Vance, revealing an unusual musical taste which has Peter Hammill rubbing shoulders with the reggae singer Dr. Alimantado's 'Reasons For Living'.

1974 JOHN LENNON was ordered to leave the USA by the Justice Department who gave him sixty days to pack his bags. Lennon immediately lodged an appeal.

1969 LED ZEPPELIN were amongst the variety of acts on offer at the Newport Folk Festival.

1966 CREAM was formed by Eric Clapton, Jack Bruce and Ginger Baker.

1959 THE COASTERS recorded 'Poison Ivy' and 'What About Us' in New York, helped out by the epic tenor sax of King Curtis.

1952 STEWART COPELAND (The Police) born, Alexandria, Virginia.

1941 DESMOND DEKKER born, Kingston, JA.

1966
'Hanky Panky'
Tommy James and the Shondells

SUNDAY
17

1974 THE MOODY BLUES opened the first quadraphonic recording studio in London.

1968 'YELLOW SUBMARINE' had its world premiere at the London Pavilion.

1967 JOHN COLTRANE, jazz 'giant of the tenor saxophone', died, NYC, of primary hepatoma, a cancer of the liver.

1959 BILLIE HOLLIDAY (Eleanora Fagen), 'Lady Blue', jazz singer, died (aged 44) of a heroin overdose, NYC.

1959 THE COASTERS recorded 'I'm A Hog For You', New York.

1952 PHOEBE SNOW born, NYC.

1949 GEEZER BUTLER (Black Sabbath and, according to the rest of the group anyway, a man with "a great brain") born.

1942 SPENCER DAVIS born, Swansea, Wales.

1939 CAB CALLOWAY recorded 'Jumpin' Jive', the first R&B million seller.

1891 HAILE SELASSIE, reggae's greatest star, born, Ethiopia.

1960
'Alley Oop'
Hollywood Argyles

J U L Y

M O N D A Y

18

1975 BOB MARLEY recorded his show at London's Lyceum, producing both the live album and the terribly sad 'No Woman No Cry' single.

1970 PINK FLOYD played a free concert in London's Hyde Park, previewing their forthcoming album, 'Atom Heart Mother'. The show was so extensively bootlegged that, by the time the official album emerged, everybody who was interested already owned a copy of the music.

1946 TIM LYNCH (Flamin' Groovies) born.

1941 MARTHA REEVES born, Detroit.

►**1939 DION** (DiMucci) born, the Bronx. If this were a just world, Dion would be Mayor of New York City or, at the very least, he would have been given the lead role in 'West Side Story'. An archetypal Italian street corner kid made good, he and the Belmonts (named after a Bronx thoroughfare) were always the sharpest, best-dressed, classiest pop doo wop singing group of the late fifties. Where others fell right back on that street corner, Dion survived. He turned down the offer of a lift in the plane that killed Buddy Holly. He came through years of junkiedom. He resisted the temptation to reform the Belmonts as a fixture on the oldies circuit. He still sings, still sounds joyfully pained. Maybe one day they'll rename it Dion and the Belmonts Avenue.

1939 BRIAN AUGER born, London.

►**1929 SCREAMIN' JAY HAWKINS** (Jalacy Hawkins) born, Cleveland, Ohio. A messenger from the underworld. A former Golden Gloves champion, he only quit the fight game when they realised he conquered the opposition by putting a hex on their mortal soul. Taking his voodoo skulls and mojo bones to Okeh, he cut 'I Put A Spell On You', a track that plays the demonic possession of Robert Johnson's 'If I Had Possession Over Judgement Day' as Grand Guignol. He appeared onstage creeping out of a coffin, he was baptized in wine, sung 'Constipation Blues', flicked a staff with snakes crawling around its stem, dallied with women who put 'the whammy' on him, ate live babies as a preparation for his shows. Personally, though, I'm inclined to doubt the latter. Toddlers would have been more his mark.

T U E S D A Y

19

1980 DAVID BOWIE made his stage acting debut in the 'Elephant Man', Denver, Colorado.

1954 ELVIS PRESLEY released his first single, 'That's Alright, Mama'/'Blue Moon Of Kentucky' (Sun 209), the only record which can truly be said to have changed the world.

►**1947 BRIAN MAY** (Queen) born, Twickenham, London.

1945 BERNIE LEADON (Eagles) born.

W E D N E S D A Y

20

1973 T. REX started a six week tour of America as support to Three Dog Night.

1968 IRON BUTTERFLY's 'In-A-Gadda-Da-Vida' entered the US album chart.

1968 JANE ASHER, appearing on BBC TV's 'Dee Time', announced that her engagement to Paul McCartney was over. This was the first McCartney — who was watching TV at a friend's — had heard about it.

1965 BOB DYLAN released his first real rock'n'roll single, 'Like A Rolling Stone'.

►**1965 THE LOVIN' SPOONFUL** released their first single, 'Do You Believe In Magic'. (Trying to remember the days that John Sebastian once made good records is indeed like trying to tell a stranger 'bout rock'n'roll.)

1947 CARLOS SANTANA born, Autlan, Mexico.

1940 BILLBOARD published their singles chart for the first time. Tommy Dorsey's 'I'll Never Smile Again' was the first number one.

►**1943 JON LODGE** (Moody Blues) born.

1872 THE FIRST RADIO PATENT was issued for 'Improvements In Telegraphing', a paper written by Dr. Mahloon Loomis on July 21, 1864 and demonstrated in October 1866.

1964
'It's All Over Now'
Rolling Stones

1975
'Give A Little Love'
Bay City Rollers

1956
'Why Do Fools Fall In Love?'
Frankie Lymon and the Teenagers.

THURSDAY

21

1948 CAT STEVENS (Stephen Georgiou) born, London.
1942 KIM FOWLEY, the greatest of all Angelano hustlers, born, Manila, the Philippines — where his parents had been interned by the Japanese army of occupation.
1931 PLAS JOHNSON, R&B sax player, born, New Orleans.

FRIDAY

22

1972 HAWKWIND's 'Silver Machine' entered the UK top twenty, the space warriors' only hit.
1969 ARETHA FRANKLIN was arrested for causing a disturbance in a Detroit car park. Having posted a $50 bond, she ran down a road sign on her way out.
➤ **1946 ESTELLE BENNETT** (Ronettes) born.
1946 DON HENLEY (Eagles) born.
1940 GEORGE CLINTON born.
1937 CHUCK JACKSON, soul singer, born, Winston-Salem, North Carolina.

SATURDAY

23

1977 LED ZEPPELIN member, John Bonham, and their manager, Peter Grant, beat up one of the security guards at the Oakland Festival, for being "rude to John Bonham's child". Both were heavily fined and given conditional discharges.
1976 THE 101'ERS released their first single, 'Keys To Your Heart', and broke up. Their singer, Joe Strummer, having seen the future — in John Rotten's performance with the Sex Pistols — decided it worked and plumped for forming The Clash with Mick Jones and Paul Simonon.
1965 THE BEATLES released 'Help', their tenth single.
➤**1962 TELSTAR**, an American satellite, made the first trans-Atlantic television transmission. It excited British record producer, Joe Meek, so much he immediately wrote an instrumental about it and phoned his band, the Tornadoes, who were backing Billy Fury at Great Yarmouth, to get them to come back to London for a recording session the following weekend. Released later that same year, it spent twenty five weeks on the British charts and sixteen on the US charts, becoming Meek's first gold disc.
➤**1947 DAVID ESSEX** (Cook) born, East London.
➤**1946 ANDY MACKAY** (Roxy Music) born.
1943 TONY JOE WHITE born, Oak Grove, Louisiana.
1937 CLEVELAND DUNCAN, lead singer on the Penguins' doo wop day dream 'Earth Angel', born.

SUNDAY

24

1972 BOBBY RAMIREZ, drummer with Edgar Winter's White Trash, died (aged 23) in a knife fight off Rush Street in Chicago. One of his assailants turned himself in and was charged with first degree murder.
1965 BOB DYLAN's 'Like A Rolling Stone' entered the US singles chart.
1964 A ROLLING STONES concert in Blackpool turned into 'Britain's biggest ever rock riot'. Held in the Empress Ballroom on the last night of the annual Glaswegian holiday fortnight, trouble began to develop during the Executives' support set. Then, during the Stones show, the more drunken members of the 9000-strong audience started to spit at Brian Jones. Keith Richards took umbrage and struck back. In the ensuing mêlée, a Steinway grand piano was dragged from the stage and prepared for a matchstick factory, chandeliers were pulled down from the ballroom's ceiling. Seventy policemen were brought in to help the ballroom's own thirty security staff. Fifty people went to hospital and the ballroom was damaged to the tune of £3000. "Later that night", Bill Wyman explained, "..our road manager went back to get our equipment. He came into our hotel room with little pieces of wood and metal. 'Here's your amp', he'd say, and give us a chip..."
➤**1942 HEINZ** (Burt), the first male peroxide blonde of British pop, born, Hargen, Germany.

J U L Y

M O N D A Y

25

1969 CROSBY, STILLS, NASH AND YOUNG played their first show as a four-piece, at the Fillmore East, NYC.

1968 JANIS JOPLIN released her second album, 'Cheap Thrills', the original cover and title of which — 'Cheap Thrills, Drugs And Sex' — had been given the bum's rush by her record company, Columbia. She and her band, Big Brother and The Holding Company, got a gold album on advance sales alone.

1965 BOB DYLAN played his first rock'n'roll set, at the Newport Folk Festival. Introduced by Peter Yarrow of Peter, Paul & Mary, Dylan surprised everyone — including the show's organisers — by bringing on with him the Paul Butterfield Blues Band and tumbling into raucous, neurotic 'Maggie's Farm', his electric guitar whining as loud as his nasal voice. Even worse, he no longer even dressed like a folk singer. Just back from a British tour, he was dressed for a night out at the Ad Lib — black leather jacket, frilly shirt, black jeans and the ultimate symbol of Swinging London, Cuban heeled boots. The audience were horrified, refused to clap even 'Like A Rolling Stone' and someone shouted out 'Go Back to the Ed Sullivan show'. Dylan stormed off stage, returning for an encore where he rammed the point of his alienation from his audience home even further by playing 'It's All Over Now, Baby Blue', albeit on acoustic guitar. "I did not have tears in my eyes", Dylan told his biographer, Anthony Scaduto, "I was just stunned and probably a little drunk."

1956 THE 'ANDREA DORIA', a passenger liner, collided with the Swedish steamer, 'The Stockholm', off Nantucket Island. Fifty four people died but Mike Stoller survived to carry on his song-writing partnership with Jerry Leiber.

1943 JIM McCARTY (Yardbirds) born.

T U E S D A Y

26

1979 THE CLASH's debut album, 'The Clash', was released in the USA, in slightly modified form, two years after it first came out in the UK. the UK.

1974 JOE POPE'S STRAWBERRY FIELDS FOREVER FAN CLUB organised the first-ever Beatle Convention, Boston, Massachusetts.

1968 JEANNIE C. RILEY recorded 'Harper Valley PTA', the first record issued on the Plantation label owned by Shelby Singleton Jr. (who, the following year, would buy Sun Records from its founder, Sam Phillips). In two weeks, it was at number one on the US charts having sold 1,750,000 copies.

1963 THE NEWPORT FOLK FESTIVAL started its annual three day stint featuring Dylan, Peter Paul & Mary, Joan Baez, Tom Paxton and Phil Ochs amongst a host of authentic Ivy League folkies. Dylan duetted on 'With God On Our Side' with Joan Baez, his latest flame and the woman who used to put librium in his coffee to calm him down.

1949 ROGER TAYLOR (Queen) born, Kings Lynn, Norfolk.

1943 MICK JAGGER born, Dartford, Kent.

1941 BOBBY HEBB, singer of 'Sunny', born, Nashville.

1941 BRENTON WOOD (Alfred Jesse Smith), singer of 'Gimme Little Sign', born, Shreveport, Louisiana.

W E D N E S D A Y

27

1974 LIGHTNIN' SLIM (Otis Hicks), Louisiana bluesman, died, aged 61, from a stomach tumour, Pontiac, Michigan.

1971 GEORGE HARRISON announced the concerts for Bangladesh, then a country being ravaged by a civil war.

1956 PAUL COOK (former Sex Pistol) born.

1944 BOBBIE GENTRY born, Chickasaw County, Mississippi.

1929 HARVEY FUQUA born, Louisville, Kentucky. The voice behind Harvey and the Moonglows' 'Ten Commandments Of Love', a doo wop epic of lost and found love (with only nine commandments) that was banned by BBC radio for being sacreligious. When the Moonglows split up in 1959, he went into record production and A&R, first with Chess, then with Motown and finally on his own.

#1 US 45
1970
'(They Long To BE) Close To You'
Carpenters

#1 UK 45
1969
'Honky Tonk Women'
Rolling Stones

#1 UK LP
1974
'Band On The Run'
Paul McCartney and Wings

THURSDAY

28 **1973 THE 'SUMMER JAM' FESTIVAL** was held at Watkins Glen, New York. A one day show featuring the Grateful Dead, the Allman Brothers Band and the Band, the music was carried by twelve sound towers and it attracted the biggest ever audience (as ratified by the Guinness Book of Records) to a pop festival, 600,000, only 150,000 of whom actually paid.

1970 'NED KELLY', the first film to be shown featuring the acting of Mick Jagger, premiered in Glenrowan, Melbourne, Australia, a small town where Kelly, an Australian Robin Hood once lived.

► **1962 RACHEL SWEET** born, Akron, Ohio.

1949 STEVE PEREGRINE TOOK (Tyrannosaurus Rex) born, London.

1948 SIMON KIRKE (Free) born, Chelsea, London.

1945 RICK WRIGHT (Pink Floyd) born, London.

FRIDAY

29 **1974 CASS ELLIOTT** (Ellen Naomi Cohen) choked on a sandwich and died (aged 33) of a heart seizure in the same London house where Keith Moon died. The coroner discovered that most of her heart tissue had turned to fat.

1972 CHUCK BERRY starred in a special in-concert show for BBC TV. For once Berry was given a backing band who actually seemed to know his music and it must have put him in a good mood — at the end of the first song, 'Roll Over Beethoven', he drawled, dry and cool as a pimp, "Thank you, we thought we'd open with a Beatles' number". The bootleg of the show, '625', remains the best live recording of The Man available.

1971 GEORGE BYINGTON, a security guard at a Who concert in Forest Hills, New York, was beaten unconscious and stabbed to death by another security guard.

1966 BOB DYLAN fell off his Triumph 500 motorbike near his Woodstock home, breaking his neck. Dylan went into seclusion, possibly using it as the best possible excuse for a rest after his blitzkreig assault on the world over the previous two years.

► **1964 'HELP'**, the Beatles' second film, had its world premiere at the London Pavilion.

SATURDAY

30 **1970 THE ROLLING STONES** announced that Allen Klein, their erstwhile manager, had no 'authority to negotiate recording contracts on their behalf in the future'.

► **1958 KATE BUSH** born.

1954 HANK BALLARD AND THE MIDNIGHTERS, at a Washington D.C. recording session, cut 'Annie Had A Baby', an answer record to Etta James' R&B hit, 'The Wallflower (Dance With Me Henry)'.

1945 DAVID SANBORNE, session sax player, born, Tampa, Florida.

1936 BUDDY GUY, Chicago blues guitarist, born, Lettsworth, Louisiana.

SUNDAY

31 **1976 THE MIAMI SHOWBAND's** van was stopped by the IRA at the Irish border. Three of the band were shot dead; the rest were wounded but survived to carry on the band.

1971 THE CONCERT FOR BANGLADESH, organised by George Harrison, was held over the next two nights. Helping George out were Leon Russell, Eric Clapton, Ringo Starr, Billy Preston and Bob Dylan.

1970 THE ROLLING STONES' contract with Decca Records expired.

1967 MICK JAGGER AND KEITH RICHARDS' drug convictions came before London's Appeal Court. Richards' conviction for allowing his house to be used for smoking marijuana was set aside and Jagger's three months was altered to a conditional discharge.

► **1964 JIM REEVES**, country singer, died, 39, when his light plane failed to avoid a Tennessee mountain.

1946 BOB WELCH (Fleetwood Mac) born, California.

1941 PAUL ANKA born, Ottawa, Canada.

A U G U S T

M O N D A Y

1

1980 HAZEL O'CONNOR released her most successful single, 'Eighth Day'.

1970 'PERFORMANCE', Mick Jagger's film acting debut, had its world premiere. Also the directing debut of Donald Cammell and Nicholas Roeg — who's since worked with other rock 'n' roll singers, David Bowie in 'The Man Who Fell To Earth' and Art Garfunkel in 'Bad Timing'. It was made in 1968 but held up for two years by potential distributors, Warner Brothers, who were dismayed at the film's contents. Almost shockingly direct for a big budget sixties feature film, it described with lingering matter-of-factness the sexual and pharmaceutical adventures of the twin spirits of Jagger — who plays a faded rock star, living out a decadent, hermitic-like existence in a West London house — and James Fox — who arrives at Jagger's house as a small-time, anal retentive gangster. Certainly, the film was explicit enough for Roeg to be forced to cut out Jagger fucking both Michele Breton and Anita Pallenberg — which was the last nail in the coffin of the relationship between Pallenberg and Brian Jones. Although this scene was later shown, at the Amsterdam Wet Dream Festival, the film is edited with such kaleidoscopic fury and deliberate confusion, it's quite possible that *no* definitive print of the film exists, that Roeg issued different versions on different occasions. While it's undoubtedly a remarkable film, it's quite likely that there's a lot less going on than there appears to be. Equally, given its subject matter and treatment, it's hardly surprising that it was a resounding financial failure, condemned to the untesting zombie world of late night circuit cult status.

1964 JOHNNY BURNETTE, rockabilly legend and pop star, died when he fell off a boat in Clear Lake.

1958 JOHNNY CASH left Sun Records of Memphis for the bright lights and big cheques of Columbia in New York.

1942 JERRY GARCIA (Grateful Dead) born, San Francisco.

1927 THE CARTER FAMILY, the first people to record the ancient hillbilly folk songs which formed the basis of early country music, recorded for the first time, in a temporary studio using portable equipment in Bristol, Tennessee. This, the 'original' Carter Family comprised A.P. Carter, bass vocalist, his wife Sarah Carter, lead singer and autoharp player, and her first cousin, Maybelle Carter, alto singer and lead guitarist. Later versions of the Carter family included their daughter, June, who eventually married Johnny Cash (see above).

T U E S D A Y

2

1980 DEEP PURPLE topped the UK album charts with a greatest hits compilation, 'Deepest Purple', four years after they'd split up.

1972 BRIAN COLE, an original member of the Association, died of a heroin overdose in Los Angeles.

1969 MAX ROMEO's 'Wet Dream' entered the UK singles chart, reaching number ten, despite a ban by BBC radio who decided the song was an obvious piece of filth. Max begged to differ, claimed it was about trying to sleep in a hut with a leaky roof. Nobody believed him; he probably didn't even believe himself.

1969 BOB DYLAN attended his hometown reunion of the Hibbing High School Class of 1960 with his wife, Sarah. Echo Helstrom, his childhood sweetheart, told Anthony Scaduto, Dylan's biographer "He stayed about an hour. And then some dumb-dumb guy tried to start a fight with him and all of a sudden Bob was gone. That town, really impossible."

1937 GARTH HUDSON (The Band) born, London, Ontario.

W E D N E S D A Y

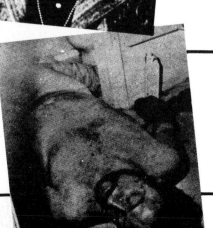

3

1971 PAUL McCARTNEY announced he was forming a band to be called Wings.

1966 LENNY BRUCE (Leonard Alfred Schneider), rock mythologists' favourite comic martyr, died of a morphine overdose in the bathroom of his New York apartment.

1963 THE BEATLES made their final, 294th, appearance at the Cavern.

1956 KIRK BRANDON (Theatre Of Hate) born.

T H U R S D A Y

4 1980 **PINK FLOYD** started a week of concerts at London's Earls' Court, the first live presentation of 'The Wall'.
1972 **10 CC** released their first single, 'Donna'.
► 1970 **JIM MORRISON** fell asleep on an elderly woman's porch in Los Angeles and was charged with public drunkeness — just one day before his trial in Miami for indecent exposure started.
1966 **BEATLES'** records were banned by radio stations in six American cities following John Lennon's casual remark to a British journalist that the Beatles were probably more famous than Jesus Christ.
1940 **FRANKIE FORD**, singer of the hit version of 'Sea Cruise', born, Gretna, Louisiana.
1939 **BIG DEE IRWIN**, singer (with Little Eva) of the hit revival of 'Swinging On A Star', born, New York.
1936 **ELSBERRY HOBBS** (Drifters) born.
1927 **JIMMIE RODGERS**, 'The Singing Brakeman', founder of the Blue Yodelling school of country music, was recorded for the first time, by RCA Victor scout, Ralph Peer, in Bristol, Tennessee, just three days after he'd captured the Carter Family on tape for the first time. Together, the two events made for the week that country music moved out of its hill country hiding place.

F R I D A Y

5 1980 **THE JAM** released 'Start', their tenth single.
1978 **PETE MEADON**, the Who's first manager and writer of their first single, 'Zoot Suit' (which they recorded as the High Numbers), died of barbiturate poisoning at his parents' North London home.
► 1967 **PINK FLOYD** released their first album, 'Piper At The Gates Of Dawn', taking its title from the one chapter of Kenneth Grahame's classic children's fantasy, 'Wind In The Willows' that no child ever manages to read.
1966 **THE BEATLES** released 'Revolver', their seventh UK album.
1957 **AMERICAN BANDSTAND**, hosted from Philadelphia by Dick Clark, became the first networked TV rock'n'roll show. The very first group it presented was the Chordettes.
1957 **JOE HILL LOUIS**, one man blues band who recorded for — amongst a host of other labels — Sun, died (aged 325) of tetanus.
1946 **JIMMY WEBB** born, Elk City, Oklahoma.

S A T U R D A Y

6 1977 **THE SECOND ANNUAL EUROPEAN PUNK FESTIVAL** — and the last, as it happened — opened in the bull ring at Mont de Marsan in the South of France. On the bill were most of the new English punk bands, including the Damned who were introducing their second guitarist, Lu, and the Clash whose set was interrupted by stink bombs courtesy of the Damned's Captain Sensible. The organiser, Mark Zermatti, gave up trying to handle it on the first evening and returned to his four poster bed for the remainder of the weekend. The Jam, when not allowed to top the bill on their night, refused to play and returned to London in a sulk.
1973 **MEMPHIS MINNIE**, Chicago blues singer of 'Me And My Chauffeur Blues', died, Memphis, Tennessee.
1973 **STEVIE WONDER** was seriously injured when his car collided with a logging truck in North Carolina. And he can't say no-one had told him not to drive.
1965 **THE SMALL FACES** released 'Watcha Gonna Do About It', their first single.
1940 **MIKE SARNE**, film director and singer of 'Come Outside', born, London.
► 1938 **ISAAC HAYES** born, Covington, Tennessee.

S U N D A Y

7 1952 **ANDY FRASER** (Free) born.
1936 **CHARLES POPE** (Tams) born, Atlanta, Georgia.
1926 **STAN FREBURG**, creator of the funniest record ever made about pop music, 'The Old Payola Roll Blues', born, Los Angeles.

A U G U S T

M O N D A Y

8

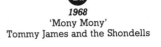

1980 THE GREATER LONDON COUNCIL stopped
the Plasmatics exploding a car onstage, three hours
before their British debut at Hammersmith Odeon.
1978 PETER BARDENS left Camel.
1976 BOSTON released their debut album. The tapes —
which the band had recorded in their home studio — had
been turned down by every record company in New York.
When Epic finally agreed to put out the tapes, they
discovered — probably as much to their own surprise as the
other record companies' — they'd a phenomenon on their
hands. The album, a horrid mish-mash of overproduced
pomp, went platinum in eleven weeks, becoming the fastest-
ever selling debut album.
1973 WEA RECORDS combined the Elektra and Asylum
labels together under the control of David Geffen while
Elektra's founder, Jac Holzman, was promoted to Vice
President of Warner Communications.
1973 STEVE PERRON, lead singer of Chillen and writer of
Z.Z. Top's hit 'Francene', died when he inhaled his vomit
after taking too much of something.
1967 GEORGE HARRISON visited San Francisco's hippie
ghetto, Haight Ashbury.
1965 THE FIFTH NATIONAL JAZZ AND BLUES FESTIVAL,
was held at Richmond-On-Thames, Surrey. On the bill were
the Yardbirds, the Who, the Moody Blues, Georgie Fame,
Manfred Mann, the Spencer Davis Group and, bottom of the
bill, Stempacket featuring Brian Auger, Julie Driscoll, Long
John Baldry and Rod Stewart. Tickets were ten shillings
(50p).
1958 CHRIS 'CHRISSY BOY' THOMPSON (Madness) born,
London.
► **1956 DAVID GRANT** (Linx) born, Hackney, London.
1933 JOE TEX born, Baytown, Texas.
The preacher. Elemer Gantry in black face and on
humanity's side for once. Stax singer with gospel throat and
country philosophy, forever caught between bumping with a
big fat woman and giving the agony aunt advice of 'You
Better Hold What You Got'.

T U E S D A Y

9

1978 MUDDY WATERS played a set at the White
House Lawn Picnic. President Carter had specifically
requested "some of those darkie tunes".
1973 LILLIAN ROXON died, 41, of an asthma attack,
NYC. Rock encyclopedist and woman without whom this
book...etc. etc.
1969 THE MANSON MURDERS, Beverly Hills. Sharon Tate,
eights months pregnant, died with four friends, who were
hanging around her house as company while her film
director and jailbait fancier husband, Roman Polanski, was
away filming in Europe.
1963 'READY STEADY GO', the most over-rated TV pop
show of all time was first broadcast on British TV. The
weekend started here...till December 1966, when the show
was killed off.
► **1962 CHARLIE RICH** recorded the original version of the
country boozers' classic, 'Sittin And Thinkin'', Sam Phillips
Studio, Nashville.

W E D N E S D A Y

10

1972 THE McCARTNEYS were arrested for
possessing drugs in Sweden.
1972 DEREK AND THE DOMINOES' 'Layla'
entered the UK singles chart.
1969 MARLON RICHARDS, a son to Keith Richards and
Anita Pallenberg, born.
1968 THE BAND's first album, 'Music From Big Pink',
entered the US charts.
1968 DEEP PURPLE played their first major UK show, at the
Sunbury Festival.
► **1947 IAN ANDERSON** (Jethro Tull) born, Blackpool.
► **1943 RONNIE SPECTOR** (Veronica Bennett) born, NYC.
1940 BOBBY HATFIELD (Righteous Brothers) born, Beaver
Dam, Wisconsin.
1928 JIMMY DEAN (Seth Ward), singer of 'Big Bad John',
born, Plainview, Texas.

THURSDAY

11

1978 THE JAM released their fifth single, 'David Watts'/"A" Bomb In Wardour St.'.
1963 THE ROLLING STONES played the first Jazz and Blues Festival to be held in Richmond, eighth on a bill topped by Acker Bilk.
1949 ERIC CARMEN born, Cleveland, Ohio.
1914 BUSTER BROWN, R&B singer of 'Fannie Mae', a 1960 pop hit, born, Criss, Georgia.

FRIDAY

12

1970 JANIS JOPLIN sang her final concert before her death, at Harvard Stadium, Cambridge, Massachusetts.
1967 PETER GREEN'S FLEETWOOD MAC played their first live show, at that year's Richmond Jazz and Blues Festival.
1966 THE BEATLES started a US tour, at the Chicago Amphitheatre. Although it was never a conscious decision to abandon playing live altogether, this turned out to be the last series of shows the Beatles ever played.
► **1964 'A HARD DAY'S NIGHT'**, the Beatles' first film, opened simultaneously in five hundred American cinemas.
1949 MARK KNOPFLER (Dire Straits) born.

SATURDAY

13

1978 BEBOP DELUXE, the band formed by serious young guitarist, Bill Nelson, split up.
1976 THE CLASH played their very first show, an invitation only performance at their Rehearsal Rehearsals studio in London's Camden Town.
1972 JOHN LENNON AND YOKO ONO played a benefit show for retarded children at Madison Square Gardens, raising $250,000, supplemented by $300,000 from ABC for the film rights and $60,000 of John and Yoko's own money.
1971 KING CURTIS (Ousley), rock'n'roll's finest and loudest sax player, was stabbed to death outside an apartment block he owned in New York City. He was 37.
1958 FERGAL SHARKEY (Undertones) born, Derry, Northern Ireland.
1952 WILLIE MAE THORNTON cut the original 'Hound Dog' in Los Angeles. Written by white boys Leiber & Stoller in under half an hour, it was an R&B hit, hitting number one in the Spring of 1953, giving Willie Mae her only chart record in a twenty year career. Three years later, Elvis covered it after hearing a bar band play it somewhere.
1921 JIMMY McCRACKLIN, R&B guitarist who hit with 'The Walk', born, St. Louis, Missouri.

I'VE GOT MY BEATLES MOVIE TICKET — HAVE YOU?

SUNDAY

14

1976 STIFF RECORDS released its first single, Nick Lowe's 'Heart Of The City'/'So It Goes', recorded as a publishers demo for a total of £45 with everything played by Lowe, except the drums (played by the Rumour's Steve Golding). Stiff got the money to issue it by borrowing £600 from Dr. Feelgood's manager. As they noted at the time, Motown, started out with about the same amount of cash.
1970 THE FAMILY DOGG, the San Francisco rock venue, closed down, marking — according to those who know — the end of the much vaunted San Francisco sound.
► **1970 STEVE STILLS** was arrested in a San Diego motel when he was found crawling down a corridor, incoherent. He was set free on $2500 bail.
1965 JAMES BROWN's 'Papa's Got A Brand New Bag' topped the US R&B chart.
1958 BIG BILL BROONZY, country blues singer, died of cancer in Chicago.
1958 GLADYS PRESLEY, Elvis's beloved, overweight mother and the woman he shared a bed with till he was thirteen, died of a heart attack.
1956 BERTOLT BRECHT, German Marxist playright and composer of pop hits for Bobby Darin and Louis Armstrong ('Mack The Knife'), the Doors and David Bowie (both 'Alabama Song/Whisky Bar'), died.
1944 TIM BOGERT born, New York.
► **1941 DAVID CROSBY** born, Los Angeles.

A U G U S T

M O N D A Y

15

1980 GEORGE HARRISON published his 'autobiography', 'I, Me Mine', in a limited, signed edition at £148 a copy.

1974 'JOHN, PAUL, GEORGE, RINGO...AND BERT', a musical about a fifth imaginary member of the Beatles by Liverpudlian writer, Willy Russell, opened at London's Lyric Theatre.

➤ **1969 WOODSTOCK MUSIC & ART FAIR**, billed as '3 Days of Peace & Music', opened at Max Yasgur's farm near Bethel, upstate New York. The first night's bill offered Joan Baez, Arlo Guthrie, Tim Hardin, Richie Havens, Incredible String Band, Ravi Shanker and Sweetwater.

1967 THE MARINE OFFENCES ACT became law, making it illegal to operate pirate radio ships and, more tellingly, illegal for British based firms to buy advertising space on the stations. Overnight, pirate radio ships disappeared — with the exception of Radio Caroline which continued its fitful existence for nearly another fifteen years.

1958 BUDDY HOLLY married Maria Elena Santiago in Lubbock, Texas only two weeks after they'd started walking out together.

1950 TOMMY ALDRIDGE (Black Oak Arkansas) born, Nashville.

1877 THOMAS EDISON recorded the words 'Mary had a little lamb' on his 'phonograph or speaking machine' — a hand-operated cylinder covered with tin foil — in Menlo Park, New Jersey. The first recording of sound.

T U E S D A Y

16

1980 JAH WOBBLE left Public Image limited.
1980 BILL WARD left Black Sabbath.
1980 JOOLS HOLLAND left Squeeze.
1980 COZY POWELL left Rainbow.

1977 ELVIS PRESLEY died of a heart attack, aged 42, in his Memphis mansion. With a collection box on his grave for the upkeep of his resting place, Gracelands has come to resemble an efficiently-run shrine for the faithful. A Lourdes or Santiago de Compestela for all those who would be Americans.

➤ **1975 ROBERT PLANT** and his wife Maureen were badly injured in a car crash on a Greek holiday.

1974 THE RAMONES played their first show at CBGBs, the cradle of New York punk. The band had finally come to assume the shape we know and love — Tommy had switched from manager to drummer while Joey had switched from drummer to singer and placard carrier.

1969 WOODSTOCK's second day presented Keef Hartley, Canned Heat, Creedence Clearwater Revival, the Grateful Dead, Janis Joplin, Jefferson Airplane, Mountain, Santana and the Who.

1966 SANDY POSEY, the forgotten heroine of the sixties, released the devastatingly accepting 'Born A Woman'.

1962 THE BEATLES sacked their drummer, Pete Best, replacing him with Ringo Starr, who was until then one of Rory Storme's Hurricanes.

➤ **1945 KEVIN AYERS** born, Herne Bay, Kent.
1945 GARY LOIZZO (American Breed) born.
1941 CHRIS CURTIS (Searchers) born.

W E D N E S D A Y

17

1980 JOHN PHILIPS, formerly of the Mamas and Papas, was accused of running a drug ring in Los Angeles.

1973 PAUL WILLIAMS, of the original Temptations, was found in his car dressed only in his swimming trucks with a bullet through his head. Suicide was assumed.

1969 WOODSTOCK's third night presented The Band, the Jeff Beck Group, Blood, Sweat & Tears, Joe Cocker, Crosby, Stills and Nash, Jimi Hendrix, Iron Butterfly, the Moody Blues and Johnny Winter.

1964 THE KINKS released 'You Really Got Me'.

1963 BOB DYLAN was introduced as a special guest by Joan Baez at her Forest Hills concert in front of 14,000 people, probably the event which broke Dylan out of the New York folk ghetto into the world-wide folk ghetto.

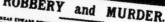

£8000 REWARD

ROBBERY and MURDER.

THURSDAY
18

1979 NICK LOWE married Carlene Carter in Los Angeles.

1978 SIOUXSIE AND THE BANSHEES released their debut single, 'Hong Kong Garden'.

1976 SNIFFIN' GLUE, the first punk fanzine, published its first issue.

1975 DAVID BOWIE released 'Fame', his most successful single and the only one to get him a hit on the soul charts.

► **1969 MICK JAGGER**, while doing location work on 'Ned Kelly' in Australia, was accidentally shot.

1945 NONA HENDRYX born. Street corner singer with the Del Capris, she then sang as one of Patti Labelle's Blue Belles ('I Sold My Heart To The Junkman') who turned into LaBelle, a much camper, much more chic proposition ('Voulez Vouz Coucher Avec Moi Ce Soir') whose shows looked like Dan Dare joins the Black & White Minstrels. In the eighties her harsh, no messing voice resurfaced on Material's 'Bustin' Out' and eventually a new solo career helped by British dilettante, Rusty Egan.

1944 CARL WAYNE (Move) born, Birmingham.

1941 JOHNNY PRESTON, singer of 'Running Bear', born, Port Arthur, Texas.

FRIDAY
19

1977 THE SEX PISTOLS, under the nom de punk, the Spots, played a show in Wolverhampton, one of the dates on a very short, very secret tour.

1977 THE ADVERTS released their second single, 'Gary Gilmore's Eyes' which became their biggest chart success.

1972 DAVID BOWIE finished his Ziggy Stardust tour of Britain at the Rainbow Theatre, London.

► **1951 JOHN DEACON** (Queen) born, Leicester.

1945 IAN GILLAN born, Hounslow, Middlesex.

1943 BILLY J. KRAMER (William Ashton) born, Bootle, Lancashire.

1940 JOHNNY NASH born, Houston, Texas.

1939 GINGER BAKER born, Lewisham, London.

SATURDAY
20

1980 JOHN AND YOKO ONO LENNON began recording the 'Double Fantasy' album at the Record Plant in New York.

1980 THE BRITISH PHONOGRAPHIC INDUSTRIES (BPI) brought 19 people to court for counterfeiting albums, describing them as 'one of the biggest counterfeiting syndicates operating in the UK'.

1977 THE TOM ROBINSON BAND signed to EMI Records.

1965 THE ROLLING STONES released 'Satisfaction' in Britain, four months after it came out in the USA.

► **1951 PHIL LYNOTT** (Thin Lizzy) born.

1947 ROBERT PLANT born, Birmingham, Warwickshire.

1943 ISAAC HAYES born, Covington, nr. Memphis, Tennessee.

1924 JIM REEVES born, Panola County, Texas.

SUNDAY
21

1980 'BREAKING GLASS', the movie that introduced the world to Hazel O'Connor's teeth, opened in London.

1980 LINDA RONSTADT appeared as Mabel in the opening of the revival of Gilbert & Sullivan's 'Pirates Of Penzance' on Broadway.

1976 THE ROLLING STONES head-lined the annual Knebworth summer one-dy festival in the Hertfordshire countryside, supported by amongst others 10 CC and Todd Rundgren. As expected the Stones went on absolutely hours late.

1976 THE FIRST ANNUAL FRENCH EUROPEAN PUNK ROCK FESTIVAL was held at Mont de Marsan in the South of France — without the Sex Pistols who the promoters had thrown off the bill for going 'too far'.

1957 BUDGIE (Siouxsie And The Banshees) born, St. Helens, Lancashire.

► **1952 JOE STRUMMER** (The Clash) born.

1944 JACKIE DeSHANNON (Sharon Myers) born, Hazel, Kentucky.

A U G U S T

M O N D A Y

22

1969 ELVIS PRESLEY made his first public appearance since 1961 when he started a series of shows at the International Hotel, Las Vegas. The show was recorded over the next four nights and released as the live half of the 'From Memphis to Vegas/From Vegas To Memphis' album.

1965 'HELP', the Beatles' second movie, had its US premiere.

► **1956 'LOVE ME TENDER'**, Elvis Presley's first film, went into production.

1938 DALE HAWKINS, the 'Suzy Q' man, born, Goldmine, Louisiana.

1917 JOHN LEE HOOKER born, Clarksdale, Mississippi. Coarse, untutored country bluesman who notched up the bizarre achievement of a UK single hit — 'Dimples' which reached number twenty one in June 1964.

1906 THE VICTOR TALKING MACHINE CO. of New Jersey marketed the first Victrola, a gramophone with a speaker in its cabinet, at a cost of $200.

T U E S D A Y

23

1980 DAVID BOWIE's 'Ashes To Ashes' became his first UK number one single since the re-issued 'Space Oddity' in 1975.

1979 MADNESS released 'The Prince', on 2 tone (TT3). It was one of three tracks they'd recorded at North London's Pathway Studios for two hundred pounds. They'd been lent the money by Warner Brothers Publishing after an earlier session had been abandoned when the drummer couldn't find the studio. 'Madness' and 'My Girl' were the other two tracks cut. In fact, 'The Prince' was a last minute addition, "a sideline, an experiment", as drummer Woody described it.

► **1978 JET BLACK**, a Strangler, was fined £25 for a breach of the peace, Glasgow.

1973 THE READING FESTIVAL, an annual event in the mud of the Thames Valley police authority's manor, presented a bill headed by Traffic, Focus and Eric Burdon.

1970 LOU REED played his last show with the Velvet Underground, at Max's Kansas City, New York, providing six tracks for the Velvet's 'Live At Max's' recorded by Brigid Polk on a cheapie machine. Lou left without saying a word about quitting but never returned, going into a year's seclusion at his parent's Lond Island house, only re-emerging to begin his solo career under David Bowie's jealous eye.

1963 THE BEATLES released 'She Loves You'.

1962 JOHN LENNON married Cynthia Powell at Liverpool's Mount Pleasant Registry Office.

1960 EDWYN COLLINS (Orange Juice) born.

1949 JIM SOHNS born, Prospect Heights, Illinois. Lead singer with the Shadows of Knight who had the big American hit with Van Morrison and Them's barely rstrained sexual fantasy, 'Gloria'.

► **1946 KEITH MOON** born, Wembley, London.

1936 RUDY LEWIS (Drifters) born.

W E D N E S D A Y

24

1965 THE ROLLING STONES met Allen Klein for the first time, in London's Hilton Hotel. Within days he took over the Stones' financial affairs, leaving Andrew Loog Oldham to concentrate on 'personal management'. For the first time, the Stones according to Keith Richards, had enough money to go shopping.

1961 MARK 'BEDDERS' BEDFORD (Madness) born, North London.

1956 STUDIO 51, London's first rock'n'roll club, opened in a Great Newport Street basement — just a spit away from Leicester Square — with Rory Blackwell's Rock'n'Rollers.

1945 KEN HENSLEY (Uriah Heap) born.

1943 JOHN CIPOLLINA (Quicksilver Messenger Service) born, Berkeley, California.

1942 FONTELLA BASS born, St. Louis, Missouri.

1938 MASON WILLIAMS, player and writer of 'Classical Gas', born, Abilene, Texas.

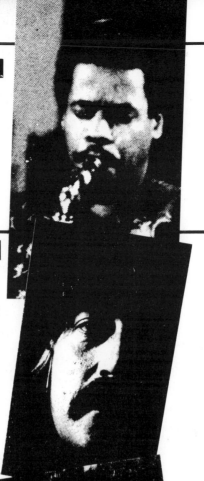

T H U R S D A Y

25

1979 GARY NUMAN released his 'Cars' single.
1978 READING FESTIVAL switched from head-banging to a polite pogo, including on the new wavish bill Sham 69, the Tom Robinson Band, John Ottway and Patti Smith — who informed the crowd that she'd checked out Pope John Paul I on their behalf and found out he was "cool"; he died shortly after.
1973 WINGS lost two members just as they were about to leave for a recording stint in Lagos, Nigeria — guitarist Henry McCullough and, five days later, drummer Denny Siewell.
➤ **1933 WAYNE SHORTER** (Weather Report) born, New Jersey.

F R I D A Y

26

1981 LEE HAYS, co-writer of 'If I Had A Hammer' with Pete Seeger, died of a heart attack, 67.
1977 IAN DURY released the first fruits of his solo career, the 'Sex & Drugs & Rock & Roll' single. Surprisingly, given its later elevation to the anthem of wallies everywhere, it got lousy reviews on release and achieved absolutely no chart success.
1970 THE THIRD ISLE OF WIGHT POP FESTIVAL started with a bill including Jimi Hendrix, the Doors, Richie Havens and Emerson Lake & Palmer.
1967 JIMI HENDRIX's debut album, 'Are You Experienced' entered the US charts.
1967 THE BEATLES journeyed by train to Bangor, North Wales, to sit at the feet of champion giggler Maharishi Mahesh Yogi (aka 'Sexy Sadie').
1967 THE FESTIVAL OF THE FLOWER CHILDREN, the first UK hippie pop festival was held at Woburn Abbey, the stately home of the Duke of Bedford whose wife, according to The People Newspaper, claimed "I thought it was going to be a flower show, with competitions, prizes and lots of flowers."
1957 JOHN O'NEILL (Undertones) born, Derry, Northern Ireland.
1941 CHRIS CURTIS (Searchers) born, Oldham, Lancashire.
1926 GEORGIA GIBBS born.

S A T U R D A Y

27

➤ **1978 JON LORD** joined Whitesnake.
1975 HAILE SELASSIE, Lion of Judah, King of Kings, Jah Rastafari, reggae's master toaster, died. Or, on the other hand, if you're a Rastafarian, he didn't.
1967 BRIAN EPSTEIN, the Beatles manager, took an overdose of Carbitol, anti-depressants, and died at his London home. Whether it was accidental or suicide has never been established beyond doubt. The Beatles returned immediately from Bangor, North Wales where they'd been spending the weekend listening to the priceless dribble of the Maharishi Yogi.
1965 BOB DYLAN released his sixth album and first all rock'n'roll collection, 'Highway 61 Revisited'. Less than a year later, he'd had a close encounter with a different highway near his Woodstock home when he fell of his Triumph 500. (Or didn't, if you're a conspiracy theorist.)
➤ **1956 GLEN MATLOCK** born, Paddington, London.
1950 WILLY DEVILLE born.
1949 SIMON KIRKE (Free) born.

S U N D A Y

28

1978 TELEVISION, following bad reviews of their second album, split up.
1969 MARY, a daughter, born to a Mr. and Mrs. McCartney of London.
1965 THE ROLLING STONES signed a management deal with New York businessman, Allen Klein, and a new recording contract with Decca Records, the same day 'Satisfaction' became their sixth UK top twenty hit.
➤ **1965 BOB DYLAN** was booed for playing an electric set at Forest Hill, New York. In his band were Levon Hulm, Robbie Robertson on guitar, Harvey Brooks on bass and Al Kooper on organ.
1948 DAN SEREPHINE (Chicago) born.

AUGUST

MONDAY

29

1976 THE CLASH made their public debut, at the Screen on the Green cinema, Islington, London, a late night show supporting the Sex Pistols. Also on the bill were Buzzcocks, described by one reviewer as 'rough as a bear's arse'.

1966 THE BEATLES played their last live show before a paying audience, Candlestick Park, San Francisco.

1958 GEORGE HARRISON joined the Quarrymen, the skiffle group started by John Lennon.

► **1958 MICHAEL JACKSON** born, Indiana. That wonderful thing, a black male dizzy blonde. Able to sing just as sweetly, just as powerfully either side of his voice breaking, Michael Jackson had the dumb canary routine down pat. Interviewed, he spouts seamless gabble, all 'love talk', all well-meant banality, with just a little astrology to confuse the enemy. In a recording studio, he can invest the simplest tune, the utter nonsense of 'ABC', the dance floor litany of 'Off The Wall', with a wealth of meanings that can never have occured to the writers. He ven makes McCartney's specious 'Girlfriend' sound profound, an achievement on a par with the Dixie Cups elevation of the deliberately idiotic 'Chapel Of Love' to the highest realms of teenage lovers' prayers. A black, male Marilyn Monroe for the dance floor...and teenage girls' bedroom walls.

► **1924 DINAH WASHINGTON** (Ruth Jones) born, Tuscaloosa, Alabama.

► **1920 CHARLIE PARKER**, the inventor of modern jazz, born, Kansas City, Kansas.

TUESDAY

30

1972 JOHN AND YOKO ONO LENNON played two shows at Madison Square Gardens, New York, for the 'One-to-One' charity for handicapped children.

1968 THE BEATLES released 'Hey Jude', the first single on their own Apple label.

1954 SIR HORACE GENTELMAN (Horace Panter) born, Coventry. Bass player with the Specials — from a background in thick, heavy South Midlands soul — who survived the split which formed the Fun Boy Three only to sink even deeper into the morass of his favourite self-improvement therapy, Exegesis, a cult which numbers Mike Oldfield amongst his adherents. Only believe in yourself, says Exegesis, and everything you wish will come about. Horace's rewards were sneers from the rest of the band and, eventually, his cards from the Specials' toothless Fuhrer, Jerry Dammers. Obviously, Exegesis would argue, this was Horace's most secret desire.

1941 JOHN McNALLY (Searchers) born, Liverpool.

► **1939 JOHN PEEL** (Ravenscroft) born, Liverpool. Somehow he became the only truly important British DJ. As a programmer, he's always hopping on to the latest phase — albeit very quickly, very accurately. After, by his account, a less than happy adolescence, he gained his radio experience working as an American AM DJ in the mid-sixties when *anything* English was fashionable, moving back to England to create the country's first 'progressive' show, 'The Perfumed Garden', on the Radio London pirate ship, finally transferring a more professional version of the same format to Radio One where he's remained ever since. An unreconstructed enthusiast, he's jumped from adoring Jefferson Airplane to the Sex Pistols to D.A.F., never sensing the chasms between the leaps.

1935 JOEN PHILLIPS, formerly of the Mamas & Papas, born, Parris Island, South Dakota.

1919 KITTY WELLS, country singer, born, Nashville.

WEDNESDAY

31

1969 BOB DYLAN played at the second Isle of Wight pop festival, scooping up £38,000 cash for a one hour show. The show was recorded for a live album but, eventually, only four songs were officially released, on the double 'Self Portrait' album.

► **1945 VAN MORRISON** born, Belfast, Northern Ireland.

1939 JERRY ALLISON (Crickets) born.

SEPTEMBER

THURSDAY

1

1980 KEN HENSLEY left Uriah Heep, leaving Mick Box as the only remaining member of the original band.

1979 JIMMY PURSEY reformed Sham 69 after a brief alliance with former Sex Pistols, Steve Jones and Paul Cook.

1972 DAVID BOWIE released his most sexually ambiguous record, 'John, I'm Only Dancing'.

1967 BOZ SCAGGS returned from working as a folk-singer in Denmark to join the Steve Miller Band in time to work on their debut album, 'Children Of The Future'.

➤**1955 BRUCE FOXTON** (Jam) born, Woking, Surrey.

1947 BARRY GIBB born, Douglas, Isle of Man.

1941 ROY HEAD born, Three Rivers, Texas. White soul man from Swamp Country who worked with Crazy Cajun Huey Meaux, Despite churning out a stream of smokey rhythmic grooves, his only hit was the New Orleans pulse of 'Treat Her Right' in 1964.

1933 CONWAY TWITTY (Harold Jenkins) born, Friars Point, Mississippi.

1927 TOMMY EVANS (Drifters) born.

1965 EMI RECORDS announced that they'd sold one million copies in the UK alone of the Beatles' second album, 'With The Beatles'.

1979
'We Don't Talk Anymore'
Cliff Richard

FRIDAY

2

1980 SELECTER members Charley Anderson (bass) and Desmond Brown (keyboards) left the band. Those remaining commented "The situation had not been right for some time".

1971 THE ROLLING STONES started suing their former managers — Andrew Oldham, Eric Easton and Allen Klein — for unpaid recording royalties.

1965 THE ROLLING STONES took over the TV pop show, 'Ready Steady Go', retitled for the evening 'Ready Steady Goes Live'. Apart from playing a Stones set, Mick and Andrew Oldham did a take-off of Sonny & Cher's 'I Got You Babe' with Oldham taking Cher's part.

1943 ROSALIND ASHFORD (Martha and the Vandellas) born, Detroit.

1943 JOE SIMON born, Simmesport, Louisiana. A typical full-throated Southern soul singer with one foot in the black church and one in country music. Despite a clutch of R&B hits in the mid-sixties, he only reached out for a mass audience in the seventies. Under the guidance of Gamble & Huff, he had one of the first hits in their new Philly soul vein, 'Drowning In A Sea Of Love', a rich melodrama sung with almost more expressiveness than it needed. His 'Step By Step' was, of course, a perfect dance floor record, there to be revived as long as DJs are around to play it.

1939 BOBBY PURIFY (Robert Lee Dickey) born, Tallahassee, Florida.

1972
'You Wear It Well'
Rod Stewart

SATURDAY

3

1970 AL WILSON, Canned Heat's slide guitarist, was found dead in the Topanga Canyon garden of Canned Heat singer Bob Hite with a bottle reds in his pack pocket. Suicide was assumed.

1948 DON BREWER (Grand Funk Railroad) born.

➤**1944 GARY LEEDS** (Walker Brothers) born, Glendale, California.

➤**1942 AL JARDINE** (Beach Boys) born, Los Angeles.

1925 HANK THOMPSON, country singer of 'The Wild Side Of Life', born, Waco, Texas.

1916 MEMPHIS SLIM (Peter Chatman) born, Memphis.

1966
'Sunshine Superman'
Donovan

SUNDAY

4

1980 YES, with the added wonder ingredient of Buggles, played the first of three nights at Madison Square Gardens, New York.

1971 FRANCISCO CARRASCO, a sandwich seller at a Wishbone Ash concert in Texas, was murdered for refusing to give someone a free sandwich.

➤**1951 MARTIN CHAMBERS** (Pretenders) born, Hereford.

1976
'Dancing Queen'
Abba

SEPTEMBER

MONDAY

5 **1978 THE DOOMED**, the short-lived group which prefigured the reformation of the Damned, played their first show at the Electric Ballroom, Camden Town, London, with Motorhead's Lemmy helping out on bass.

1969 JOSH WHITE, blues singer, died during heart surgery.

1964 THE ROLLING STONES started a British tour, at London's Finsbury Park Astoria, supported by Charlie and Inez Foxx, Mike Berry, the Mojos, Billie Davis, Simon Scott and the LeRoys.

1958 SAL SOLO (Classix Nouveaux) born.

1946 BUDDY MILES born, Omaha, Nebraska.

1946 DEAN FORD (Marmalade) born.

1946 LOUDON WAINWRIGHT III born, Chapel Hill, North Carolina.

1939 JOHN STEWART born, San Diego, California.

1964
'House Of The Rising Sun'
Animals

TUESDAY

6 **1978 'THE BUDDY HOLLY STORY'** had its British premiere.

1974 GEORGE HARRISON launched his own Dark Horse record label, issuing an album by Splinter.

1965 THE ROLLING STONES released their album, 'Out Of Our Heads', the first to be recorded entirely in America and the first to contain a substantial number of Jagger-Richards compositions.

► **1958 BUSTER BLOODVESSEL** (Doug Trendle) born. Who can eat thirty two Big Macs at one sitting? Who dresses up as Henry VIII just to know what it feels like to be a self-made king? Who mixes it with the Boot boys on football terraces? Who sticks his tongue out so far he can polish the buttons on his jacket? Who puts on petticoats to dance the Can Can because it's the perfect excuse to moon on prime time TV? Buster Bloodvessel, of course, the public face of Bad Manners. Doug Trendle, his alter ego, is a much more serious character, given to worrying about his future, about his audience's secret dreams, about grown men prancing about in Can Can skirts. But Buster Bloodvessel is the Charlie Brown the Coasters sung about, the nasty little boy with 'a heart of gold', the one who puts worms down girls' dresses, the one who — if he was still at school — would undoubtedly call the English teacher 'Daddy-O'.

1954 STELLA BARKER (Belle Stars) born, Scunthorpe, Lincolnshire.

► **1946 FREDDIE MERCURY** (Bulsara) born, Zanzibar.

1944 ROGER WATERS born, Great Bookham, Cambridgeshire.

1925 JIMMY REED, blues singer, born, Leland, Mississippi.

1975
'Sailing'
Rod Stewart

WEDNESDAY

7 **1979 THE SLITS** released their debut album, 'Cut', on Island Records.

1979 KENNY MORRIS AND JOHN MACKAY left Siouxsie and the Banshees at the start of a British tour just before the opening show in Aberdeen. Without telling the rest of the band, they caught the train back to London, leaving pillows stuffed under their blankets to give the impression — as demonstrated in a hundred POW escape movies — that they were still there, having a quick nap.

1979 MUSICIANS UNITED FOR SAFE ENERGY (MUSE) started five nights of concerts at Madison Square Gardens.

► **1978 KEITH MOON**, after spending the previous evening at the 'Buddy Holly Story' premiere, woke up early, had breakfast, went back to bed where he was found dead six hours later with 32 Heminevrin pills in his stomach, part of a prescription given him to help wean him off his alcoholism.

1974 THE 101'ERS, the band formed by Clash front man, Joe Strummer, played their first show, at the Telegraph pub, Brixton, London.

1963 BOB DYLAN had his first chart entry, with his 'Freewheelin'' album.

► **1951 CHRISSIE HYNDE** (Pretenders) born, Akron, Ohio.

1936 BUDDY HOLLY (Charles Hardin Holley) born, Lubbock, Texas.

1934 LITTLE MILTON (Campbell), blues singer, born, Inverness, Mississippi.

1979
'In Through The Out Door'
Led Zeppelin

THURSDAY

8
1978 PUBLIC IMAGE LIMITED released their first record, the 'Public Image' single.
1972 ZEKE SNODGRASS YOUNG, was born to Mr. Neil Young and Miss Carrie Snodgrass of Santa Cruz, California.
1972 MOTT THE HOOPLE released the 'All The Young Dudes' single, the revival of their career under the guidance of their new-found sugar Daddy, David Bowie.
1972 THE ANN ARBOR JAZZ AND BLUES FESTIVAL was held in a field commemorating the memory of Chicago blues pianist, Otis Spann. On the bill organised by John Sinclair, once manager of the MC5, were Dr. John, Muddy Waters, Howlin' Wolf, Bonnie Raitt, Sun Ra, Junior Walker, Freddie King, Otis Rush, Luther Allison and Bobby 'Blue' Bland.

1946 PIG PEN (Ron McKernan) of the Grateful Dead, born, San Bruno, California.
1932 PATSY CLINE, country singer, born, Winchester, Virginia.

FRIDAY

9
1979 CAT STEVENS, calling himself Yusef Islam since his conversion to Muhammedanism, married Fouzia Ali at the Kensington Mosque, London.
1975 WINGS started a world tour which lasted till October 21, 1976, covered ten countries and drew an audience of two million. Beginning and ending in Britain — with three nights at the Empire Pool, Wembley — it was documented as 'Wings Over The World'.
1961 'THANK YOUR LUCKY STARS', the British TV pop show, was first broadcast.
1946 BILLY PRESTON born, Houston, Texas.
1942 INEZ FOXX born.
1941 OTIS REDDING born, Dawson, Georgia.
1927 ELVIN JONES, drummer, born, Pontiac, Michigan.

SATURDAY

10
1980 CHEAP TRICK announced that Tom Peterson (bass) had been replaced by Peter Comita.
1973 BBC RADIO banned the Rolling Stones' 'Star Star' when they noticed that the chorus included the word 'starfucker'.
▶ **1956 JOHNNIE FINGERS** (Boomtown Rats) born.
▶ **1950 DON POWELL** (Slade) born, Bilston, Staffordshire.
1945 JOSE FELICIANO born, Puerto Rico.
1939 ARTIE TRIPP (Mothers Of Invention, Captain Beefheart's Magic Band) born.
1925 ROY BROWN, R&B pianist and singer, born, New Orleans.

SUNDAY

11
1974 CROSBY, STILLS, NASH AND YOUNG, THE BAND AND JONI MITCHELL played a show at London's Wembley stadium.
1969 THE GREAT WHITE WONDER, the world's first rock'n'roll bootleg, appeared in Los Angeles stores. The Basement Tapes section of it was cut in the period following his motorbike accident two years earlier which prompted rumours that Dylan had been a victom of and LBJ-Pentagon-CIA conspiracy; that he'd turned into a vegetable and been put in the monsters hospital, next bed to Buddy Holly; or maybe he'd spent the time away cleansing his system of Mandrax, of Quaaludes, of Methamphetamine Sulpate, of monkey glands. My friend Gerry reckons Dylan didn't even exist. The name was owned by a circle of New York businessmen who, each year, scoured the campuses for the likeliest songwriter, recorded him, then dispatched the corpse to Poet's Corner. How else, Gerry argues, can you explain the incessant changes in Dylan's style?
1962 THE BEATLES went up to London to record their first single, 'Love Me Do'.
1961 BOB DYLAN played his first New York City show, at Gerde's Folk City, playing 'House Of The Rising Sun', 'Song To Woody' and some dusty old folk tunes.
1944 PHIL MAY (Pretty Things) born.

GREAT WHITE WONDER

1960
'Apache'
Shadows

1972
'Mama Weer All Crazee Now'
Slade

1966
'You Can't Hurry Love'
Supremes

1964
'You Really Got Me'
Kinks

SEPTEMBER
M O N D A Y

▶ **12** **1980 DAVID BOWIE** released his 'Scary Monsters And Super Creeps' album.
▶ **1970 WOODY GUTHRIE MEMORIAL CONCERT** at the Hollywood Bowl with Bob Dylan, Joan Baez, Grumbling Jack Elliott and Arlo Guthrie on the bill.
1966 'THE MONKEES' show started on American TV.
1957 DONNY OSMOND born.
1955 JAY OSMOND born.
1943 MARIA MULDAUR (Maria Grazia Rosa Domenica d'Amato) born, Greenwich Village, NYC.
▶ **1931 GEORGE JONES**, country singer, born, Beaumont, Texas. Equal first with Dean Martin in any list of The World's Best-Known Drunks, Jones must have recorded more songs about life viewed through the bottom of a bottle of Pabst Blue Label than anyone else. Right through his on/off/on and off again C&W marriage with singer, Tammy Wynette, he drank and sang, sang and drank. Always bar-room ballads with titles like 'Tarnished Angel', 'She Thinks I Still Care', 'Cup Of Loneliness' and, best title of all, 'A Man Can Be A Drunk But A Drunk Can't Be A Man'. Brought up in the South-Eastern urban sprawl of Texas, Jones embodies all the aspirations of the city poor with their roots still in the backwoods. He wants respect above everything else but continually screws up his chances of getting it. Too obviously commercial to get the 'American working class poet' tag that hung around Merle Haggard for a while, Jones has a wonderful voice — full of hurt pride and failed dreams — and a facial expresson so bemused, so lost, he could be watching from another planet. Then, if you'd re-enacted your wedding onstage every night for half a dozen years, you'd probably look that way too.

T U E S D A Y

13 **1969 THE PLASTIC ONO BAND** played their first live show at the Toronto Rock'n'Roll Revival Show. The event was recorded and released as 'Live Peace In Toronto' on December 12 that year.
1960 THE FCC AMENDMENT ON PAYOLA became law, forbidding radio personnel to take money or presents in return for playing records on the station. Radio stations were held resonsible for their employees' misdemeanours.
1944 PETER CETERA (Chicago) born.
1941 DAVID CLAYTON-THOMAS (Blood, Sweat & Tears) born, Surrey.

W E D N E S D A Y

14 **1981 WALTER 'FURRY' LEWIS**, bottle-neck blues guitarist, died of heart failure, 88, Memphis — where he'd been a street cleaner for forty-four years.
▶ **1955 LITTLE RICHARD** recorded his first side for Specialty records, at Cosimo Matassa's J&M studio, New Orleans — a dirty blues by local songwriter Dorothy La Bostrie he'd been humming to himself during a break, cleaned up and dubbed 'Tutti Frutti'. Whoooo, my soul...
1950 PAUL KOSSOFF born, Hampstead, London.
1912 ARCHIBALD (Leon T. Gross) born, New Orleans. The least-known of the crscent City's R&B piano thunderers. Fats just about owned the *Billboard* charts through the fifties. *Everyone* knows Huey Smith's 'Rockin' Pneumonia And The Boogie Woogie Flu'. Professor Longhair, his off-key whistle and his Mardi Gras poetry, they all have their fans. But Archibald never quite made the transition from whorehouse boogie woogie to rock'n'roll. When he cut his version of 'Stack-O-Lee' in 1950 — divided into Parts One and Two — it already sounded old-fashioned, a song so far out of its time, it belonged almost to the days before the New Orleans red light district was torn down in 1917. Shortly after it hit he had to cancel a West Coast tour because of illness. This crucial failure to follow up consigned him to the New Orleans tourist ghetto, carressing the ivories in the Poodle Patio Club on Bourbon Street night after night, recreating the mythical encounter between Stock and Billy Lyon for drunken lawn-mower salesmen from Minneapolis. He died of a heart attack in 1973.

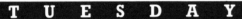

#1 UK 45
1970
'Tears Of A Clown'
Smokey Robinson and the Miracles

#1 US LP
1980
'Hold Out'
Jackson Browne

#1 UK 45
1963
'She Loves You'
Beatles

THURSDAY

15

1980 BILL EVANS, jazz pianist, died of a bleeding ulcer, 51, NYC.

1974 GARY THAIN, Uriah Heep bass player, was electrocuted onstage in Dallas, Texas, sending him into early retirement.

1970 BING CROSBY was presented with a platinum disc for having sold over 300M records.

1966 BRIAN EPSTEIN was rushed to hospital after taking an overdose of pills.

1965 THE BEATLES played Shea Stadium in front of over 55,000 people, grossing $304,000.

► **1903 ROY ACUFF**, country singer and founder of Acuff-Rose publishing house, born, Maynardsville, Tennessee.

FRIDAY

16

1972 FRAMPTON'S CAMEL debuted at the New York Academy of Music supporting J. Geils Band.

1972 JOHN LENNON released his 'Sometime In New York City' double album.

1961 THE MARVELETTES' 'Please Mr. Postman' was released, taking fifteen weeks to hit the number one spot on the *Billboard* charts.

1948 KENNY JONES (Small Faces, Faces, Who) born, Stepney, London.

1944 BETTY KELLY (the Vandellas) born, Detroit.

1925 B.B. KING born, Itta Bena, Mississippi.

SATURDAY

17

► **1977 MARC BOLAN** died when the Mini his girlfriend, Gloria Jones, was driving skidded off the road on to a tree on Barnes Common, London.

1970 RANDY NEWMAN started recording his shows over the next three nights at the Bitter End East, New York, producing his 'Live' album.

1958 CHARLIE RICH recorded the rockabilly tracks, 'Whirlwind' and 'Rebound' for Sun Records at their Memphis studio.

1947 LOL CREME born, Manchester.

1931 RCA VICTOR RECORDS demonstrated their 33⅓ rpm long-players at the Savoy Plaza Hotel, New York, an innovation on which they caught rather a bad financial cold. It wasn't till the war helped the development of vinylite, a superior substance for manufacturing discs, that microgroove records were a viable proposition. Even then, when Columbia Records came to develop them, they found they not only had to construct new records but re-design the playback equipment from top to bottom, from woofer to tone arm.

1929 SIL AUSTIN, fifties sax session player, born, Dunellon, Florida.

► **1926 BILL BLACK** born.

► **1923 HANK WILLIAMS** born, Mount Olive, Alabama.

SUNDAY

18

1979 THE TENNESSEE MEDICAL EXAMINERS BOARD filed charges against Elvis Presley's personal physician, Dr. George Nichopolous, claiming that he had been guilty of "gross malpractice in the indiscriminate prescribing of prescription drugs" in the period leading up to Presley's death. Indicating that such over-prescribing might have been a contributory factor in the heart attack which killed Presley, Nichopolous' actions were described as "the worst case of over-prescribing in the history of the Tennessee Medical Examiners Board".

1970 JIMI HENDRIX died, 28, London. He went to sleep with a stomach full of downers and booze and choked on his own vomit. Pronounced DOA at St. Mary Abbott's Hospital, Kensington, his death certificate states that death was due to 'Inhalation of vomit; Barbiturate intoxication (quinalbarbitone); Insufficient evidence of circumstances; open verdict'.

► **1951 DEE DEE RAMONE** (Douglas Colvin) born, Fort Lee, Virginia.

SEPTEMBER
MONDAY

19

1973 GRAM PARSONS died, 26, Joshua Tree Motel, Joshua Tree National Monument. The cause was listed as 'multiple drug use' — cocaine, morphine, alcohol and amphetamines were found in his corpse. As his wishes had been that he be cremated at Cap Rock, a quartz monzonite outcrop in the park where he died, his personal roadie, Phil Kaufman 'executive nanny services' (now with Emmylou Harris' band), stole the body from Los Angeles International airport where it was being readied to be flown back to his Southern gentry parents. His ashes were scattered in the park and Kaufman and an associate were charged with theft of the coffin and fined $300.

1968 RED FOLEY, country singer, died of a heart attack, 58, Fort Wayne, Indiana.

1958 ELVIS PRESLEY sailed from Brooklyn naval base to join his army unit in Germany.

► **1957 RUSTY EGAN** born.
Mr. All Mouth And Trousers. Drummer with The Rich Kids turned clothes horse turned DJ at the Blitz (cradle of The New Romantics) turned member of Visage turned inspiration of Metropolis Records. A man with more taste than sense.

1946 JOHN COGHLAN (Status Quo) born.

1945 DAVID BROMBERG born, Tarrytown, New York.

1941 CASS ELLIOTT (Mamas & Papas) born, Baltimore.

1940 BILL MEDLEY (Righteous Brothers) born, Santa Ana, California.

1934 BRIAN EPSTEIN born, Liverpool.

1921 BILLY WARD (Dominoes) born, Los Angeles.

TUESDAY

20

1981 WIGAN CASINO held the last of its Northern Soul Nights, the holy mass of the true believers — Defenders of the Faith, they call themselves — in the living power of frantic soul, the faster the better, the more obscure the betterer. No more would the lame be caused to dance, the crippled to perform back flips.

1976 THE 100 CLUB PUNK FESTIVAL's first night. On the bill were the Sex Pistols, the Clash and Slaughter and the Dogs.

► **1973 JIM CROCE** died with five other people when their light plane hit a tree on take-off, Natchitoches, Louisiana. His greatest fame came after his death with 'Bad Bad Leroy Brown' and 'Time In A Bottle' which topped the US singles chart at the end of that year.

1972 PAUL McCARTNEY was charged with growing marijuana on his farm in Campbelltown, Scotland.

1970 JIM MORRISON was cleared by a Miami court of 'lewd' behaviour but found guilty of indecent exposure and profanity, copping a $500 dollar fine and six months hard labour on the first charge and sixty days hard labour on the second. When he died in the middle of the following year, the case was still on appeal.

1969 ATV (Associated Television) spent a million pounds to gain control of the Beatles' publishing company, Northern Songs.

1966 GEORGE HARRISON flew to India to study under the Maharishi Mahesh Yogi.

1966 SIMON & GARFUNKEL's 'Parsley, Sage, Rosemary & Thyme' album was released.

WEDNESDAY

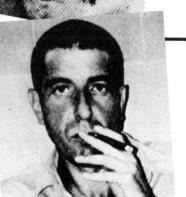

21

1971 THE OLD GREY WHISTLE TEST was broadcast on BBC TV for the first time. The 'serious' 'rock' programme — a boring, living embodiment of the laughable notion that rock is about musicianship. Essential viewng only for fans of Bill Nelson or the Grease Band and those who derive spiritual satisfaction from compiling lists of 'Greatest Living Bassists'.

1953 BETTY WRIGHT born, Miami.

1940 DICKY LEE, country writer of 'She Thinks I Still Care', born, Memphis.

► **1934 LEONARD COHEN** born, Montreal, Canada.

1932 DON PRESTON (Mothers Of Invention) born, Michigan.

THURSDAY

22

1962 BOB DYLAN played Carnegie Hall, a 'Hootenanny', performing five songs, including 'Talking John Birch Society Blues'.
▶ **1949 DAVID COVERDALE** (Deep Purple, Whitesnake) born, Saltburn, Yorkshire.
1942 MIKE PATTO (McCarthy) born, Glasgow.

FRIDAY

23

1977 THE CLASH released their third single, 'Complete Control'.
1977 DAVID BOWIE released his 'Heroes' single, making it available in English, French and German versions.
▶ **1974 ROBBIE McINTOSH**, Average White Band drummer, died in Los Angeles when he took too much of what he thought was cocaine but was in fact heroin. Later, someone confessed that it was a revenge killing.
1969 PAUL McCARTNEY was suspected to be dead for the first time when an article appeared in the *Northern Star*, the Illinois University newspaper, headlined 'Clues Hint At Beatle Death'.
1966 THE ROLLING STONES released 'Have You Seen Your Mother Baby', their densest, most driven single and compounded its confusions by appearing in drag for the promo photos.
1957 THE CRICKETS' 'That'll Be The Day', their first single, peaked in the *Billboard* charts, reaching number one on the Hot Hundred and number two on the R&B chart.
1954 ELVIS PRESLEY made his debut at 'the home of country music', the Grand Ole Opry in Nashville.
1949 BRUCE SPRINGSTEEN born, New Jersey. If ever a rock'n'roll singer deserved to be discussed in religious terms, it's Springsteen. With his heavy-lidded, distant eyes, he even looks like one of the icons of saints they sell down South America way — a style popularised by the most famous poster image of Che Guevara. As a saviour, though, he's strictly second-rate. When he brings his audience together for the sacrament of his Mitch Ryder medley, it's a sham miracle, a raising of the dead when they're better off staying in the their fine and private place.
1942 BARBARA ALLBUT (Angels) born.
1940 PHYLLIS ALLBUT (Angels) born.
1940 TIM ROSE born, Washington D.C.
▶ **1939 ROY BUCHANAN** born, Ozark, Arkansas.
▶ **1930 RAY CHARLES** born, Albany, Georgia.
1926 JOHN COLTRANE born, Hamlet, North Carolina.
1921 JOE HILL LOUIS, one man blues band, born, Whitehaven, Tennessee.

SATURDAY

24

1980 THE 'SON OF STIFF' TOUR, the third national Stiff tour, started with a bill of fare that read King Carasco, Tenpole Tudor, the Equators, Any Trouble and Dirty Looks.
1946 JERRY DONAGHUE (Fairport Convention) born.
1942 GERRY MARSDEN born, Liverpool.
▶ **1942 LINDA McCARTNEY** (nee Eastman) born.
1931 ANTHONY NEWLEY born, Hackney, London.

SUNDAY

25

1980 JOHN BONHAM, Led Zeppelin drummer, died, 32, London. After knocking back forty shots of vodka, he asphyxiated on his own vomit. About to embark on a US tour, Led Zeppelin cancelled and — eventually — dissolved the band.
1975 CHARLIE MONROE died, 72, of cancer. Brother of Bill Monroe, Charlie helped him from the Monroe Brothers hillbilly/bluegrass vocal group with the third brother, Birch. After recording sixty sides for Bluebird in the late thirties, the brothers went their separate ways, each forming their own band. Bill, the most notable of the three, started up the Bluegrass Boys who gave the music its name.
1964 BRIAN EPSTEIN refused an offer of £3,500,000 for the Beatles' management contract from a syndicate of American businessmen.

SEPTEMBER

MONDAY

26

1969 THE BEATLES released the last album they recorded, 'Abbey Rd.'.

1968 BRIAN JONES was found guilty of cannabis possession at Inner Court Sessions, London, and fined £50 with £105 costs.

1955 EDDIE FISHER AND DEBBIE REYNOLDS, two fifties mainstream pop singers, were married. Three years later, Eddie left Debbie for Liz Taylor.

► **1948 OLIVIA NEWTON JOHN** born, Cambridge.

1947 LYNN ANDERSON born, Grand Forks, North Dakota.

► **1945 BRYAN FERRY** born, Washington, County Durham. Peter York, author of 'Style Wars', a neurotic guide to the switchbacks of fashion, nailed Ferry perfectly. '...the best possible example of the ultimate art-directed existence...He should hang in the Tate (Gallery), with David Bowie.'

1937 BESSIE SMITH, 'Empress Of The Blues', died in a car crash near Coahama, Mississippi. The belief that she bled to death when refused admittance to a whites-only hospital — while providing a nice myth for the white liberal conscience — is almost certainly a fiction created by Edward Albee's play 'The Strange Death Of Bessie Smith'. She was buried in Philadelphia on October 4, an event described by the *Chicago Defender*, 'In a gorgeous flesh lace gown with pink slippers...in an expensive open silver metallic casket trimmed in gold and draped in two-tone velvet lining.' But despite the opulence of her passing, her grave remained unmarked until the price was raised by a small group of fans including Janis Joplin who said of Bessie Smith, "She showed me the air and taught me how to fill it."

1934 DICK HECKSTALL-SMITH born.

1925 MARTY ROBBINS born, Glendale, Arizona.

1889 GEORGE GERSHWIN born, NYC.

1887 EMILE BERLINER obtained the first US patent on a flat disc gramophone.

TUESDAY

27

1972 RORY STORME, leader of the Mersey beat group the Hurricanes which provided the Beatles with Ringo Starr, took an overdose of sleeping pills the same day as his mother — a suicide pact was assumed. Later, the character played by Billy Fury in the rock film 'That'll Be The Day', was based on Rory Storme.

1962 BOB DYLAN was reviewed in the *New York Times*, his first appearance in a major newspaper.

1942 ALVIN STARDUST/SHANE FENTON (Bernard Jewry) born, Muswell Hill, London.

1941 DON NIX, original Mar-Key, producer and songwriter, born, Memphis, Tennessee.

1920 HAL HARRIS, rockabilly, born, Pike County, Alabama.

WEDNESDAY

28

1979 JIMMY McCULLOCH, former guitarist with Thunderclap Newman, Stone The Crows and Wings, was found dead in his North London flat, aged 26.

1977 DAVID BOWIE & BING CROSBY recorded a duet medley of 'Little Drummer Boy' and 'Peace On Earth' for a Crosby TV special. It was originally planned as a Christmas show but, when Crosby died that autumn, it was rescheduled and shown on US TV in November.

1972 DAVID BOWIE made his New York debut, at Carnegie Hall.

► **1958 THE TEDDY BEARS'** 'To Know Him Is To Love Him' topped the US singles chart. Phil Spector's first hit production, it took its title from his father's gravestone. Although it only cost $40 to make, it took in $20,000 — $17,000 of which Spector still claims he's owed.

1956 RCA RECORDS announced that in the previous year they'd sold ten million Elvis Presley records, sixty percent of their entire output.

► **1956 BILL HALEY** had five singles in the UK top thirty.

1946 HELEN SHAPIRO born, Bethnal Green, London.

1938 BEN E. KING (Benjamin Nelson) born, Henderson, North Carolina.

THURSDAY

29

1970 THE ROLLING STONES released 'Get Your Ya-Yas Out', the live album recorded on their 1969 tour of America, the coast-to-coast drag which elevated them to mythical status in the American rock critics' eyes. No longer were they just a rock'n'roll band, they were the 'Greatest Rock'n'Roll Band In The World'. Music took second place to myth as they came to epitomise a decadent chic based on hard drugs, cheekbones so hollow you could park an ocean liner in them, tequila sunrises and invocations of demon brothers. A member of the audience on the album unwittingly pin-pointed their new stature when, as they lumbered into 'Sympathy For The Devil', she screamed out "Paint It Black,' 'Paint It Black', you devils".

1963 THE ROLLING STONES started their first major UK tour, supported by the Everly Brothers and Bo Diddley, playing London's New Victoria theatre. Out of deference to the man "shooting tombstone bullets on balls and chains", the Stones cut all their Bo Diddley covers from their set. But, despite the Stones' new fame, box office returns were not good enough: Little Richard was flown in October 5 to improve the draw of the package.

➤ **1948 MARK FARNER** (Grank Funk Railroad) born, Flint, Michigan.
1948 MIKE PINERA (Iron Butterfly) born.
1935 JERRY LEE LEWIS born, Ferriday, Louisiana.

FRIDAY

30

1977 IAN DURY released his first solo album, 'New Boots And Panties'.
1967 RADIO ONE, Britain's first official pop music station, made its first broadcast, starting with Tony Blackburn spinning the Move's 'Flowers In The Rain'.
➤ **1946 MARC BOLAN** born, East London.
1945 MIKE HARRISON (Spooky Tooth) born, Carlisle, Cumberland.
1942 FRANKIE LYMON born, Washington Heights, NYC.

OCTOBER

SATURDAY

1

➤ **1979 ELTON JOHN** played the first of eight nights at New York's Madison Square Gardens.
1977 RAT SCABIES resigned from the Damned...but was back in the anarchic fold within two years.
1970 JIMI HENDRIX was buried at Greenwood Cemetery, Seattle.
1967 PINK FLOYD started their first American tour.
1956 BILL HALEY's live album 'Rock'n'Roll Stage Show' was released in the UK.
1944 SCOTT McKENZIE born, Arlington, Virginia.
1944 HERBERT RHOAD (Persuasions) born, Bamberg, South Carolina.
1944 BARBARA PARITT (Toys) born, Wilmington, North Carolina.

SUNDAY

2

1979 THE JAM released 'The Eton Rifles', the fullest ever discourse on class war in Woking.
1978 DAVID BOWIE released his second double live album, 'Stage'.
1971 JOHN LENNON released his second and most financially lucrative solo album, 'Imagine'.
1967 THE GRATEFUL DEAD's communal house at 710 Ashbury St., San Francisco, was raided by narcotics agents who arrested eleven people including the Dead's Pigpen and Bob Weir then had to let them go because they'd forgotten the formality of obtaining a warrant before smashing through the front door.
1965 BOB DYLAN's 'Highway 61 Revisited', his first all rock'n'roll album entered the US chart. At last, he'd vindicated his graduation book promise that he wa off 'to join Little Richard'.
➤ **1955 PHIL OAKLEY** (Human League) born.
➤ **1951 STING** (Gordon Sumner) born, Wallsend, Northumberland.

1958
'It's All In The Game'
Tommy Edwards

1961
'Michael (Row The Boat Ashore)'
Highwaymen

1972
'How Can I Be Sure'
David Cassidy

#1 UK LP
1971
'Every Picture Tells A Story'
Rod Stewart

OCTOBER
MONDAY

THE MIRACLES
Tamla Recording Artists

3
1980 ROCKPILE, the band formed by Dave Edmunds and Nick Lowe, released their debut — and as it turned out, only — album, 'Seconds Of Pleasure', five years after the band had started. Previously, they'd been kept from working as a unit by the fact that Edmunds had been under contract to Swan Song while Lowe had been with, successively, Stiff, Radar and F Beat in the UK and Columbia in the USA.

1969 SKIP JAMES died, 67. A keening country blues whiner and spidery guitarist who wrote 'I'd Rather Be The Devil' and 'I'm So Glad', once turned into raw electric mush by Cream.

1968 THE ROLLING STONES relented to pressure from Decca Records over the intended sleeve for their 'Beggars Banquet' album. The Stones had offered a lavatory wall covered with graffiti to spread right across the gate-fold sleeve. Decca, bastions of British propriety, refused the offer and stalled the album's release. The Stones eventually compromised with the almost bare cream sleeve which is on the released album but the row was a big factor in the Stones' refusal to re-sign with Decca when their contract came up for renewal two years later.

1967 WOODY GUTHRIE, folk singer and Bob Dylan's adenoidal inspiration, died of Huntington's Chorea, aged 55.

► **1960 THE MIRACLES** released their first single, 'Shop Around'.

1938 EDDIE COCHRAN born, Albert Lea, Minnesota.

TUESDAY

4
1980 STIFF RECORDS lost their appeal against a fine of £50 plus £50 costs for selling their famous t-shirt bearing the label's founding motto: 'If it ain't stiff, it ain't worth a fuck'.

1974 THIN LIZZY played their first show with the twin guitars of Scott Gorham and Brian Robertson, Aberystwyth University, Wales.

► **1970 JANIS JOPLIN** died, aged 27, of a heroin overdose at the Landmark Hotel, Hollywood.

1929 LEROY VAN DYKE born, Spring Fork, Missouri. Farm boy turned farm boy myth and two-hit wonder with a pair of unrepeatably perfect country songs, 'The Auctioneer' and 'Walk On By' — not the Dionne Warwick song but a similar tale of the difficulties of love; in this case, the problems faced by adulteress — soap opera with solid rather than cardboard sets. Whether 'Walk On By' was written from experience is not known but 'The Auctioneer' certainly was. Growing up working on his daddy's farm and in his trucking business, Leroy, via a degree in agriculture at the University of Missouri and a stint with the US Army in Korea — graduated from Auctioneering School in Decatur, Illinois and became a professional livestock auctioneer with a sideline in writing for the Midwest stock newspaper chain, *Corn Belt Dailies*. Hustling his way into talent contests, he wrote 'The Auctioneer' with is friend Buddy Black. Dot Records signed him and pushed his speedfreak gabble hard enought for it to sell two and a half million copies and become a staple of children's radio shows.

WEDNESDAY

5
1962 THE BEATLES released their first single, 'Love Me Do'.

1957 LEE THOMPSON (Madness) born, St. Pancras, London.

► **1954 BOB GELDOF** (Boomtown Rats) born.

1950 ELEKTRA RECORDS was launched by Jac Holzman. Starting out as almost a hobby run from Holzman's room at St. John's College, it became the first home of the obscure and ethnic, then the less obscure with — in the early sixties — Judy Collins and Phil Ochs and eventually, the straight rock 'n' roll pop of the Doors, Love, Tim Buckley and the MC5. Holzman sold out to Warner Brothers in 1973.

1944 DINAH SHORE became the first woman to top the US charts, with 'I'll Walk Alone'.

► **1941 CHUBBY CHECKER** (Ernest Evans) born, Philadelphia.

THURSDAY

6

1980 JOHN LYDON (nee Rotten) was sentenced to three months jail on an assault charge by a Dublin court. He was acquitted on appeal.

1980 THE BEE GEES sued their manager, Robert Stigwood, and their record company, Polygram, for a total of $200m, claiming the sum wa due to them because of fraud, misrepresentation and unfair enrichment at their expense.

1979 THE KNACK's 'My Sharona' ended its record-breaking run at the top of *Billboard's* Hot Hundred.

1967 SAN FRANCISCANS mounted a 'Hippie Funeral', intended to be a final nail in the coffin of a movement that they saw as hopelessly compromised by commercialism.

► **1960 RICHARD JOBSON**, former Skid, born.

1942 MILLIE SMALL, singer of the first Jamaican-based single to enter the UK charts, born, Clarendon, JA.

1962
'Telstar'
Tornadoes

FRIDAY

7

1970 JANIS JOPLIN was cremated at the West Village Mortuary, Los Angeles County. In accordance with her wishes, her ashes were scattered by air along the Marin County coast-line.

1966 SMILEY LEWIS (Overton Amos Lemons), New Orleans R&B singer and guitarist, died of cancer, New Orleans.

1966 JOHNNY KIDD (Frederick Heath) died in a car crash. One of the very few great British rockers before the Beatles. Hidden behind an eye patch and backed by the Pirates, he growled through a handful of great tracks, notably 'Shakin' All Over', the best British record made before 'With The Beatles'.

1945 KEVIN GODLEY born, Manchester, Lancashire.

1942 GARY PUCKETT born.

1960
'Only The Lonely'
Roy Orbison

SATURDAY

8

1980 BOB MARLEY collapsed in New York's Central Park and was rushed to hospital. Rumours that he was suffering from either a brain tumour or a cancer were denied, the blame being laid on 'complete exhaustion'. Nonetheless, shortly after, he flew to the spiritual homeland of Rastafarians, Ethiopa, and eventually it was revealed that he was in a controversial German cancer clinic.

► **1976 THE SEX PISTOLS** signed to EMI Records.

1976 L.B.C., London's all news radio station and Britain's first commercial station, broadcast for the first time.

► **1948 JOHNNY RAMONE** (John Cummings) born, Long Island.

1977
'Silver Lady'
David Soul

SUNDAY

9

1980 JOHN LENNON released 'Starting Over' on his fortieth birthday, signalling his return from a wilderness of child-rearing and fur coat collecting. Yoko Ono celebrated the event by hiring a sky-writer to display 'Happy Birthday, John' across the New York skies.

1978 JACQUES BREL died. The Belgian born son of a cardboard manufacturer, he was the best-known and most admired French language songwriter of his generation. Surprisingly for one so successful, he wrote of the nastier side of life, creating a nightmare of a First World War military brothel in 'Next', a vision of human beings rotting as quickly and messily as the fish in the port of 'Amsterdam'. Almost over-typically French in his despair, Brel observed the underbelly of France with the inflinching eye of a twentieth century Villon.

1975 SEAN ONO LENNON, the only child of John and Yoko's marriage, born, NYC.

1973 ELVIS AND PRISCILLA PRESLEY were divorced in Santa Monica, California, she having deserted the Memphis Flash for the more obvious physical attractions of her karate instructor.

1964 THE ROLLING STONES announced that they'd cancelled their forth-coming tour of South Africa following the embargo by the Musicians' Union.

1953 TELECLUB, the first British TV show to be aimed specifically at teenagers, was broadcast for the first time.

1948 JACKSON BROWNE born, Heidelberg, West Germany.

1946 JOHN ENTWHISTLE born, Chiswick, London.

1940 JOHN LENNON born, Liverpool (during an air raid).

1971
'Maggie May'/'Every Picture Tells A Story'
Rod Stewart

OCTOBER

MONDAY

10

1980 BRUCE SPRINGSTEEN started a world tour to promote his fifth album, 'The River'.
1978 STIFF RECORDS started their second national package tour of the UK. The 'Be Stiff' tour — where everyone travelled by train — started at Bristol University with a bill of five: Wreckless Eric, Mickey Jupp, Jona Lewie, Lena Lovich and Rachel Sweet.
1978 SMASH HITS went on sale for the first time. The first issue — dated November — featured a cover story on Blondie.
1969 FRANK ZAPPA released his first solo album, 'Hot Rats'.
1965 EARL BOSTIC died.
► **1961 MARTIN KEMP** (Spandau Ballet) born, North London.
1959 KIRSTY McCOLL born.
1957 JULIAN COPE born, South Wales.
1953 MIDGE URE (Slik, Rich Kids, Ultravox) born, Cambuslang, Glasgow.
1946 KEITH REID (Procol Harum) born.
1945 ALAN CARTWRIGHT (Procol Harum) born.
1939 GRACE SLICK born, Chicago, Illinois.

TUESDAY

11

1974 SLIK released their first single, 'The Boogiest Band In Town', two years before they scored their first and only real success with 'Forever And Ever.
► **1969 MUDDY WATERS** was seriously injured in an Illinois car crash which killed three other people.
1963 EDITH PIAF (Edith Giovanna Gassion), the gutsiest French chanteuse, died, aged 48.
1963 EMI RECORDS announced that they'd sold a million copies of the Beatles' 'She Loves You' in the UK.
1949 GREG DOUGLAS (Steve Miller Band) born.
1946 GARY MALLABER (Steve Miller Band) born.
1941 LESTER BOWIE born, Frederick, Maryland.
1931 LITTLE WILLIE LITTLEFIELD, R&B singer, born, El Campo Texas. Stomping piano player and husky-throated, fine and mellow singer, Little Willie Littlefield cut the original version of Leiber & Stoller's 'K.C. Lovin'', perhaps better known as 'Kansas City' — a big hit under that title for Wilbert Harrison in the late fifties. One of the main men of the Bihari Brothers' Los Angeles based Modern Records, Littlefield drawled his way through the blues like he was just about holding on to life — and soared through the steady rock of 'Ain't A Better Story Told' (which he sang with Laura Wiggins(like a man just released from a five to ten stretch in San Quentin. In the words of one of his own songs, a truly Mello Cat.

WEDNESDAY

12

1978 NANCY SPUNGEN, Sid Vicious' girlfriend, died of a knife wound in the stomach in their room at New York's Chelsea Hotel.
► **1975 PHIL SPECTOR** launched Warner Spector, a new label which flourished briefly for the tycoon of teen in the mid-seventies, putting out an unbalanced mix of pale echoes of Spector's greatest days and exaggerated, decadent memories of what he could achieve — Dion's 'Born To Be With You', Jerri Bo Keno's 'Here I Come'.
► **1971 GENE VINCENT** died, aged 36, of a heart attack aggravated by a bleeding ulcer, Newhall, California. No more Thunderbird wine, no more sad Virginia whisper. No more white face, black shirt, white socks, black shoes, black hair, white strap, lead white, dyed black.
1962 RITCHIE BLACKMORE played his final show with Screamin' Lord Sutch, in Putney, London. He'd been working in Sutch's Outlaws for six months, a stint which included going out as backing band for American stars touring Britain — Jerry Lee Lewis and Gene Vincent.
1948 RICK PARFITT (Status Quo) born.
1935 SAM MOORE (Sam and Dave) born, Miami. With partner, David Prater, Sam Moore honestly was Double Dynamite. Pleading, screaming, kneeling, hollering for forgiveness, redemption, a woman's love, Stax Records and, of course, the Lord.

1964
'Oh, Pretty Woman'
Roy Orbison

1980
'Don't Stand So Close To Me'
Police

1980
'Zenyatta Mondatta'
Police

1968
'Cheap Thrills'
Big Brother and the Holding Company

THURSDAY

13

1963 THE BEATLES appeared on the TV variety show, 'Sunday Night At The London Palladium', whizzing round with all the other guests on the roundabout, waving goodbye at the end of the show.

1962 THE BEATLES' 'Love Me Do' entered the UK singles chart. Their first single, their first hit and the first Merseybeat record to chart.

1959 MARIE OSMOND born.

1947 SAMMY HAGAR, the Johnny Weissmuller of heavy rock, born.

1944 ROBERT LAMM (Chicago) born.

1941 PAUL SIMON born, Newark, New Jersey.

1940 CHRIS FARLOWE (John Deighton) born, London.

1979
'Eat To The Beat'
Blondie

FRIDAY

14

1972 JOE COCKER and six of his band were charged with possession of illegal drugs in Adelaide, Australia.

1964 CHARLIE WATTS married Shirley Ann Shepherd in Bradford, Yorkshire.

1955 BUDDY HOLLY — as a member of the Buddy, Bob and Larry trio — supported Bill Haley and his Comets in a show at the Fair Park Coliseum, Lubbock, Texas.

1940 CLIFF RICHARD (Harry Roger Webb) born, Lucknow, India.

1930 ROBERT PARKER, R&B sax player, born, New Orleans.

1926 BILL JUSTIS, composer of 'Raunchy', born.

1972
'Ben'
Michael Jackson

SATURDAY

15

1973 KEITH RICHARD AND ANITA PALLENBERG received suspended sentences and a £500 fine for drug offences from a court in Nice, France.

1969 HOWLIN' WOLF, the baaadest bluesman, had a heart attack but recovered to growl for another six years.

1966 PINK FLOYD AND THE SOFT MACHINE played at the launch party for 'International Times', the London 'underground' newspaper.

1965 COUNTRY JOE AND THE FISH released their first record, an EP, 'Fire In The City'/'Superbird', which they handed out at a protest march in Oakland, California.

1964 SCREAMIN' LORD SUTCH, the most wilfully eccentric early British rocker, stood for election to Parliament. To the eternal shame of the nation, not only did his Youth Party not rack up enough votes to retain his deposits but the publicity couldn't even get Sutch a chart record.

1953 TITO JACKSON born, Gary, Indiana.

1945 RICHARD CARPENTER born, Connecticut.

1938 MARV JOHNSON born, Detroit. The voice on the first Tamla release, 'Come To Me', which — although it actually appeared on the United Artists label — was the start of the Motown organisation.

1935 BARRY McGUIRE, New Christy Minstrel and singer of 'Eve Of Destruction', born, Oklahoma City.

1925 MICKY 'GUITAR' BAKER (Micky & Sylvia) born, Louisville, Kentucky.

1966
'Reach Out, I'll Be There'
Four Tops

SUNDAY

16

1976 THE JAM, in search of a little publicity, played a free lunchtime show on the pavements of London's Soho Market.

1973 CAPITAL RADIO, Britain's first official commercial station, went on air.

1969 LEONARD CHESS, co-founder of the grittiest blues label Chess, died of a heart attack, Chicago, at the age of 52.

1965 'A TRIBUTE TO DR. STRANGE' was held at the Longshoreman's Hall, San Francisco (which later became famous as the Fillmore West). Probably the first psychedelic dance show, it had a bill which included Jefferson Airplane and the Charlatans.

1960 GARY KEMP (Spandau Ballet) born, North London.

1947 BOB WEIR (Grateful Dead) born, San Francisco.

1923 BERT KAEMPFERT, band leader and record company executive, born, Hamburg, West Germany.

1976
'Mississippi'
Pussycat

OCTOBER

MONDAY

17

1975 CAMEL presented their rock opera treatment of Paul Gallico's novelette, 'The Snow Goose', at London's Royal Albert Hall.
1962 THE BEATLES made their first appearance on television, slotted into Manchester-based Granada TV's early evening show, 'People And Places'.
1942 GARY PUCKETT born, Hibbing, Minnesota.
► **1934 RICO** (Rodriquez), ska and reggae trombonist, born, Mark Lane, Kingston, JA.
► **1928 COZY COLE**, drum soloist, born.

TUESDAY

18

1979 PENETRATION, the Newcastle-based punk group, split.
1979 THE ADVERTS, the West Country based punk group, split.
1973 AL GREEN was badly injured by Mary Woodson, whose advances he'd spurned, when she tipped boiling grits over him and then shot herself. A turning point of his life, it prompted him to gradually withdraw from the secular life, reconstructing himself as the Reverend Al Green, the sexiest preacher on the Southern holy roller circuit.
1969 JOHN LENNON AND YOKO ONO's London flat was raided by police who found cannabis for which Lennon was eventually fined £150 plus £21 costs.
1969 PAUL KANTNER was charged with possession of cannabis in Oahu, Hawaii.
1969 RICHARD NADER promoted the first of his Rock'n'Roll Revival Shows, at the Felt Forum, NYC, with a bill including Bill Haley, Chuck Berry, the Platters and the Shirelles.
1968 LED ZEPPELIN played their first British shows under that name, at London's Marquee Club.
► **1967 'HOW I WON THE WAR'**, the Dick Lester film which includes John Lennon's only dramatic role, premiered at the London Pavilion.
1956 DICK CRIPPEN (Tenpole Tudor) born, Malta.
1956 CLIFF GALLUP, legendary guitarist, played his last session with Gene Vincent's Blue Caps, cutting three tracks including 'Red Blue Jeans And A Pony Tail'. Although Gallup retired after this, sticking to local, amateur groups, the twenty or so tracks he recorded with Vincent have remained an inspiration to guitarists as disparate as Dave Edmunds and Ritchie Blackmore. Thanks to the researches of rock'n'roll chartered surveyor, Pete Frame, we now know that Gallup used a Gibson Les Paul Duo-Jet pancake model guitar with a Bigsby tremolo arm and, for recording dates, a leather covered Standell amp.
1926 CHUCK BERRY, THE MAN, born, East St. Louis, Illinois. (He claims it was 1931 but then he also claims he's never been to jail.)

WEDNESDAY

19

1979 THE SPECIALS released their Elvis Costello-produced debut album, 'The Specials', their second single, 'A Message To You, Rudy', and played the first date of the 2 Tone national tour, at Brighton Top Rank, supported by Madness and the Selector.
► **1973 DAVID BOWIE** released his tribute to the spirit of Swinging London, 'Pin Ups', with an advance order of 150,000.
1968 PETER FRAMPTON sat in on a Small Faces show, getting on very well with Small Faces' singer, Steve Marriott. So well in fact that within a year the two of them had joined forces to form Humble Pie.
1966 THE YARDBIRDS arrived in America for their first tour of the USA. They started out with the twin guitars of Jeff Beck and Jimmy Page but Beck returned home after two dates, claiming illness.
1960 WOODY (Madness) born, London.
1947 WILBERT HART (Delfonics) born, Philadelphia.
1945 JEANNIE C. RILEY born, Anson, Texas.
► **1944 PETER TOSH** (Winston Hubert McIntosh), reggae singer, born, Church Lincoln, Westmoreland, JA.

THURSDAY

20

1973 VAN MORRISON returned to Ireland for the first time in seven years. He'd left Belfast with Them and never looked back. Although only on a visit on this occasion, he came back again the following year for two shows in Dublin.

1971 'JESUS CHRIST SUPERSTAR' opened in New York, at the Mark Hellinger Theater.

1965 EARL BOSTIC, R&B sax player, died.

1964 THE ROLLING STONES played in Paris for the first time, at the Olympia. There were 150 arrests and £1400 worth of damage to the hall.

1954 LAVERN BAKER cut "Tweedle Dee" at the Atlantic studios, NYC.

1945 RIC LEE (Ten Years After) born, Gannock, Staffordshire.

➤ **1937 WANDA JACKSON**, singer of the breathless rocker 'Let's Have A Party', born.

1979
'Video Killed The Radio Stars'
Buggles

FRIDAY

21

1978 THE CLASH ceased to be managed by their mentor, Bernard Rhodes, situationist and second-hand Renault dealer, claiming all kinds of financial mismanagement. (They returned to his arms two years later.)

1971 JADE JAGGER, the only child of Mick and Bianca Jagger, born, Paris.

1965 BILL BLACK, bass player on Presley's earliest records and leader of the Bill Black combo, died, aged 39, Memphis, Tennessee.

1958 BUDDY HOLLY attended his last studio session before his death the following February, at Pythian Temple Studios, New York. Helped out by Sam 'The Man' Taylor on tenor sax, he cut four tracks — 'True Love Ways', 'Moondreams', 'Raining In My Heart' and 'It Doesn't Matter Anymore'.

➤ **1957 JULIAN COPE** (The Teardrop Explodes) born, Deri, Glamorgan.

1941 STEVE CROPPER (MGs and session guitarist) born, Ozark Mountains, Missouri.

➤ **1940 MANFRED MANN** (Lubowitz) born, Johannesburg, South Africa.

1972
'My Ding-A-Ling'
Chuck Berry

SATURDAY

22

1965 THE ROLLING STONES released 'Get Off My Cloud', their eighth single and fifth consecutive UK number one.

1964 THE WHO were turned down by EMI Records' Mr. John Burgess who was unable to decide whether the High Numbers — the Who's name at the time — had 'anything to offer'.

➤ **1945 LESLEY WEST** born, Queens, NYC.

1942 ANNETTE FUNICELLO, Mousketeer and everyone's dream date for the beach party, born, Utica, New York.

1955
'Love Is A Many Splendoured Thing'
Four Aces

SUNDAY

23

1978 SID VICIOUS attempted suicide, slashing his wrists.

1977 HENRY BOWLES, art student and friend of the Clash was thrown into a plate glass window by a bouncer at a pub in London's Kings Cross. He died two weeks later of his head injuries. Although the bouncer was initially sentenced to twelve months jail for manslaughter, the sentence was quashed on appeal.

1976 THE CLASH played a show at London's Institute of Contemporary Arts. In town for some shows, Patti Smith popped in for a look and was reportedly extremely impressed by Paul Simonon's cheek bone structure.

1969 TOMMY EDWARDS, singer of 'It's All In The Game', died, Richmond, Virginia.

1953 PAULINE BLACK, former Selecter singer, born, Coventry, Warwickshire.

1941 GREG RIDLEY (Humble Pie) born, Cumberland.

1939 CHARLIE FOXX, singer — with his sister, Inez, of 'Mockingbird' — born, Greensboro, North Carolina.

1939 ELLIE GREENWICH, writer of scores of teen dreams including 'Be My Baby' and 'River Deep, Mountain High', born, Long Island, New York.

1961
'Runaround Sue'
Dion

OCTOBER

MONDAY

24

1978 KEITH RICHARD was sentenced in Toronto on the heroin trafficking charge which resulted from a Mounties raid on his hotel room the previous year. To everyone's surprise he was let off extremely lightly. He was ordered to visit his probation officer, try to keep off heroin and play a charity concert for the blind within six months. At a press conference later the same day, he claimed he'd kicked heroin because 'It got boring'. The following day he flew down to New York and celebrated his luck by jamming — totally out of tune — with Rockpile on a couple of Chuck Berry numbers at the Bottom Line.

1973 KEITH RICHARD was fined £205 at London's Marlborough St. Magistrates' Court for possession of marijuana, heroin, Mandrax and two guns — a Smith & Wesson .38 and an antique shotgun.

➤ **1969 JOHN LENNON** released his second solo single, 'Cold Turkey'.

1962 JAMES BROWN recorded the First Commandment of Soul, 'Live At The Apollo'...the hardest working man in show business, Mr. Dynamite, the amazing Mr. 'Please, Please' himself, the star of the show, James Brown and his Famous Flames...now everybody shout and shimmy.

1948 DALE 'BUFFIN' GRIFFIN (Mott The Hoople) born, Ross-On-Wye, Harefordshire.

➤ **1948 PAUL AND BARRY RYAN** born, Leeds, Yorkshire.

1947 EDGAR BROUGHTON born.

1944 TED TEMPLEMAN, member of Harpers' Bizarre and producer, born.

1930 BIG BOPPER (J.P. Richardson) born, Sabine Pass, Texas.

TUESDAY

25

1974 NICK DRAKE, English songwriter and singer, died of a drug overdose which was recorded as deliberate - something his friends have always disputed.

1973 JOHN LENNON filed a case at Manhattan's Federal Court claiming that wire taps and surveillance had been used against him and his lawyer in the battle over his threatened deportation from the USA.

1964 THE ROLLING STONES appeared on the Ed Sullivan show.

1944 JON ANDERSON (Yes) born, Accrington, Lancashire.

1942 HELEN REDDY born, Melbourne, Australia.

WEDNESDAY

26

1967 PINK FLOYD played the Fillmore West, San Francisco, third on the bill behind Big Brother and the Holding Company and Richie Havens. Part of an eight-day tour of the Americas, the most intriguing moment of which must have been their appearance on Dick Clark's Bandstand, miming to 'See Emily Play' — singer Syd Barrett decided not to move his lips.

1965 THE BEATLES were invested with their MBEs at Buckingham Palace...after they'd partaken of a little draw in the gents.

1965 FONTELLA BASS topped the *Billboard* R&B charts with 'Rescue Me'.

➤ **1963 BOB DYLAN** played New York's Carnegie Hall, writing a poem, 'My Life In A Stolen Moment', for the program notes.

➤ **1956 TOMMY STEEL's** first single, 'Rock With The Cavemen', entered the UK charts.

1944 FLORENCE FOSTER JENKINS, 'the world's worst singer', hired Carnegie Hall for a farewell performance. Probably her most acclaimed performance, it was truly awful. Born in Pennsylvania in 1864, she didn't make her debut till she was forty, old enough to have inherited her parents' considerable wealth. Her chosen metier was opera though her voice was such that deciding whether she was a sopramo or a mezzo soprano was a task that would have occupied a bevvy of musicologists for more than a handful of years. Convinced that her audiences thought she was a truly great singer, she'd hurl basketfulls of rosebuds into the audience during her theme tune, the Spanish song, 'Cavelitos'.

1964
'(There's) Always Something
There To Remind Me'
Sandie Shaw

1980
'Woman In Love'
Barbra Streisand

1974
'Everything I Own'
Ken Boothe

THURSDAY

27

1977 LYNYRD SKYNYRD was decimated when three of the band — singer Ronnie Van Zant, guitarist Steve Gaines and backing singer, Cassie Gaines — died in the crash when their plane ran out of fuel coming in to land in Florida.

1960 BEN E. KING, working in the Bell Studios, W54th St., New York, cut 'Spanish Harlem' and 'Stand By Me'. Leiber and Stoller were producing while Phil Spector was hanging around in a corner somewhere.

▶ **1958 SIMON LE BON** (Duran Duran) born.

1933 FLOYD CRAMER, country pianist who hit with 'On The Rebound', born, Shreveport, Louisiana.

#1 UK LP
1973
'Hello'
Status Quo

FRIDAY

28

1977 THE SEX PISTOLS released their long-awaited and extraordinarily disappointing debut album, 'Never Mind The Bollocks...' If Pepsi Cola had ever gone in for anarchy in a big way, it would have sounded like this — smooth, poppy with a slight aroma of trying too hard.

1964 THE TAMI SHOW was filmed in Los Angeles, featuring the Beach Boys (who don't appear in the film), the Barbarians, Chuck Berry, Marvin Gaye, Gerry and the Pacemakers, Lesley Gore, Jan and Dean, Billy J. Kramer and the Dakotas, Smokey Robinson and the Miracles and the Supremes. Although the Rolling Stones were technically top of the bill, they refused to go on after James Brown's epic knee-drop and golden cape routine.

1945 WAYNE FONTANA (Glyn Geoffrey Ellis), born, Manchester, Lancashire.

▶ **1941 HANK B. MARVIN** born, Newcastle, Northumberland.

1941 CURTIS LEE, singer of 'Pretty Little Angel Eyes', born.

1938 KOKO TAYLOR (Cora Walton), Chicago blues singer of 'Wang Dang Doodle', born, Memphis.

#1 UK 45
1973
'Daydreamer'
David Cassidy

SATURDAY

29

1976 ELVIS PRESLEY recorded 'Way Down', the last hit he had before he passed on to the great hamburger joint cum pharmacy in the sky, cutting it in a studio in his Gracelands mansion.

▶ **1971 DUANE ALLMAN** died, aged 25, in a motorbike crash in Macon, Georgia.

1967 'HAIR' opened, off-Broadway, at the Public Theater, East Greenwich Village.

1966 EMI RECORDS chairman, Sir Joseph Lockwood, told the *Sun* that, even if commercial radio were introduced in Britain, he would refuse to allow his records to be played o it.

1965 THE WHO released 'My Generation'.

1946 PETER GREEN (the original Fleetwood Mac) born, Bethnal Green, London.

1944 DENNY LAINE (Brian Arthur Haynes) born on a boat off the coast of Jersey.

1940 MICKY GALLAGHER (Blockheads) born, Newcastle, Northumberland.

#1 US 45
1966
'96 Tears'
? and the Mysterians

SUNDAY

30

1981 THE FUN BOY THREE, the pop faction that emerged from the Specials' split, released their debut single, 'The Lunatics Have Taken Over The Asylum'.

1975 BOB DYLAN's Rolling Thunder Revue played its first show, in Plymouth, Massachusetts.

1970 HOTLEGS, the fore-runner of 10 CC, played their first show, supporting the Moody Blues at London's Festival Hall.

1968 THE MC5 recorded their debut album, 'Kick Out The Jams', live at Russ Gibb's Grande Ballroom, the occasion being the 'Zenta New Year'.

1967 BRIAN JONES, found guilty of possession of marijuana, was sentenced to nine months and taken to London's Wormwood Scrubs jail.

1943 GRACE SLICK born, Chicago.

1939 EDDIE HOLLAND born, Detroit. The first — or maybe it's the third, I can never remember — part of Holland-Dozier-Holland, Motown's most productive and prolific writing and producing team.

#1 UK 45
1971
'Imagine'
John Lennon

MONDAY

31

1980 SPANDAU BALLET released their first single, 'Cut A Long Story Short'. Overnight, every other 'concerned' rock writer confessed to having been a soul boy all along, having only been attracted to the *spectacle* of punk.

1975 QUEEN released their biggest-selling single, the cod operatic 'Bohemian Rhapsody'.

1967 BRIAN JONES was released from Wormwood Scrubs, pending appeal, on £750 bail.

► **1965 ANNABELLA LWIN** (Bow Wow Wow) born. A pop manipulator's dream, a Trilby to Malcolm McLaren's Svengali. The image is so obvious that the ironies pretty much collapse it into farce. When she sings 'I'm a rock 'n' roll puppet' who's she kidding? Herself? McLaren? Those outraged at a young girl so obviously used? The delicious confusion, of course, is just what gives the band its piquancy. That and their sexy songs which first found favour with the ageing and knowing but eventually cut through to Annabella's own age group. Even better, like all child actors, Annabella has a pushy mother who swings wildly between moral outrage and claiming all the credit for herself. Elizabeth Taylor would understand.

1965 THE MINDBENDERS parted company with Wayne Fontana.

► **1964 BOB DYLAN** played New York's Carnegie Hall, taping the show for a possible — but never released — live album.

1947 RUSS BALLARD, former member of Argent and songwriter, born.

1944 KINKY FRIEDMAN born, Rio Duckworth, Texas.

1937 TOM PAXTON born, Chicago.

NOVEMBER

TUESDAY

1

1980 GRAHAM BONNET left Rainbow.

1974 QUEEN released their third album, 'Sheer Heart Attack', surely the worst pun ever to grace a record sleeve.

1973 SALVATION — later to turn into teeny bop product, Slik in the cynical hands of Martin & Coulter — player the Glasgow Apollo, as support to Sweet.

1969 THE BEATLES released the last album they recorded together, 'Abbey Road'.

1968 GEORGE HARRISON released 'Wonderwall Music', the first Beatles solo record of any kind.

1968 THE DEVIANTS released their sensitive, subtle theme tune, 'Let's Loot The Supermarket'.

1967 FAMILY played their first show.

1963 THE ROLLING STONES released their second single and first top twenty hit, 'I Wanna Be Your Man', one of Lennon and McCartney's less developed compositions.

1962 THE BEATLES started their fourth season at the Star Club, Hamburg.

1953 THE DRIFTERS' 'Money Honey' topped the *Billboard* R&B chart.

1945 RIC GRECH (Family, Blind Faith, Gram Parsons' band) born, Bordeaux, France.

WEDNESDAY

2

1978 CLASH manager, Bernard Rhodes, obtained a court order, stipulating that all Clash earnings were to be paid direct to him.

► **1974 GEORGE HARRISON** started a fifty date tour of North America in Vancouver, Canada.

1968 CREAM appeared in New York for the last time, in front of 21,000 at Madison Square Gardens.

1966 MISSISSIPPI JOHN HURT, country blues singer, died, 74, Grenada, Mississippi.

1961 JOHN COLTRANE, jazz saxophonist colossus, recorded his 'Live At The Village Vanguard' album in New York City over the next two nights.

1955 BILLBOARD began publishing the Hot Hundred. Before that, their chart had varied in size from ten to thirty records.

1947 DAVE PEGG (Fairport Convention) born.

1944 KEITH EMERSON born.

► **1941 BRUCE WELCH** (Shadows) born, Bognor Regis, Sussex.

1941 JAY BLACK, of Jay and the Americans, born.

#1 US 45
1964
'Baby Love'
Supremes

#1 UK 45
1957
'That'll Be The Day'
Crickets

#1 UK 45
1963
'You'll Never Walk Alone'
Gerry and the Pacemakers

THURSDAY

3

1979 2 TONE staked its claim to being that year's dominant British musical fashion. 'The Specials', the band's debut, entered the UK album charts at number four and the Madness debut, 'One Step Beyond', slotted in a little lower, at number sixteen.

1972 JAMES TAYLOR AND CARLY SIMON were married in her Manhattan apartment. Later that evening, she joined him onstage, taking a bow at his Radio City Music Hall show.

1962 PAUL RAVEN, the future Gary Glitter, released a cover of Gene McDanciels' US hit, 'Tower Of Strength'. Raven's luck had yet to arrive — Frankie Vaughan had the UK hit with the song.

► **1961 JIMMIE RODGERS**, 'The Singing Brakeman' who'd died in 1933, was unanimously elected as the first member of Nashville's Country Music Hall of Fame.

► **1954 ADAM ANT** (Stuart Goddard) born, London. A mess of confusion who both had fame thrust upon him and reached out for it with two, greedy hands. Hustling around the fringes of punk, he was a bad, silly joke. But, by surviving while others disintegrated, he gained a large cult following of sorts; one impressed by his 'Sex' talk and unworried by his Nazi chic. Starting over with the massed drums of the Burundi, his simple rhythms and crass but exciting slogans attracted the very young. Sadly, like all the worst teeny stars, Adam turned 'entertainer' spurning both his audience and his own slight but undeniable talent for danceable fairy stories.

1948 LULU (Marie McDonald McLaughlin Lawrie) born, Glasgow.

1943 BERT JANSCH, folk singer, born, Glasgow.

1941 BRIAN POOLE born, London.

1932 ANDY WILLIAMS born, Wall Lake, Iowa.

FRIDAY

4

1968 CREAM played their final US show, in Providence, Rhode Island.

1967 THE DOORS' second album, 'Strange Days', entered the US chart.

1963 THE BEATLES played the Royal Command Performance at London's Prince of Wales theatre. "Those of you in the cheaper seats, clap" John Lennon advised the audience, "the rest of you can rattle your jewellery."

1961 BOB DYLAN played a show at the small Chapter Hall in the Carnegie Hall building, New York. Not quite small enough though — only fifty people, mostly friends, showed and paid two dollars apiece. The promoter lost money...but Dylan still got his twenty dollar fee.

► **1956 JAMES HONEYMAN-SCOTT** (Pretenders) born, Hereford.

► **1954 CHRIS DIFFORD** (Squeeze) born, Greenwich, London.

SATURDAY

5

1973 RONNIE LANE'S SLIM CHANCE played their first show, in Chipperfield's Circus big top on Clapham Common, London.

1972 MISS CHRISTINE, member of the GTOs, cover girl of Zappa's 'Hot Rats' and the subject of Gram Parsons' 'Hot Burrito No. 2' (I'm Your Toy'), died of a drugs overdose.

1947 HERMAN/PETER NOONE born, Manchester, Lancashire.

1946 GRAM PARSONS born, Winterhaven, Florida.

1941 ART GARFUNKEL born, NYC.

► **1931 IKE TURNER** born, Clarksdale, Mississippi.

SUNDAY

6

1979 THE BEAT released their first single, 'Tears Of A Clown'/'Ranking Full Stop', on the Specials' 2 Tone label.

1972 BILLY MURCIA, the New York Dolls' original drummer, died in London, aged 21, when — after a night's indulgence at the Speakeasy — he suffocated when a girl tried to revive him by pouring coffee down his throat.

1950 CHRIS GLEN (Sensational Alex Harvey Band) born.

1946 GLENN FREY (Eagles) born, Detroit.

1941 DOUG SAHM born, San Antone, Texas.

1938 P.J. PROBY (James Marcus Smith) born, Houston, Texas.

1962
'He's A Rebel'
Crystals

1972
'I Can See Clearly Now'
Johnny Nash

1965
'Get Off My Cloud'
Rolling Stones

1977
'Name Of The Game'
Abba

NOVEMBER

MONDAY

7

1980 DEXY'S MIDNIGHT RUNNERS, split. The majority formed the Bureau, taking a brave leap into obscurity while the rump — singer and writer, Kevin Rowland, and trombonist/arranger Big Jim Patterson — retained the name and the 'passion'.

1975 STEVE ANDERSON set a new world record for continuous guitar plucking, in Los Angeles — 114 hours and 17 minutes, a jump of four hours over the previous record.

1969 THE ROLLING STONES played the first date — Fort Collins, Colorado — on the US tour which transformed them from musicians to legends, supported by Ike & Tina Turner and Terry Reid. On later dates, they were sometimes joined by Chuck Berry or B.B. King.

1960 A.P. CARTER died, Maces Springs, Virginia. The head of the Carter Family who were the first people to record the old folk tunes which formed the basis of hillbilly and, eventually, country music.

➤ **1943 JONI MITCHELL** (Roberta Joan Anderson) born, McLeod, Alberta, Canada.

1942 JOHNNY RIVERS born, New York.

1938 DEE CLARK, R&B singer, born, Blythesville, Arkansas.

➤ **1937 MARY TRAVERS** (Peter, Paul & Mary) born, Louisville, Kentucky.

TUESDAY

8

1975 DR. FEELGOOD recorded their show at the Southend Kursaal, providing the second side of their chart-topping album, 'Stupidity'.

1974 IVORY JOE HUNTER, R&B singer and pianist, died, Houston, Texas. Texan Ivory Joe started out recording for his own, modestly-named Ivory Records in the mid-forties but despite relocating in California, his biggest success came with King Records of Cincinnati, Ohio, for whom he cut a series of big hits backed by the Duke Ellington orchestra. His rich, deep, sweet voice gave a distinctive distance to his music, always he sounded like he was trying very hard not to care. Like many Southern R&B musicians, he was as close to country music as he was to the blues, seeing both as just different sides of the same raised-in-poverty-and-isolation set of emotions. Right back in the early fifties, he cut Hank Williams' songs for MGM, nearly ten years before Ray Charles supposedly crashed through the racial boundaries with 'Modern Sounds In Country And Western Music.'

1968 JOHN AND CYNTHIA LENNON were divorced in London after six years of marriage.

1961 SEAN OLIVER (Rip, Rig & Panic) born.

1958 TERRY DE MIALL HARRON (Adam and the Ants) born, London.

1950 BONNIE RAITT born, Los Angeles.

1946 ROY WOOD born, Birmingham, Warwickshire.

➤ **1944 BONNIE BRAMLETT** (Lynn) born, Acton, Illinois.

WEDNESDAY

9

➤ **1980 BOB DYLAN** started his first tour of the US as a card-carrying 'born again' fundamentalist. Praise the Lord and pass the thesaurus.

1975 DAVID BOWIE's US TV debut on the Cher was broadcast. Taped in October, it featured Bowie singing 'Fame' and duetting with Cher — first on Bowie's 'Can You Hear Me' and then on a medley which ran: 'Young Americans', Neil Diamond's 'Song Sung Blue', Harry Nilsson's 'One', 'Da Doo Ron Ron', 'Wedding Bell Blues', 'Maybe', 'Day Tripper', 'Ain't No Sunshine', 'Youngblood' and back to 'Young Americans'. (Incidentally, Cher's very first recording session had been as a backing singer on the Crystals' original version of 'Da Doo Ron Ron'; for the TV show with Bowie, Darlene Love, singer of the original, was in the background chorus.)

1967 'ROLLING STONE' published its first issue, giving away a roach holder as a promotional freebie with every copy.

1961 BRIAN EPSTEIN saw the Beatles play for the first time, at a lunchtime session at the Cavern. According to later reports, he was particularly struck by John Lennon's trousers.

THURSDAY

10

1978 THE CLASH's second album, 'Give 'Em Enough Rope, produced by Blue Oyster Cult's father figure, Sandy Pearlman, was released.
1967 DAVID BOWIE made his first TV appearance on the Dutch show, 'Fan Club'.
1965 THE FILLMORE WEST held its first rock'n'roll concert. On the bill were the Grateful Dead, Jefferson Airplane and the Charlatans. Promoter Bill Graham paid sixty dollars rent for the hall.
1948 GREG LAKE born, Bournemouth, Hampshire.
► **1944 TIM RICE**, writer of musicals, born, Amersham, Buckinghamshire.
► **1940 SCREAMIN' LORD SUTCH** born.
1939 TOMMY 'BUBBA' FACENDA born, Virginia. In 1959 he recorded twenty eight local versions of 'High School USA' but even this sterling effort gained him no more than a minor hit.

1967
'Baby Now That I've Found You'
Foundations

FRIDAY

11

1972 BERRY OAKLEY, an Allman Brother, crashed his motor bike into a bus in Macon, Georgia, three blocks from where Duane Allman died on his bike. Oakley refused hospital treatment and died later of a brain haemorrhage.
1970 BOB DYLAN's only novel 'Tarantula', was finally published. Most reviewers agreed that waiting for Godot would have been more fruitful.
1969 JIM MORRISON was arrested on a Continental Airlines flight from Los Angeles to Phoenix, Arizona where he planned to see a Rolling Stones show. He — and his friend Tom Baker — were charged with interfering with the hostesses, a federal charge carrying a possible ten year sentence and $10,000 fine. After the initial fuss, the stewardess whose complaints had been crucial to the case, withdrew her accusations and the case against Morrison was dropped.
► **1958 HANK BALLARD** and his Midnighters cut the original version of 'The Twist' in the King Studios, Cincinnati, Ohio.
1956 IAN CRAIG MARSH (Heaven 17) born.
1953 ANDY PARTRIDGE (XTC) born, Malta.
1928 LAVERN BAKER, R&B singer, born, Chicago.
1927 MOSE ALLISON, jazz singer, pianist and writer of 'parchman Farm', born, Tippo, Mississippi.

1972
'Claire'
Gilbert O'Sullivan

1977
'Never Mind The Bollocks...Here's The Sex Pistols'

SATURDAY

12

1979 SNOWY WHITE joined Thin Lizzy.
1979 JOHN SLOMAN joined Uriah Heep.
1972 BOBBY JAMESON a singer once produced by Keith Richard was talked down from the roof of the Hollywood Theater...three months after being talked down from the roof of the Hyatt House hotel and two months after an epileptic seizure at the Troubadour. As he was walking out the Hollywood Theater, he fell on the steps, breaking both his legs.
1973 QUEEN started their first national tour, supporting Mott The Hoople in Leeds.
1945 NEIL YOUNG born, Toronto, Canada.
1944 BOOKER T. JONES born, Memphis.
► **1943 BRIAN HYLAND** born, Queens, NYC.
1917 STORYVILLE, the red light district of New Orleans, was closed down by the military authorities, forcing all the jazz musicians chopping out a living in brothel parlours to leave town, introducing jazz to the rest of the world.
1902 CARUSO recorded the first record to become a million seller, 'Vesta La Guibba', in Italy, later recutting in the USA with a full orchestra.

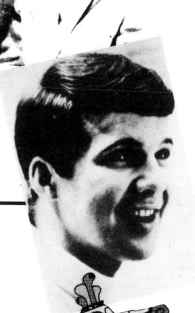

SUNDAY

13

► **1968 'YELLOW SUBMARINE'** had its US premiere.
1968 BRIAN JONES bought Cotchford Farm in Sussex, the house where A.A. Milne wrote *Winnie The Pooh*.
1949 TERRY REID born, Paxton Park, Huntingdonshire.
1934 TIMMY THOMAS, singer of 'Why Can't We Live Together', born, Evansville, Indiana.

1971
'Coz I Luv You'
Slade

NOVEMBER
M O N D A Y

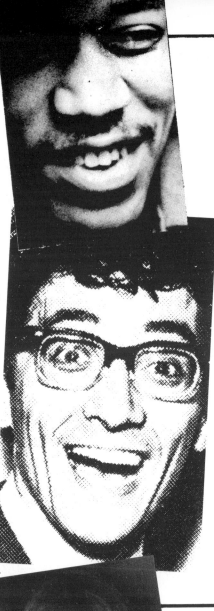

14
1975 **QUEEN** released 'A Night At The Opera', an album reported to have cost somewhere between thirty and forty thousand pounds to record.
1969 **DAVID BOWIE** released his debut album, on Phillips.
➤ 1967 **THE JIMI HENDRIX EXPERIENCE** head-lined the first night of a Tito Burns package tour at London's Royal Albert Hall. Hendrix got forty minutes. Down the bill were The Move (thirty minutes), Pink Floyd (seventeen minutes), Amen Corner (fifteen minutes), The Nice (twelve minutes), Heir Apparent and Outer Limits (eight minutes each).
1966 **BRIAN EPSTEIN** denied rumours that the Beatles were about to part company.
1952 **THE NEW MUSICAL EXPRESS** published the first UK charts. At number one was Al Martino's 'Here In My Heart' which stayed there for eight weeks.
➤ 1940 **FREDDIE GARRITY** born, Manchester. A fool from Manchester who hoisted himself into the charts on the tails of the Merseybeat Boom. Freddie and the Dreamers appealed greatly to the scarcely sophisticated tastes of the pre-teens. By introducing their dance craze for dorks, 'The Freddie', they were even bigger in the States than they were in their home country — undoubtedly some kind of odd benchmark of the depth of the USA's Anglophilia in the mid-sixties. Presumably, their fans saw them as an alternative Betles composed entirely of five Ringos. Their split in the late sixties, because of 'musical differences', still prompts passionate argument amongst pop scholars, dividing them into two, terminally hostile camps — those who consider Freddie, wanting to move with the times, wished to recut their earlier hit, 'Short Shorts', as 'Crazy Kaftans', and those who are convinced that the bulk of the Dreamers, inspired by the May 1968 uprising in Paris, wanted to reconstitute themselves as an autonomous anarcho-syndicalist commune, drawing heavily on the philosophies of Situationism, using it as a forward base for intervention in the pre-teen market with a musical mime show entitled 'If You Gotta Make A Fool Of Somebody, Make It Of Yourself'. Freddie, in their vision, would have become a dialectical interlocutor who combined the best elements of black-face minstrel show and Mao's musings on industrialisation in the province of Hunan. History, cruel as ever, smashed their dreams and pushed Freddie into the kid's TV show, 'Little Big Time'.
1938 **CORNELL GUNTER** (Flairs, Coasters) born, Los Angeles.
1922 **THE BBC** made its first regular broadcast, from Alexandra Palace, London, under the call sign, 2 LO.

T U E S D A Y

15
1975 **J. GEILS** started recording their 'Blow Your Face Out' live double at the Boston Gardens. The rest of the album was taped at the Cobo Hall, Detroit, four nights later.
1969 **JANIS JOPLIN** was arrested in Tampa, Florida for using 'vulgar and indecent language' and released on a $50 bond.
➤ 1945 **ANNI-FRID LYNGSTAD-FREDRIKSSON** (Abba) born, Norway. (She grew up in Toshalla, Sweden.)
1942 **DAVE CLARK** born, Tottenham, London.
1937 **LITTLE WILLIE JOHN** (William J. Woods), teenage R&B star, born, Camden, Arkansas.
➤ 1933 **PETULA CLARK** born, Epsom, Surrey.
1932 **CLYDE McPHATTER**, R&B singer, born, Durham, North Carolina.

W E D N E S D A Y

16
1974 **MIKE LEADBITTER**, blues collector and publisher/editor of 'Blues Unlimited', died.
1973 **RONNIE LANE** released his first solo single, 'How Come'.
1956 **RORY BLACKWELL**, possibly the first British rocker, had his show in Brixton, London, interrupted by 'Teddy Boy disturbances'.
1949 **PATTI SANTOS** (It's A Beautiful Day) born.
1938 **TONI BROWN** (Joy Of Cooking) born.
1938 **TROY SEALS**, session musician, born, Bill Hill, Kentucky.

T H U R S D A Y

17

1979 JOHN GRASCOCK, former Jethro Tull bass player, died in London, aged 27. He'd left the band after having heart surgery from which he never recovered.

1968 DAVID BOWIE's mime troupe, Feathers, made their first appearance, at the Country Club, Hampstead, London.

1947 ROD CLEMENTS (Lindisfarne) born.

1942 BOB CREWE (Four Seasons) born, the Bronx, NYC.

➤ **1941 GENE CLARK** (Byrds) born, Tipton, Missouri.

1938 GORDON LIGHTFOOT born, Orillia, Ontario, Canada.

F R I D A Y

➤ **18**

1976 RICHARD HELL AND THE VOIDOIDS made their world debut at CBGBs, the New York club.

1972 DANNY WHITTEN, Crazy Horse guitarist, died of a heroin overdose. Neil Young commemorated his death on the sprawling, painful, brutally honest 'Tonight's The Night'.

1971 LITTLE JUNIOR PARKER, R&B singer, died during a brain operation in St. Francis Hospital, Chicago. From the backstreets of West Memphis, Herman Parker got into the blues as a harmonica player, eventually graduating to Howlin' Wolf's band in the late forties, where he shared the blowing and sucking duties with James Cotton. Around the same time he worked with his main stylistic influence Sonny Boy Wiliamson, then a regular on King Biscuit Hour.

In 1952, he formed his own band, the Blue Flames, and cut a couple of sides for the Modern label under the direction of its A&R scout and arranger, Ike Turner. But it was his next venture for which he's best remembered. Still in Memphis, he cut two singles for Sun Records, then strictly a blues label. One of them was the rumbustious boasting of 'Feeling' Good', where Parker sneered with just the kind of street-wise sassiness the lyrics demanded and whipped out the best whoop of joy ever put on record. The other single, though, was even better. A black version of the Carter Family's white hillbilly song, 'Worried Man Blues', 'Mystery Train' was full of menace, like a story without an explanation. Two years later, in Elvis Presley's hands, it became a cry of utter desparation, an exorcism of unseen devils, the most astounding, maybe even the best rock'n'roll record ever made.

1963 EMI RECORDS' chariman, Sir Joseph Lockwood, presented the Beatles with a silver disc for 250,000 sales of 'Please Please Me'.

➤ **1960 KIM WILDE** (Smith) born, Chiswick, London. The finest flower of a family affair. Daddy used to be greasy pop singer. Brother Ricky writes and produces. Kim sings the results. A truly rare pop star. The only intelligent, assertive female British pop singer since the sixties. Only through her lips would 'Cambodia' not have sounded silly.

S A T U R D A Y

19

1979 CHUCK BERRY was released from Lamproc Prison Farm, California where he'd served two thirds of a four month sentence for tax evasion. While inside, he'd played a concert for the inmates. It was, in fact, his third spell behind bars. In his youth he'd been sent to borstal. And then, in the late fifties, he'd been jailed on a trumped-up charge under the Mann Act — transportation of a female across a state boundary for immoral purposes.

1954 ANNETTE GUEST (First Choice) born.

1937 RAY COLLINS (Mothers Of Invention) born.

S U N D A Y

➤ **20**

1966 'CABARET' opened at the Imperial Theater, New York.

1950 GARY GREEN (Gentle Giant) born.

1946 DUANE ALLMAN born, Nashville, Tennessee.

1944 MIKE VERNON, producer and founder of Blue Horizon records, born, Harrow, London.

1942 NORMAN GREENBAUM, singer of 'Spirit In The Sky', born, Malden, Massachusetts.

NOVEMBER

MONDAY

21 **1980 DON HENLEY**, the Eagles drummer, was arrested when medical services were called to his Los Angeles home to cope with a naked sixteen year old girl suffering from the effect of too many drugs. Later, he was given two years' probation, a £2000 fine and two years attendance at a drug counselling scheme.

1976 CHELSEA, one of the first punk bands, played their last show with their original line-up, guitarist Billy Idol and bassist Tony James going off to form Generation X.

1968 THE BEATLES released their double white album, at the bargain price of £3.70.

➤ **1968 YOKO ONO** miscarried in a London hospital with John Lennon by her side, an event later commemorated on the sleeve of 'Unfinished Music No. 2'.

1959 ALAN FREED, DJ and self-proclaimed 'King Of Rock'n'Roll', was dropped by WABC New York when he refused to sign an affidavit stating he never took money to play records. Freed took off for KDAY Los Angeles but only lasted till the Spring of the following year when the payola investigators brought an indictment against him, claiming he'd taken $30,650 in bribes.

1964
'Baby Love'
Supremes

TUESDAY

22 **1969 'JOE COCKER'** entered the US album chart.

1965 BOB DYLAN married Sarah in Nassau County. (The event didn't reach the papers until the following February.)

➤ **1955 ELVIS PRESLEY** signed an official management contract with Colonel Tom Parker, former fairground hustler, and signed to RCA Records, his former label, Sun, receiving £35,000 plus £5000 in back royalties.

1946 ASTON 'FAMILY MAN' BARRETT (Wailers) born, Kingston, JA.

1899 HOAGY CARMICHAEL, composer of 'Stardust', born, Indiana.

1975
'D.I.V.O.R.C.E.'
Billy Connolly

WEDNESDAY

23 **1979 MARIANNE FAITHFUL** was arrested at Oslo Airport, Norway, for possession of marijuana. After she signed a confession, she was allowed to proceed on her tour of the country.

1964 THE ROLLING STONES were banned by the BBC for arriving late fro the radio programmes 'Saturday Club' and 'Top Gear'.

➤ **1936 ROBERT JOHNSON**, the Prometheus of the blues, recorded for the first time, in a San Antonio hotel, cutting five tracks including 'Come On In My Kitchen' and 'Rambling On My Mind'.

1899 LOUIS GLASS, who held the West Coast franchise for the North American Phonograph Company, installed the first-ever coin-operated phonograph in the Palais Royal hotel, San Francisco. The machine, the first jukebox, had four tubes to listen through and a coin slot on each — it could bring in up to twenty cents a play. The machine was so successful that, by the time of the phonograph manufacturers annual convention the following year, Glass was able to boast that all his income came from coin operated machines. Although, of course, these very early machines only contained one record, they were the beginning of the American juke box boom. Within a couple of years, several diferent companies were operating the new-fangled — and profitable — record players. Felix Gottschalk of the Metropolitan Phonograph Company set up a deal with North American to supply machine parts and formed the Automatic Phonograph Exhibition Company on a capital base of a million dollars. The Columbia Phonograph Company — which, after many, many changes became the Columbia Records of toady — went into the pay as you play phonograph business and the Louisiana Phonograph Company took the innovative step of changing the one record on their machines twice daily. But, despite North American's lead in the manufacture and distribution of jukeboxes, its founder, Thomas A. Edison, took the decision to wind up the company's affairs in 1894, preferring to concentrate on machines for the home.

1959
'Mack The Knife'
Bobby Darin

T H U R S D A Y

24

1978 THE CLASH released 'Tommy Gun', their sixth single.
1972 DAVID BOWIE released 'Jean Genie', a song all about his friend, Iggy Pop.
1964 MANX RADIO, on the Isle Of Man, became Britain's first land-based commercial station. (The Isle Of Man is outside the jurisdiction of British broadcasting legislation.)
1945 LEE MICHAELS born, Los Angeles.
► **1944 BEV BEVAN** (ELO) born, Birmingham, Warwickshire.
1943 ROBIN WILLIAMSON (Incredible String Band) born, Glasgow.
1941 DUCK DUNN, former MG and session bassist, born, Memphis, Tennessee.
1868 SCOTT JOPLIN, composer of the music used much later in the film, 'The Sting', born.

#1 US 45
1958
'It's Only Make Believe'
Conway Twitty

F R I D A Y

25

1972 THE ROLLING STONES started recording in Byron Lee's studio in Kingston, Jamaica. The results became 'Goat's Head Soup'.
1970 ALBERT AYLER, avant garde jazz saxophonist was found floating near Brooklyn's Congress St. Pier in New York's East River. No-one knew for sure how long he'd been dead — he hadn't been seen for twenty days before his corpse was discovered.
1969 JOHN LENNON returned his MBE to the Queen 'with love', as a protest against British involvement in the Vietnam and Nigerian civil wars...and his 'Cold Turkey' slipping down the charts.
1955 BILL HALEY'S 'Rock Around The Clock' topped the UK singles chart, the first rock'n'roll record to do so.
► **1945 JOHN McVIE** (Fleetwood Mac) born, London.
1945 MILES DAVIS made his first recording date — with Charlie Parker's band.

#1 UK 45
1972
'My Ding-A-Ling'
Chuck Berry

S A T U R D A Y

26

1976 THE SEX PISTOLS released their first record, 'Anarchy In The UK'.
1975 REVEREND CHARLES BOYKIN of Lakewood Baptist Church, Florida, got his youth group to collect more than $2000 worth of rock'n'roll records, stuffed them in garbage cans outside the church and set fire to them. The reason for this excess was that Brother Charlie — as *Rolling Stone* referred to him — said of 1000 girls who got pregnant out of wedlock, 984 got that way doing it to a background of rock'n'roll.
1973 JOHN ROSTILL, a Shadow, was found electrocuted in his own home. The jury at the coroner's court returned an open verdict, indicating the possibility of his having been responsible for his own death in some way.
► **1968 CREAM** played their last concert, at the Royal Albert Hall, London. The event was filmed for BBC TV by Tony Palmer who edited the results into a particularly noxious piece of sycophancy.
1946 BURT REITER (Focus) born, Holland.
► **1938 TINA TURNER** (Annie Bullock) born, Brownsville, Tennessee.

#1 UK 45
1961
'Take Good Care Of My Baby'
Bobby Vee

S U N D A Y

27

1973 JIMMY WIDENER, Hank Snow's lead guitarist, was mugged and shot dead.
1972 'GREASE' opened at the Royale Theater, NYC, eventually becoming the longest running Broadway show in December 1979 after 3243 performances.
1970 GEORGE HARRISON released his first solo album of music — as opposed to the aural scribbling of 'Wonderwall' — the triple set, 'All Things Must Pass'.
1969 THE ROLLING STONES — over the next two nights — recorded 'Get Your Ya Yas Out' at New York's Madison Square Gardens.
1965 KEN KESEY hosted the first public acid test, as immortalised in Tom Wolfe's book, 'The Electric Kool Aid Acid Test'.
1964 THE BEATLES released their fourth album, 'Beatles For Sale', and their ninth single, 'I Feel Fine'.
1942 JIMI HENDRIX born, Seattle, Washington.
1934 AL JACKSON, MG and session drummer, born, Memphis, Tennessee.

#1 UK 45
1965
'The Carnival Is Over'
New Seekers

NOVEMBER

M O N D A Y

28

1976 DAVID BOWIE was interviewed on Russel Harty's British TV show, live by satellite. Franco had died that day and American TV asked if they could have Bowie's time. He refused.

1968 JOHN LENNON was fined £150 for possession of marijuana.

► **1949 HUGH McKENNA** (Sensatonal Alex Harvey Band) born.

► **1943 RANDY NEWMAN** born, Los Angeles.

1940 CLEM CURTIS (Fortunes) born.

1940 BRUCE CHANEL born, Jacksonville, Texas.

1929 BERRY GORDY, founder of Motown, born, Detroit. The most important Black American businessman ever. Where others set up record labels, Gordy formed a corporation, as much a high capacity, high speed production line as the car factories on the other side of Detroit. As a songwriter and producer he'd had 18 Hot Hundred hits by th end of the fifties. As the head of Motown, he must have had twenty times that number, all of them sounding less like individual records than excerpts from the same, endless story.

T U E S D A Y

29

1979 ANITA PALLENBERG was cleared of complicity in the death of Scott Cantrell, the young man who died in her American house.

1968 VAN MORRISON released 'Astral Weeks'.

1968 JOHN LENNON released his first solo album, 'Two Virgins', featuring a full-frontal nude cover shot of John and Yoko.

1963 THE BEATLES released 'I Want To Hold Your Hand', their fifth single.

1944 FELIX CAVALIERE (Rascals) born, Pelham, New York.

1941 DENNIS DOHERTY (Mamas & Papas) born, Halifax, Nova Scotia, Canada.

► **1933 JOHN MAYALL** born, Manchester, Lancashire. A British eccentric who was convinced that he was imbued with the living spirit of THE BLUES. Although he'd been obsessed with the music since an early age, when he came down to London to form his first professional blues band, he was already a decade older than most of his fellow musicians. There's also little doubt that none of them — unlike him — had lived in a tree house to cut down on expenses. Nor it is likely that they had quite such extensive collections of blues records and erotica. As a musician, he blew a fairly thin harmonica, all puff and gasp, little power. As a singer, he was just the wrong side of adequate. And as a songwriter, he was pleased with himself when he worked out which key to play in\. But, somehow, God knows how, he collected around him the finest of the young British blues musicians\. Right through the sixties, he ran a series of bands under the umbrella name of the Bluesbreakers, each one of themincluding fresh, grasping talent. (If Mayall had turned his talents to an even older profession, he would undoubtedly have made an excellent Madame.) Eric Clapton worked with him for one album (Mayall's best effort by far.) John McVie stayed with him for several albums before going off to form Fleetwood Mac. Mick Taylor left him for the Rolling Stones. At one time, it seemed every other new British band was formed by John Mayall alumni. As his proteges superceded his fame, Mayall emigrated to the Promised Land where he settled into the semi-retirement of the occasional solo album and cataloguing his record collection.

W E D N E S D A Y

30

1972 WINGS relesed 'Hi Hi Hi' which the BBC banned because of its 'unsuitable lyrics'.

1963 BILLBOARD ceased publishing an R&B chart, not re-instating it until January 1965.

1958 DAVID McLYMONT (Orange Juice) born.

1957 RICHARD BARBIERI (Japan) born.

1956 CLARENCE PALMER AND THE JIVE BOMBERS recorded the thunderous doo wop of 'Bad Boy', NYC.

1953 SHUGGIE OTIS born, Los Angeles.

1945 ROGER GLOVER (Deep Purple) born, Brecon, South Wales.

1943 LEO LYONS (Ten Years After) born, Standbridge, Bedfordshire.

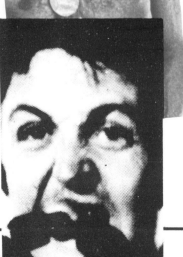

DECEMBER
THURSDAY

1
▶ **1978 IAN DURY** released his biggest seller, 'Hit Me With Your Rhythm Stick'.
▶ **1976 THE SEX PISTOLS** appeared on Bill Grundy's early evening British TV show. An — edited — extract.
GRUNDY: I'm told you have received £40,000 from a record company. Doesn't that seem...er...to be slightly opposed to your anti-materialistic view of life?
GLEN MATLOCK: No, the more the merrier.
GRUNDY: Well, tell me more then.
STEVE JONES: We've fuckin' spent it, ain't we?
GRUNDY: Really?
GLEN: Down the boozer.
(Grundy propositions Siouxsie Sioux, a member of the Pistols' entourage.)
STEVE: You dirty sod, you dirty old man.
GRUNDY: Well, keep going, chief, keep going, Go on, you've got another five seconds. Say something outrageous.
STEVE: You dirty bastard.
GRUNDY: Go on, again.
STEVE: You dirty *fucker!*
GRUNDY: *Whaaat* a clever boy.
STEVE: What a fucking rotter.
And so, with that rivetting dialogue, suburban Britain plunged into a moral panic it hadn't experienced since Mods and Rockers stopped whacking each other on Brighton Esplanade.
1969 MAGIC SAM (Maghett), Chicago bluesman, died, 32.
1959 STEVE JENSEN (Batt), member of Japan, born.
1946 GILBERT O'SULLIVAN born, Waterford, Eire.
1945 BETTE MIDLER born, Paterson, New Jersey.
1944 JOHN DENSMORE (Doors) born, Santa Monica, California.
▶ **1938 SANDY NELSON**, the sticks behind the way cry 'Let There Be Drums', born, Santa Monica, California.
1934 BILLY PAUL, soul singer, born, Philadelphia.

FRIDAY

2
1976 PINK FLOYD, photographing the cover of 'Animals', 'accidentally' let slip a giant inflatable pig over London's Bettersea Power Station.
1971 TAJ MAHAL played a show for the inmates on death row at Washington State Penitentiary.
1941 TOM McGUINNESS (Manfred Mann, McGuinness Flint, Blues Band) born.

SATURDAY

3
1965 THE BEATLES released 'Day Tripper' and their sixth album, 'Rubber Soul'.
1956 THE MILLION DOLLAR QUARTET recording at Sun studios, Memphis. Elvis Presley dropped by a year after he'd left for RCA New York and spent two and a half hours harmonising his way through the gospel catalogue with follow Fundamentalists, Jerry Lee Lewis, Carl Perkins and Johnny Cash.
▶ **1948 OZZY OSBOURNE** born.

SUNDAY

4
1979 A WHO concert in Cincinnati was the scene of eleven people being trampled to death in the rush to get to the best of the — unreserved — seats.
1976 BOB MARLEY was shot in the arm in his Kingston house in what was almost certainly an assassination attempt, part of the run up to that year's Jamaican elections.
1976 TOMMY BOLIN, Ritchie Blackmore's replacement in Deep Purple, died of a heroin overdose before a Miami concert.
1944 DENNIS WILSON (Beach Boys) born, Hawthorne, California.
1942 CHRIS HILLMAN (Byrds) born, Los Angeles.
1940 FREDDIE CANNON (Picariello) born, Lynn, Massachusetts.
▶ **1926 LEE DORSEY**, New Orleans soul singer, born, Portland, Oregon.

1968
'Love Child'
Diana Ross and the Supremes

1072
'Papa Was A Rolling Stone'.
Temptations

1977
'Mull Of Kintyre'
Wings

1971
'Family Affair'
Sly and the Family Stone

DECEMBER
MONDAY

5 **1971 KILBURN AND THE HIGH ROADS**, Ian Dury's first band, played their first show, getting twenty pounds for an appearance at the end of term ball at Canterbury Art College — where Ian was a lecturer.
1968 THE ROLLING STONES released 'Beggars Banquet', marking the occasion with a party at London's Elizabethan Rooms, cheering all the guests up by lobbing custard pies at them.
► **1959 GENE VINCENT** arrived at London's Heathrow airport to be met by an official welcoming committee which included TV producer Jack Good. Horrified by Vincent's very unlegendary mild southern manners and neat casual clothes, Good quickly stuffed Vincent into black leather with a heavy silver medallion swinging from his neck, later admitting that he swiped the image from 'Hamlet'
1947 JIM MESSINA born, Haywood, California.
► **1940 JOHN CALE** born, Wales.
1932 LITTLE RICHARD (Penniman) born, Macon, Georgia.

1959
'What Do You Want'
Adam Faith

TUESDAY

6 **1981 MICHAEL DEMPSEY**, publisher and manager of the Adverts, fell off a chair while changing a light bulb. He was found the next morning and taken to hospital where he died of a punctured liver and internal bleeding.
1970 'GIMME SHELTER', the film of the Stones 1969 tour of America, opened in New York on the first anniversary of its completion when...
1969 MEREDITH HUNTER was stabbed to death by Hell's Angels in front of the stage at the Rolling Stones free concert at the Altamont Speedway, near San Francisco, an event recorded in 'Gimme Shelter'.
► **1955 TENPOLE TUDOR** born, Waterloo, London.
Star of the Sex Pistol's 'Rock 'N' Roll Swindle', it all went to his head. He thinks he's a potential star, a keeper of the Holy Spirit of Punk. In fact, he's a slightly amusing novelty; he and his band are undoubtedly the Freddie and The Dreamers of the eighties.
1955 RICK BUCKLER (Jam) born, Woking, Surrey.
1949 LEADBELLY (Huddie Ledbetter), blues and folk singer, died, aged 64, of Gehrig's disease (Huntington's Chorea).
► **1944 JONATHAN KING** born, London.
1942 LEN BARRY, singer of '1-2-3', born, West Philadelphia.

1979
'Walking On The Moon'
The Police

WEDNESDAY

7 **1979 THE CLASH** released their ninth single, 'London Calling'.
1976 SIR JOHN REED, the chairman of EMI, made some comments 'on the content of records' at the company's AGM. 'Sex Pistols have acquired a reputation for aggressive behaviour...There is no excuse for this. Our...experience of working with the group, however, is satisfactory...whether EMI does in fact release any more of their records will have to be carefully considered.'
1967 THE BEATLES opened the notoriously unsuccessful Apple shop at 94 Baker St., London.
1963 THE BEATLES were the entire jury on British TV's 'Juke Box Jury'.
1963 THE BEATLES' 'I Want To Hold Your Hand' became the first of their records to enter the UK chart at number one, where it remained for the next five weeks.
1963 'JOHN FITZGERALD KENNEDY — A MEMORIAL ALBUM' was released. Retailing at 99 cents, it sold four million copies in the next six days, establishing itself as the world's fastest-selling album.
1963 THE SINGING NUN's 'Dominique' was top of the US singles chart with the Kingsmen's gumbie anthem 'Louie Louie' tucked right in below it.
► **1956 TOMMY STEELE AND THE STEELMEN** played London's Finsbury Park Astoria.
1949 TOM WAITS born, Pomona, California.
1942 HARRY CHAPIN born, Greenwich Village, NYC.
1877 THOMAS EDISON demonstrated the first phonograph — built to his design by his mechanic, John Kruesi — in the New York offices of *Scientific American*.

1974
'You're My First, My Last, My Everything'
Barry White

THURSDAY

8

1980 JOHN LENNON was shot five times with a .38 pistol by 25 year old Mark Chapman, in the courtyard of New York's Dakota building where Lennon lived in several apartments. The only musician ever to have been the victim of an assassination, the only rock star to have been killed because he was a rock star.
1978 PUBLIC IMAGE LTD. released their debut album.
1975 GARY THAIN, Uriah Heep bassist, died in his bath of a drugs overdose.
1949 RAY SHULMAN (Gentle Giant) born.
1947 GREG ALLMAN born, Nashville, Tennessee.
1946 GRAHAM KNIGHT (Marmalade) born.
1943 JIM MORRISON born, Melbourne, Florida.
1939 JERRY BUTLER, R&B singer, born, Sunflower, Mississippi.
1925 SAMMY DAVIS JR. born, NYC.
1925 JIMMY SMITH born. The fingers behind the jazz organ of the theme to 'Walk On The Wild Side'.

FRIDAY

9

1972 'TOMMY' was produced live onstage at London's Rainbow by Lou Reizner.
1967 CREAM's second album, 'Disraeli Gears', entered the US chart.
1967 JIM MORRISON was busted for the first time. Establishing relations with a girl in a backstage showeroom before a show in New Haven, Connecticut, Morrison was turfed out by a cop. Later, onstage Morrison told the crowd about the incident, badmouthing the cops in less than restrained terms. Off went the lights and Morrison was arrested onstage, charged with breach of the peace and that old standby, resisting arrest.
1964 JOHN COLTRANE recorded 'A Love Supreme'.
1957 DONNY OSMOND born, Ogden, Utah.
► **1950 JOAN ARMATRADING** born, St. Kitts, West Indies.
1932 JUNIOR WELLS, Chicago Blues harmonica player, born, West Memphis, Arkansas.

SATURDAY

10

1976 GENERATION X played their first show, at London's Central School of Art.
1972 FRANK ZAPPA broke a leg, an ankle and fractured his skull when a young man, jealous of Zappa because his girlfriend was enamoured with the Los Angeles cynic, pushed him into the orchestra pit at London's Rainbow Theatre.
►**1967 OTIS REDDING** and three of his backing band, the Bar Kays, died when their plane, carrying them from a show in Cleveland, Ohio, crashed into a frozen Wisconsin lake.
1954 GEOFF DEANE (Modern Romance) born.
1943 CHAD STUART (Chad & Jeremy) born, Durham.

SUNDAY

11

1972 GENESIS played their first US show, at Brandeis University, near Boston, Massachusetts.
1971 JOHN LENNON AND YOKO ONO played at a benefit in Ann Arbor, Michigan, for former MC5 manager, John Sinclair, Mr. Ten For Two himself, in jail on a drugs charge.
1970 JOHN LENNON released 'Plastic Ono Band', his first studio solo album of *songs*.
►**1964 SAM COOKE**, 29 year old sweet soul singer, was shot three times by Bertha Franklin, an employee of the Hacienda Motel, Los Angeles. Cooke had taken Elisa Boyer there after a party with friends and when she fled their room, Cooke chased her, finally arriving in the motel office where Bertha Franklin pumped the bullets into him as he lunged at her — in self protection? The papers had a field day with the fact that he was in his underwear and the jury took fifteen minutes to decide it was justifiable homicide, that he'd been shot in 'protection of life, limb and property'.
1954 GERMAINE JACKSON born, Gary, Indiana.
►**1944 BRENDA LEE** (Tarpley) born, Atlanta, Georgia.
1940 DAVID GATES (Bread) born, Tulsa, Oklahoma.
►**1926 WILLIE MAE 'BIG MAMA' THORNTON**, R&B singer of the original 'Hound Dog', born, Montgomery, Alabama.

#1 UK LP
1973
'Stranded'
Roxy Music

#1 UK 45
1967
'Hello Goodbye'
Beatles

#1 US 45
1966
'Good Vibrations'
Beach Boys

#1 US 45
1061
'Please Mr. Postman'
Marvelettes

D E C E M B E R
M O N D A Y

12

1974 THE ROLLING STONES announced that Mick Taylor was leaving the band.

1968 THE ROLLING STONES filmed their legendary, never shown, TV show, 'Rock And Roll Circus'. As well as the Stones, a classical pianist and violinist and the Robert Fossett Circus with the lovely Luna, the guests were The Who, Jethro Tull, Eric Clapton, John Lennon and Yoko Ono, Jimi Hendrix's drummer, Mitch Mitchell, Marianne Faithful and Taj Mahal.

1967 BRIAN JONES' sentence of nine months for marijuana possession was set aside.

1949 PAUL RODGERS (Free) born, Middlesborough, Yorkshire.

1943 DICKIE BETTS (Allman Brothers) born.

1942 MIKE PINDER (Moody Blues) born, Birmingham, Warwickshire.

1942 MIKE HERON born.

► **1941 DIONNE WARWICKE** born, East Orange, New Jersey. The main mouthpiece for the songs of Burt Bacharach and Hal David. Maybe a little more than that but no much. Although she had a big hit in 1974 when she teamed up with the Spinners for 'Then Came You', Philly soul with uptown emotion, it's her work with Bacharach and David that's given her a lifetime's gainful employment on the cabaret circuit. Brought up in a family of gospel singers (who didn't use the 'e' on their surname), she studied music from the age of six, graduating to the Hart College of Music in Hartford, Connecticut, where she still moonlighted for the Lord every Sunday. Her work as a backing singer for Garnett Mimms and the Drifters in New York City brought her to the attention of Bacharach and David, a pair of songwriters whose work trod the most careful of lines between teen beat psychodrama and showbiz schmaltz. Her light, unemotional voice was a perfect foil to the anguished love of their lyrics and melodies. Her readings of their songs — which were amongst the most polished ballads of the sixties — were simply definitive but, while she had the hits in the States, the British record buyer often had to be content with vastly inferior versions, notably Cilla Black's appalling overstated interpretation of 'Anyone Who Had A Heart'.

1938 CONNIE FRANCIS born, Newark, New Jersey.

► **1915 FRANK SINATRA** born, Hoboken, New Jersey.

1901 MARCONI transmitted and received the first radio signal.

T U E S D A Y

13

1978 DOLPHIN TAYLOR, a drummer, left the Tom Robinson Band.

1963 THE BEATLES finished their third UK tour, at the Southampton Gaumont.

► **1950 DAVID O'LIST** (Nice, Roxy Music, Jet) born.

1940 TONY GOMEZ (Foundations) born.

W E D N E S D A Y

14

1980 YOKO ONO asked for ten minutes silence in memory of John Lennon at 2 p.m.

1979 THE CLASH released their third album, 'London Calling'.

1969 THE WHO played 'Tommy' at London's Coliseum Opera House.

1963 DINAH WASHINGTON (Ruth Jones), a 'sultry siren of song', died when, after drinking heavily, she took too many sleeping pills.

1956 ROCK AND ROLL took hold of the UK singles chart. Tommy Steele's 'Singing The Blues', Bill Haley's 'Rudy's Rock' and Little Richard's 'Rip It Up' all enterd the chart.

► **1942 DAVE CLARK** born, Tottenham, London.

1934 CHARLIE RICH born, Colt, Arkansas. Country music's perpetual outsider. Sam Phillips thought he could replace the departed Elvis Presley. He thought he wanted to be a jazz musician. The public — despite 'Mohair Sam' and 'The Most Beautiful Girl In The World' — thought he couldn't make up his mind about stardom. They were right, he'd rather be home with his children and his songwriting wife, Margaret Ann.

#1 US 45
1968
'I Heard It Through The Grapevine'
Marvin Gaye

#1 US 45
1970
'Tears Of A Clown'
Smokey Robinson and the Miracles

#1 UK 45
1968
'Lily The Pink'
Scaffold

THURSDAY

15

1978 THE FALL recorded their 'Live At The Witch Trials' album at London's Camden Sound Suite, mixing it the following day.

1969 JOHN LENNON AND YOKO ONO played a 'War Is Over' concert at London's Lyceum, being joined onstage by George Harrison and Delaney & Bonnie.

1955 JOHNNY CASH released his original version of 'Folsom Prison Blues'.

► **1955 PAUL SIMONON** (Clash) born.

1949 PAUL WILLIAMS recorded the original version of 'The Hucklebuck', NYC.

1946 CARMINE APPICE born, Staten Island, NYC.

1946 HARRY RAY (Moments) born.

► **1944 GLENN MILLER**, the first Sultan of Swing, died in a plane crsh over the English Channel.

1943 FATS WALLER, boogie woogie piano played, died of alcoholic poisoning on the Sante Fe Superchief.

1939 CINDY BIRDSONG (Supremes) born.

1933 JESSE BELVIN, doo wop singer, born, Texarkana, Arkansas.

1922 ALAN FREED, the coiner of the phrase 'rock'n'roll' and the most important ever DJ, born, Johnstown, Pennsylvania.

1910 JOHN HAMMOND born, NYC. Self-proclaimed discoverer of Bessie Smith, Billie Holliday, Bob Dylan and Bruce Springsteen.

1979
'Another Brick In The Wall'
Pink Floyd

FRIDAY

16

► **1967 PINK FLOYD** played their first show at London's Middle Earth, an 'underground' club.

1946 BENNY ANDERSON (Abba) born, Stockholm, Sweden.

1943 TONY HICKS (Hollies) born.

1899 NOEL COWARD born.

1972
'Me And Mrs. Jones'
Billy Paul

SATURDAY

17

1981 CHRISTOPHER TYRER, a fifteen year old heavy metal fan of Wednesfield, Staffordshire, attended a Saxon concert in nearby Wolverhampton, spending the evening in a frenzied session of three hours' 'head banging'. The next morning he woke up paralysed on one side and unable to speak, dying eight days later on Christmas Day. The coroner returned a verdict of death by misadventure.

1977 'OH BOY!' a British teenage girls' magazine, ran a feature headlined 'Who's A Pretty Punk, Then?'. 'Ravishing Rotten' was placed in their top three dishy punks with the comment, 'He's so cute you can forget all those stupid spittin' and swearin' scenes the Pistols staged just to get noticed'.

1950 CHARLIE BARRETT (Wailers) born, Kingston, JA.

► **1943 DAVE DEE** (Harman), policeman, pop singer and record company executive, born, Salisbury, Wiltshire. (He was the copper who pulled Eddie Cochran's corpse from the car wreck.)

1942 PAUL BUTERFIELD born, Chicago.

► **1939 EDDIE KENDRICKS**, Motown singer, born, Birmingham, Alabama.

1937 ART NEVILE, R&B singer/writer/musician and Meter, born, New Orleans.

1936 TOMMY STEELE (Hicks) born, Bermondsey, London.

1964
'Beatles For Sale'

SUNDAY

18

1968 YOKO ONO AND JOHN LENNON staged a 'happening' at London's Albert Hall, appearing onstage in a large white paper bag.

1960 THE MIRACLES' first record, 'Shop Around', entered the US singles chart.

1943 KEITH RICHARDS born, Dartford, Kent.

1943 BOBBY KEYES, session sax player, born, Texas.

1938 CHAS CHANDLER, former Animal and manager of both Hendrix and Slade, born.

1917 EDDIE 'CLEANHEAD' VINSON, R&B singer, born, Houston, Texas.

1914 PEE WEE CRAYTON, R&B guitarist, born, Rockdale, Texas.

1971
'Electric Warrior'
T Rex

DECEMBER
MONDAY

19

1975 THE ROLLING STONES announced that Ron Wood was their new fifth member, just over a year after his predecessor, Mick Taylor, had left.

1969 MICK JAGGER was fined £200 for possession of marijuana by a London court.

1955 LINTON BECKLESS (Central Line) born.

1955 CARL PERKINS recorded 'Blue Suede Shoes' at the Sun studios, 706 Union Avenue, Memphis, Tennessee.

1945 JOHN McEUEN (Nitty Gritty Dirt Band) born.

► **1944 ALVIN LEE** (Ten Years After) born, Nottingham.

1944 ZAL YANOVSKY (Lovin' Spoonful) born, Toronto, Canada.

1940 PHIL OCHS born, El Paso, Texas.

1918 PROFESSOR LONGHAIR (Roy Byrd), New Orleans R&B piano player, born, Bogalusa, Louisiana.

1915 EDITH PIAF (Edith Giovanna Gassion) born, Belleville, Paris, France.

1964
'Come See About Me
Supremes

TUESDAY

20

1980 MOTORHEAD drummer, Phil Taylor, broke his neck in Belfast after a show when by chance he 'bounced on his head while messing around with some friends'.

1976 CHICAGO voted to bring pinball machines back to the city where most of them were manufactured, thirty years after the city council had deemed them illegal.

► **1973 BOBBY DARIN**, fifties pop singer, died in the course of heart surgery.

1957 ELVIS PRESLEY received his draft papers for the US Army from the Memphis draft board chairman, Milton Bowers, in person.

1969
'Let It Bleed'
Rolling Stones

WEDNESDAY

21

1980 THE POLICE played the first of three charity Christmas shows in a large tent on London's Tooting Bec Common.

1978 MICKEY WALLER, a drummer, received an out of court settlement after suing Rod Stewart for unpaid royalties totalling £6000 for Stewart's 'Stealer' album.

► **1976 GENERATION X** played the preview night at London's first all-punk club, The Roxy, Covent Garden. The club, of course, became legend, the home of the mythical early days of punk. Generation X, however, were always too desperate to become myths to even get as far as becoming particularly famous. Originally, there was a band called Chelsea, one of the vry first London Punk bands that sprung up in the wake of the Sex Pistols and featuring Gene October, an undeniable wally, as lead singer. Conscious of their singer's wally-ness, Chelsea members Tony James and Billy Idol (William Broad) set out on their own, finding the other two members at a youth club dance and taking their name froma sixties paperback investigation of youth cults. The result was forever one step away from the times. If Generation X went a bit rasta, that was least week's thing. If theyopted for glossy poppy punk, they were accused of selling out. If they added a heavy metal drone guitar, they wre seen as being too orthodoxly punk. Forever unable to decide who they themselves were, they were unable to attract a similarly-confused public. After four years and some appalling records, Billy Idol gave up the chase, opted for a new career as a hoepful teeny idol in New York.

1968 JANIS JOPLIN played her first show with her new backing band, The Kozmic Blues Band, at the Stax-Volt Convention, Memphis, Tennessee.

1964 CHARLIE WATTS' book, 'Ode To A High-Flying Bird', a memorial for bebop sax player, Charlie Parker, was published.

1963 THE BEATLES premiered their Christmas show at the Gaumont, Bradford, with a cast including Rolf Harris and Cilla Black.

1946 CARL WILSON (Beach Boys) born, Hawthorne, California.

1942 CARLA THOMAS, Stax soul singer, born, Memphis, Tennessee.

► **1940 FRANK ZAPPA** born, Baltimore, Maryland.

1974
'Lonely This Christmas'
Mud

THURSDAY
22

1978 TODD RUNDGREN took the British Musicians Union to court when they stopped a radio broadcast of his London concert.

1973 STEVE STILLS lost a paternity suit against him by Harriet B. Tunis, a resident of Mill Valley, California. Stills' counsel had tried to discredit her evidence by asking the jury, "How can you believe a witness who works in the record business?"

1967 PINK FLOYD played London's Olympia, part of a show entitled 'Christmas On Earth Revisited' which also featured Jimi Hendrix, The Soft Machine and The Move. It proved to be the last important show that Syd Barrett played with the band.

1962 THE TORNADOES' 'Telstar' became the first record by a British *group* to top the US charts.

► **1949 ROBIN AND MAURICE GIBB** born, Manchester, Lancashire.

1937 ALVIN ROBINSON, R&B singer of 'Down Home Girl', born, New Orleans.

FRIDAY
23

1978 QUEEN were refused permission to play an open air show at Wimbledon by the Lawn Tennis Association.

1966 UFO, the first London 'underground' club, opened in an Irish ballroom in Tottenham Court Rd. with a show featuring Pink Floyd and The Soft Machine.

1966 'READY STEADY GO!', the British TV pop show, was broadcast for the last time.

1964 RADIO LONDON, the hippest of the priate radio ships, started broadcasting, finally closing down in August 1967 with the passage of the Marine Offences Act.

1940 LUTHER GROSVENOR (Spooky Tooth) born, Evesham, Worcestershire.

1940 JORMA KAUKONEN born, Washington D.C.

► **1939 JOHNNY KIDD** (Frederick Heath), early British rock'n'roller 'star', born, Willesden, London.

1935 LITTLE ESTHER PHILIPS, soul singer, born, Galveston, Texas.

SATURDAY
24

1964 THE BEATLES opened their Christmas show at the Hammersmith Odeon, London. Also on the bill were Freddie and the Dreamers, The Yardbirds, Elkie Brooks, Jimmy Saville, Mike Haslam and The Mike Cotton Sound. The show ran till January 18.

► **1957 IAN BURDEN** (Human League) born.

► **1946 JAN AKKERMAN** (Focus) born.

1920 DAVE BARTHOLOMEW born, Edgard, Louisiana. New Orleans R&B session player, Fats Domino's co-writer and long-time trumpeter in his band.

1906 PROFESSOR REGINALD AUBREY FESSENDEN made the first advertised radio broadcast from a 420 ft. tall mast on Brent Rock, Massachusetts, owned by the National Electric Signalling Company. Among his selections was Handel's 'Largo'.

SUNDAY
25

1978 PUBLIC IMAGE LTD. played their first live show, at London's Rainbow.

1967 PAUL McCARTNEY AND JANE ASHER announced their engagement.

1954 JOHNNY ACE (John Marshall Alexander), R&B star, waiting to go onstage at the City Auditorium, Houston, Texas, spun the chamber of his revolver for a game of Russian roulette, and lost. The late, great Johnny Ace — as Paul Simon sings of him — achieved even greater fame in death, scoring the biggest R&B hit of the following year with 'Pledging My Love'.

1945 NOEL REDDING (Jimi Hendrix Experience) born, Folkestone, Kent.

1945 TREVOR LUCAS (Fairport Convention) born, Bungaree, Australia.

1944 HENRY VESTINE (Canned Heat) born, Washington D.C.

1940 PETE BROWN, Cream's lyricist, born, London.

► **1935 LITTLE RICHARD** (Penniman) born, Macon, Georgia.

LITTLE RICHARD

DECEMBER
M O N D A Y

26
1979 QUEEN head-lined a benefit for Kampuchea at London's Hammersmith Odeon.
1967 THE BEATLES' 'Magical Mystery Tour' had its world premiere — in black and white only — on BBC 1 TV.
1942 ERNIE AND EARL CATE, the Cate Brothers, born, Fayetteville, Arkansas.
► **1940 PHIL SPECTOR** born, the Bronx, NYC.

T U E S D A Y

27
1981 HOAGY CARMICHAEL, Broadway songwriter of 'Stardust', died, aged 92, of a heart complaint at the Eisenhower Medical Center, Rancho Mirage, California.
► **1979 IAN DURY** head-lined a benefit for Kampuchea at London's Hammersmith Odeon, with the The Clash as special guests.
1978 CHRIS BELL, founder member of Big Star, died when he crashed his car into a telegraph pole near his Memphis home. Reports of the accident indicated that he was badly depressed and had been drinking heavily at the time.
1976 FREDDIE KING, electric blues guitarist, died after being taken ill with inflamed ulcers at a show in Dallas on Christmas Day.
1967 BERT BERNS died of a heart attack. Producer and song-writer, he was responsible for Them's hits — writing 'Here Comes The Night' — Van Morrison's 'Brown Eyed Girl' (and indeed all of Van's first solo album), the Isley's 'Twist And Shout', the Drifters' 'Under The Boardwalk' — all with that faint tinge of South America.
1963 THE TIMES' music critic, William Mann, hailed 'With The Beatles' as 'one of their most interesting with its chains of pandiatonic clusters.'
1958 'DIG THIS' started on BBC TV, a thin challenge to ITV's pop show 'Oh Boy!' which lasted only three months.
1944 TRACY NELSON, country singer, born, Madison, Wisconsin.
► **1931 SCOTTY MOORE**, guitarist on Presley's early sides, born, Gadsden, Tennessee.

W E D N E S D A Y

28
1979 THE WHO head-lined a benefit show for Kampuchea at London's Hammersmith Odeon, with special guests, The Pretenders and The Specials.
1967 DAVID BOWIE made his professional mime debut, at the Oxford New Theatre.
► **1950 ALEX CHILTON** born, Memphis, Tennessee. The kind of wild Southern boy who gives mothers nightmares. Like Gram Parsons, Chilton's been true to his own, very warped vision of the South. Through the white soul of the Box Tops, the deceptive pop of Big Star and his own determinedly erratic solo career, Chilton's lived the life of the unredeemable. He boasts of his own excess, telling the story that he can't re-enter the state of Tennessee for fear of irate mothers with whose daughters he's passed a night or two, and of the advantages of existing in a twilight world of empty bourbon bottles, arcane drugs and women in red dresses. With amusing inevitability, his one solo album to date was called 'Like Flied On Sherbert' and sounded like it was recorded in Jerry Lee Lewis' vision of hell.
► **1946 EDGAR WINTER** born, Beaumont, Texas.
1943 BOBBY COMSTOCK, who hit with 'Tennessee Waltz' in 1969, born, Ithaca, New York.
1932 DORSEY BURNETTE, rockabilly, born, Memphis, Tennessee.
1921 JOHNNY OTIS, R&B band-leader, born, Vallejo, California. Of Greek parentage, Otis grew up in Los Angeles' black ghettos as a white who passed for coloured. Partly his fame comes from the fact that he's survived to talk about his forty years in black music — from swing to 'Willy And The Hand Jive' to the Johnny Otis Show of the seventies — but he was also a truly innovative R&B band-leader, adding his sophisticated big band arrangements to what was often just loud, raucous dance music.

#1 US 45
1970
'My Sweet Lord'
George Harrison

#1 US LP
1969
'Led Zeppelin II'

#1 US 45
1959
'Why'
Frankie Avalon.

THURSDAY

29

1980 TIM HARDIN, folk singer, died aged 39 in Los Angeles of 'acute heroin-morphine intoxication due to overdose', after a long history of drug and alcohol problems.

1979 WINGS head-lined a benefit for Kampuchea at London's Hammersmith Odeon, with special guests Rockpile and Elvis Costello and the Attractions. For one night only, McCartney also constructed the Rockestra, a star-studded gather of too many guitars and too little rehearsal.

➤ **1979 BLONDIE** became the best selling act in the UK that year with the top selling album, 'Parallel Lines' and their three hit singles, 'Heart Of Glass', 'Sunday Girl' and 'Dreaming'.

1963 THE WEAVERS, the radical folk singing group formed by Pete Seeger, played their last show, in Chicago.

1942 RAY THOMAS (Moody Blues) born Stourbridge-on-Severn, Worcestershire.

1942 RICK DANKO (The Band) born, Simcoe, Ontario, Canada.

1930 RADIO LUXEMBURG was given permission to broadcast, quickly becoming the one English language commercial radio station that could be picked in the UK.

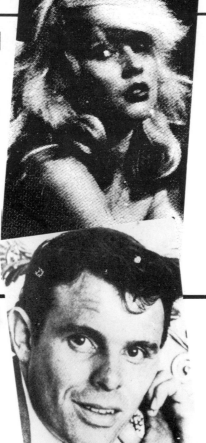

1956
'Singing The Blues'
Guy Mitchell

FRIDAY

30

1979 EMERSON, LAKE & PALMER announced that they'd gone their separate ways.

1979 RICHARD ROGERS, Broadway musical composer, died.

1977 WINIFRED ATWELL, the West Indian 'party' piano player, died, Hong Kong.

1970 PAUL McCARTNEY announced that he was suing the other Beatles.

1947 JOHN HARTFORD, writer of 'Gentle On My Mind', born.

1947 JEFF LYNNE (ELO) born, Birmingham, Warwickshire.

1946 DAVID JONES (Monkees) born, Houston, Texas.

➤ **1939 DEL SHANNON** (Charles Westover) born, Grand Rapids, Michigan.

1931 SKEETER DAVIS (Mary Francis Penick), country singer, born, Dry Ridge, Kentucky.

➤ **1928 BO DIDDLEY** (Elias McDaniel) born, McComb, Mississippi. Bo Diddley lives in a different world to the rest of us, a universe where only the bestest is powerful enough to describe their genius, where superlatives become superlativer. Greatest lover in the world, gun-slinger, lumberjack, Bossman, waited on by his faithful servants, Jerome and the Duchess. Johnny Otis claims the Bo Diddley beat is an old blues rhythm, running to the tune of 'Shave and a haircut, two bits'. We — and Bo, of course — know better. He stole it from the jungle Gods, a black Orpheus of the stock yard.

1967
'Hello Goodbye'
Beatles.

1967
'I'm A Believer'
Monkees

SATURDAY

31

1980 ROBERT PETE WILLIAMS, blues singer and former convict, died of cancer, aged 65, at his home in Maringouin, Louisiana.

1973 RADIO CLYDE in Glasgow, Britain's first provincial commercial radio station, started broadcasting.

1973 DAVID BOWIE was presented with a commemorative plaque for having five albums in the charts simultaneously for a stretch of nineteen weeks.

1971 THE BAND recorded their double live album, 'Rock Of Ages', at the New York Academy of Music.

1969 JIMI HENDRIX's Band Of Gypsies played their first show, at New York's Fillmore East, recording the event for the 'Band Of Gypsies' album.

1961 THE BEACH BOYS played their first show under that name, at the Richie Valens Memorial Center, Long Beach, California.

1956 'SHAKE, RATTLE AND ROCK', a movie featuring Fats Domino went on UK release.

1943 JOHN DENVER (John Henry Deutschendorf) born, Roswell, New Mexico.

1943 PETE QUAIFE (Kinks) born, Tavistock, Devon.

➤ **1942 ANDY SUMMERS** (Police) born, Poulton-le-Fylde, Lancashire.

1930 ODETTA (Holmes), folk singer, born, Birmingham, Alabama.

JANUARY 1984

FORWARD

WEDNESDAY
11

SUNDAY
1

MONDAY
2

TUESDAY
3

WEDNESDAY
4

THURSDAY
5

FRIDAY
6

SATURDAY
7

SUNDAY
8

MONDAY
9

TUESDAY
10

PLANNER

THURSDAY
12

FRIDAY
13

SATURDAY
14

SUNDAY
15

MONDAY
16

TUESDAY
17

WEDNESDAY
18

THURSDAY
19

FRIDAY
20

SATURDAY
21

SUNDAY
22

MONDAY
23

TUESDAY
24

WEDNESDAY
25

THURSDAY
26

FRIDAY
27

SATURDAY
28

SUNDAY
29

MONDAY
30

TUESDAY
31

THE ROCK DIARY 1983

Cramer, Floyd: (b) Oct. 27
Cramps: March 7
Cream: May 13; July 16; Nov. 2,4,26; Dec. 9
Creme, Lol: (b) Sept. 17
Crewe, Bob: (b) Nov. 17
Crickets: May 27; Sept. 23
Crippen, Dick: (b) Oct. 18
Criss, Peter: May 17
Croce, Jim: (b) Jan. 10; (d) Sept. 20
Cropper, Steve: (b) Oct. 21
Cros, Charles: April 30
Crosby, Bing: (b) May 2; June 9; Sept. 15,28
Crosby, David: (b) Aug. 14
Crosby, Stills, Nash and Young: June 28; July 9,25; Sept. 11
Crudup, Arthur: March 28
Curtis, Chris: (b) Aug. 16
Curtis, Clem: (b) Nov. 28
Curtis, Ian (Joy Division): May 17
Curtis, King: (b) Feb. 7; (d) Aug. 13
Curtis, Sonny: May 9
Czeczowski, Andy: April 23

D'Abo, Mike: (b) March 1
Daltrey, Roger: (b) March 1; April 13
Damned: Feb. 28; April 8; July 5; Oct. 1
Dammers, Jerry (Specials): (b) May 22
Dandy, Jim: (b) March 30
Danko, Rick: (b) Dec. 29
Darin, Bobby: (b) May 14,19; (d) Dec. 20
David, Hal: May 25
Davies, Cyril: Jan. 4
Davies, Ray: (b) June 21
Davis, Clive: May 23
Davis, Rev. Gary: May 5
Davis, Miles: (b) May 25; Nov. 25
Davis, Jnr. Sammy: (b) Dec. 8
Davis, Skeeter: Dec. 30
Davis, Spencer: (b) July 17
Dayton, Ronny: April 26
Deacon, John: (b) Aug. 19
Dean, Jimmy (Seth Ward): (b) Aug. 10
Deane, Geoff (Modern Romance): (b) Dec. 10
Decca Records: June 1
Dee, Dave: Dec. 7
Dee, Kiki: (b) March 6
Dee, Tommy: (b) July 15
Deep Purple April 20; Aug. 2,10
De Fleur, Zenon: March 17
Dekker, Desmond: (b) July 16
Dempsey, Michael: Dec. 6
Denny, Sandy: (b) Jan. 6; (d) April 21
Densmore, John: (b) Dec. 1
Denver, John: (b) Dec. 31
Derek and the Dominoes: June 14; Aug. 10
DeShannon, Jackie: (b) Aug. 21
Deviants: Nov. 1
Deville, Willy: (b) Aug. 27
Dexy's Midnight Runners: Nov. 7
Diamond, Neil: (b) Jan. 24
Diddley, Bo: (b) Dec. 30
Difford, Chris (Squeeze): (b) Nov. 4
Dig This: Dec. 27
Dion (and the Belmonts): June 2; July 18
Dixon, Willie: (b) April 1
Doggett, Bill: June 19
Doherty, Dennis: (b) Nov. 29
Dolenz, Mickey: (b) March 8
Domino, Fats: (b) Feb. 26; Dec. 31
Donahue, Tom: April 7,28
Donahue, Jerry: (b) Sept. 24
Donovan: (b) Feb. 10
Donner, Ral: (b) Feb. 10
Don't Look Back: May 17
Doomed: Sept. 5
Doors: Nov. 4
Dorsey, Lee: (b) Dec. 4
Douglas, Greg: (b) Oct. 11
Downey, Brian: (b) Jan. 27
Dozier, Lamont: (b) June 16
Drake, Nick: (d) Oct. 25
Drifters: April 24; Nov. 1
Dr. Feelgood: June 22; Nov. 8
Drummond, Don: April 21
Dryden, Spencer: (b) April 7
Ducks Deluxe: May 3
Dudley, Dave: (b) March 3
Duncan, Cleveland: (b) July 23
Dunn, Duck: Nov. 24
Dury, Ian: (b) May 12; (and the Kilburns) June 17; Aug. 26; Sept. 30; Dec. 1,27
Dylan, Bob: Jan. 12,18; Feb. 17; March 30; April 5, 11,12,30; May 7,22, (b) 24; June 5,7,8,9,23; July 20, 24,25,29; Aug. 2,17,27,28,31; Sept. 7,11,22,27; Oct. 2,26,30,31; Nov. 4,11,22.

Easton, Eric: April 29; May 3
Easton, Sheena: (b) April 27
Eddy, Duanne: (b) April 26
Edge, Graham: (b) March 30
Edison, Thomas: Aug. 15; Dec. 7
Edmunds, Dave: April 15
Edwards, Tommy: (b) Oct. 23
Edwin Hawkins Singers: May 18
Egan, Rusty: (b) Sept. 19
Elektra Records: Oct. 5

Elliot, Cass: (d) July 29; (b) Sept. 19
Ellison, Andy: (b) July 5
ELO: April 16; July 1
Emerson, Keith: (b) Nov. 2
Emerson, Lake and Palmer: Dec. 30
EMI Records: Jan. 26; March 31; July 5; Sept. 1; Oct. 11, 29; Nov. 18; Dec. 6
Eno: (b) May 15
Entwistle, John: June 23; (b) Oct. 9
Epstein, Brian: (d) Aug. 27; Sept. 15, (b) 19,25; Nov. 9.14
Essex, David: (b) July 23
European Punk Festival: Aug. 6,21
Evans, Bill: (d) Sept. 15
Evans, Mal: Jan. 23
Evans, Tommy: (b) Sept. 1
Evening News: May 17
Everley Brothers: July 14
Everley Don: (b) Feb. 1
Everley, Phil: (b) Jan. 19

THE FACE (magazine): May 1
Facenda, Tommy: (b) Nov. 10
Fahey, John: (b) Feb. 28
Fall, The: Dec. 15
Faith, Adam: (b) June 23
Faithfull, Marianne: May 24,28; July 8; Nov. 23
Fame, Georgie: (b) June 26
Family: Nov. 1
Family Dogg: Aug. 14
Farina, Mimi: (b) May 1
Farina, Richard: April 30
Farlowe, Chris: (b) Oct. 13
Farner, Mark : (b) Sept. 29
Faulkner, Eric: April 14
F.C.C. (Federal Communications Commission: July 1; Sept. 13
Feathers, Charlie: (b) June 12
Feliciano, Jose: (b) Sept. 10
Fessende, Professor Reginald Aubrey: Dec. 24
Festival Of The Flower Children: Aug. 26
Fillmore East: June 27; West: Nov. 10
Fingers, Johnny: Sept. 10
First Human Be-In: Jan. 14
First Radio Patent: July 20
Fisher, Eddie: Sept. 10
Fitzgerald, Ella: (b) April 25
5 Royales: Feb. 28
Flack, Roberta: (b) Feb. 2
Fleetwood Mac: Aug. 12
Fletwood, Mick: (b) June 23
Floyd, Eddie: (b) June 25
Floyd, King: Feb. 13
FM Radio: Jan. 5
Foley, Red: (b) Sept. 5
Fontana, Wayne: (b) Oct. 28
Ford, Dean: (b) Sept. 5
Ford, Frankie: (b) Aug. 4
Four Skins: July 3
Fowley, Kim: (b) July 21
Foxton, Bruce (The Jam): (b) Sept. 1
Foxx, Charlie: (b) Oct. 23
Foxx, Inez: (b) Sept. 9
Frampton, Peter: (b) April 22; Sept. 16; Oct. 19
Francis, Connie: (b) Dec. 12
Franklin, Aretha: (b) March 25; July 22
Fraser, Andy: (b) Aug. 7
Freburg, Stan: (b) Aug. 7
Fred, John: May 8
Free: May 9
Freed, Alan: Jan 20; March 21; April 13,20; May 19; Nov. 21; (b) Dec. 15
Freeman, Bobby: (b) June 13
Frey, Glenn: (b) Nov. 6
Friedman, Kinky: Oct. 31
Dry, Martin David: (b) March 3
Fogerty, John: (b) May 28
Ford, Tennessee Ernie: (b) Feb. 13
14 Hour Technicolour Dream: April 29
Froese, Edgar: (b) June 6
Fugs: July 2
Fuller, Jesse: Jan. 30
Fun Boy Three: Oct. 30
Funicello, Annette: (b) Oct. 22
Fuqua, Harvey: (b) July 27
Fury, Billy: Feb. 27; (b) April 17

Gabriel, Peter: (b) May 13
Gadd, Paul (see also Gary Glitter): Jan. 14
Gahan, Dave (Depeche Mode): (b) May 9
Gallagher, Micky: (b) Oct. 29
Gallagher, Rory: (b) March 2
Gallup, Cliff: Oct. 18
Garcia, Jerry: (b) Jan. 8
Gardner, Carl: April 29
Garfunkel, Art: (b) Nov. 5
Garland, Judy: (d) June 22
Garlow, Clarence: (b) Feb. 21
Garrity, Freddie: (b) Nov. 14
Garthwaite, Terri: (b) July 11
Gates, David: (b) Dec. 11
Gaye, Marvin: (b) April 2
Geffen, Dav id: (b) Feb. 21
Geldof, Bob: Oct. 5
Genesis: Feb. 22; March 31; June 23; Dec. 11
Gentelman, Sir Horace (Specials): (b) Aug. 30

Gentry, Bobby: (b) July 27
Gen X: Feb. 14; Dec. 10,21
George, Lowell: (b) June 29
Gershwin, George: (d) July 11, 15; (b) Sept. 26
Gibb, Barry: (b) Sept. 1
Gibb, Maurice and Robin: (b) Dec. 22
Gibbs, Georgia: (b) Aug. 26
Gillan, Ian: June 29; (b) Aug. 19
Gilliam, Michelle: (b) April 6
Gilmour, Dave: Feb. 18
Gimme Shelter: Dec. 6
Glass, Louis: Nov. 23
Glen, Chris: Nov. 6
Glitter, Gary (see also Paul Gadd and Paul Raven): Jan 26; March 3; June 16; Nov. 3
Glover, Roger: (b) Nov. 30
GM Records: May 17
Godspell: May 17
Goffin, Gerry: (b) Feb. 11
Golding, Lynval (Specials, Fun Boy Three): (b) July 7
Goldner, George: April 15
Goldsboro, Bobby: (b) Dec. 13
Gomez, Tony: (b) Dec. 13
Gordy, Berry: (b) Nov. 28
Gore, Lesley: (b) May 2
Gorham, Scott: (b) March 17
Gouldman, Graham: (b) May 10
Grand Funk Railroad: May 3; July 4
Grant, David (Linx): (b) Aug. 8
Graphophone: May 4, June 27
Grascock, John: (b) Nov. 17
Grateful Dead: May 6; Oct. 2
Grease: Feb. 14; Nov. 27
Great White Wonder: Sept. 11
Greater London Council: Aug. 8
Grech, Ric: (b) Nov. 1
Green, Al: (b) April 13; Oct. 18
Green, Gary: Nov. 20
Green, Peter: June 15,17; Oct. 29
Greenbaum, Norman: (b) Nov. 20
Greenwich, Ellie: (b) Oct. 23
Griffin, Dale: Oct. 24
Grogan, Claire Patricia (Altered Images): (b) March 17
Grosvener, Luther: (b) Dec. 23
Guest, Annette: Nov. 19
Gunter, Arthur: March 16
Gunter, Cornell: (b) Nov. 14
Guthrie, Arlo: (b) Jan. 12
Guthrie, Woody: (b) July 12; Sept. 12; (d) Oct. 3
Guy, Billie: (b) June 20
Guy, Buddy: (b) July 30

Hackett, Steve: (b) Feb. 12
Hadley, Tony (Spandau Ballet): (b) June 2
Hagar, Sammy: (b) Oct. 13
Haggard, Merle: (b) April 6
Hair: April 28; July 1; Oct. 29
Haley, Bill: Feb. 9; May 10; (b) July 6,9; Sept. 28; Oct. 1; Nov. 25; Dec. 14
Hall, Terry (Specials, Fun Boy Three): (b) March 19
Halliday, Johnny: (b) June 15
Ham, Peter: April 23
Hammond, John: March 7; (b) Dec. 15
Hancock, Herbie: (b) April 12
Hard Day's Night: July 6; Aug. 12
Hardin, Tim: (d) Dec. 29
Hardy, Francoise: (b) Jan. 17
Harper, Roy: (b) July 12
Harris, Hal: (b) Sept. 27
Harrison, George: Jan. 15, 21; Feb. 7, 25; March 31; July 27; Aug, 8,15,29; Sept. 6,20; Nov. 1,2,27
Harriso n, Mike: (b) Sept. 30
Harriso n, Wilbert: (b) Jan. 6
Harron, Terry DeMiall (Adam and the Ants): (b) Nov. 8
Harry, Debbie: (b) July 1
Hart, Wilbert: (b) Oct. 19
Hartford, John: (b) Dec. 30
Harvey, Alex: (d) Feb. 3, (b) 5.
Harvey, Les: (d) May 3
Hatfield, Bobby: (b) Aug. 10
Hathaway, Donny: (b) Jan. 10,13
Hawkins, Dale: (b) Aug. 22
Hawkins, Ronnie: (b) Jan. 10
Hawkins, Coleman: Nov. 21
Hawkins, Screamin' Jay (Jacy): April 22; (b) July 18
Hawkwind: July 22
Hayes, Bill: (b) June 5
Hayes, Isaac: (b) Aug. 6,20
Hays, Lee: (d) Aug. 26
Head, Roy: (b) Sept. 1
Headon, Nicky: (b) May 30
Hebb, Bobby: (b) July 26
Heckstall-Smith, Dick: (b) Sept. 26
Heinz (Burt): (b) July 24
Hell, Richard (& The Voidoids): Nov. 18
Helm, Levon: (b) May 26
Help!: July 29; Aug. 22
Hendrix, Jimmi: Jan 3,14; March 31; May 3; June 29; Aug, 26; (d) Sept. 18; Oct. 1; Nov. 14, (b) 27; Dec. 31
Hendryx, Nona: (b) Aug. 18

118

THE ROCK DIARY 1983

Henley, Don: (b) July 22; Nov. 21
Henry, Clarence 'Frogman': (b) March 19
Hensley, Ken: Aug. 24; Sept. 1
Heron, Mike: (b) Dec. 11
Heyward, Nick: (b) May 20
Hicks, Tony: (b) Dec. 16
Hill, Dave: (b) April 4
Hill, Louis Joe: (d) Aug. 5; (b) Sept. 23
Hillman, Chris: (b) Dec. 4
Hippies: Oct. 6
Hite, Bob: (b) Feb. 26; (d) April 5
Holder, Gene (dBs): (b) July 10
Holder, Noddy: (b) June 15
Holliday, Billie (Eleanora Fagen): (b) April 7, 20; (d) July 17
Holland, Brian: Feb. 15
Holland, Eddie: (b) Oct. 30
Holloway, Brenda: (b) June 21
Holly, Buddy: Jan. 22,26; (d) Feb 3,25; Aug, 15; Sept. 6, (b) 7; Oct. 14, 21
HMV Records: March 30; April 1
Honeyman-Scott, James (Pretenders): (b) Nov. 4
Hooker, John Lee: (b) Aug. 22
Hopkin, Mary: (b) May 3,4
Hopkins, Nicky: (b) Feb. 24
Horslips: March 17
Hotlegs: June 19; Oct. 30
Howe, Steve: (b) April 8
Howlin' Wolf: (d) Jan. 10; (b) June 10; Oct. 15
Hudson, Garth: (b) Aug. 2
Hull, Alan: (b) Feb. 20
Humperdinck, Englebert: May 22
Hunt, Marsha: June 26
Hunter, Ian: (b) June 3
Hunter, Ivory Joe: (d) Nov. 8
Hunter, Meredith (see also Gimme Shelter): (d) Dec. 6
Hunter, Tab: (b) July 11
Hurt, Mississippi John: (d) Nov. 2
Hyland, Brian: (b) Nov. 12
Hynde, Chrissie: (b) Sept. 7

Ian, Janis: (b) May 7
Immediate Records: March 18
Iommi, Tony: (b) Feb. 19
Iron Butterfly: July 20
Island Records: Feb. 13; June 2
Isle of Wight Festival: Aug. 26
Isley, Ronald: (b) May 21
Isley, Rudolph: April 1

J. Geils: Nov. 15
Jackson, Al: (b) Nov. 27
Jackson, Chuck: (b) July 22
Jackson, Germaine: (b) Dec. 11
Jackson. Mahalia: Jan. 27
Jackson, Michael: Feb. 12; (b) Aug. 29
Jackson, Tito: (b) Oct. 1'
Jackson, Wanda: (b) Oct. 22
Jagger, Mick: May 12,24,28; June 22,27,30; (b) July 26,31; Aug. 18; Oct. 21; Dec. 19
Jah Wobble: Aug. 16
Jam: March 21; April 22; May 13,29; Aug. 5,11; Oct. 2,16
James, Dick: March 11
James, Elmore: (b) Jan. 18; (d) May 23
James, Skip: (d) Oct. 3
James, Tommy: (b) April 29
Jameson, Bobby: Nov. 12
Jansch, Bert: Nov. 3
Jardine, Al: (b) Sept. 3
Jefferson Airplane: March 25; July 6; Oct. 16
Jenkins, Florence Foster: Oct. 26
Jenson, Steve: Dec. 1
Jennings, Waylon: (b) June 15
Jesus Christ Superstar: Oct. 20
Jobson, Richard: (b) Oct. 6
John, Elton: March 7, (b) 15; Oct. 1
John, Paul, George, Ringo and Bert: Aug. 15
Johnson, Kelly (Girlschool): June 20
Johnson, Linton Kwesi: March 23
Johnson, Lonnie: (d) June 16
Johnson, Marv: (b) Oct. 15
Johnson, Plas: (b) July 21
Johnson, Robert: June 20; Nov. 23
Johnston, Bruce: (b) June 27
Jones, Booker T: (b) Nov. 12
Jones, Brian: (b) Feb. 28; March 9; May 21; June 8; (d) July 3,6; Sept. 26; Oct. 30; Nov. 13; Dec. 12
Jones, David (Monkees): (b) Dec. 30
Jones, Elvin: (b) Sept. 9
Jones, George: (b) Sept. 12
Jones, John Paul: (b) Jan. 3
Jones, Kenny: (b) Sept. 16
Jones, Linda: March 14
Jones, Mick (The Clash): (b) June 26
Jones, Paul: (b) Feb. 24
Jones, Steve (Sex Pistols): (b) May 3
Jones, Tom: (b) June 7
Jones, Quincey: (b) March 14
Joplin, Janis: (b) Jan. 19; April 21; June 10; July 12,25; Aug, 12; (d) Oct. 4,7; Nov. 15; Dec. 21
Joplin, Scott: (b) Nov. 24
Jordan, Louis: Feb. 4
Justis, Bill: (b) Oct. 14
Jupp, Mickey: (b) March 6

Kaempfert, Bert: (b) Oct. 16
Kantner, Paul: Jan. 25; Oct. 18
Karoli, Michael: (b) April 29
Kath, Terry: (d) Jan. 23, (b) 31
Kaukonen, Jorma: (b) Dec. 23
Kay, Horace: (b) April 13
Kaye, John: (b) April 12
Kaylan, Howard: (b) June 22
Kelly, Betty: (b) Sept. 16
Kemble, John (Spandau Ballet): (b) July 6
Kemp, Gary (Spandau Ballet): (b) Oct. 16
Kemp, Martin (Spandau Ballet): Oct. 10
Kendricks, Eddie: (b) Dec. 17
Kennedy, President John Fitzgerald: Dec. 7
Kershaw, Doug: (b) Jan. 24
Kesey, Ken: Nov. 27
Keyes, Bobby: (b) Dec. 18
Kidd, Johnny: (d) Oct. 7; (b) Dec. 23
Kilburn & The Highroads: Dec. 5
King, Albert: (b) April 25
King, B B: (b) Sept. 16
King, Ben E: June 18; (b) Sept. 28; Oct. 27
King Crimson: April 9
King, Earl: (b) Feb. 7
King, Jonathan: Dec. 6
King, Phil: April 27
Kinks: May 5; Aug. 17
Kirke, Simon: (b) July 28
Klein, Allen: Jan. 29; March 9
Knack: Oct. 6
Knight, Gladys: (b) May 28
Knight, Terry: April 9
Knopfler, Mark: (b) Aug. 12
Korner, Alexis: (b) April 19
Kossoff, Paul: March 19; (b) Sept. 14
Kramer, Billy J: (b) Aug. 19
Kreutzmann, Bill: June 7
Krieger, Robbie: (b) Jan. 8
Kristofferson, Kris: (b) June 22

Labelle, Patti: (b) May 24
La Flame, David: (b) April 5
Laine, Denny: April 25; (b) Oct. 29
Laine, Frankie: May 26
Laing, Corky: (b) Jan. 26
Lake, Greg: (b) Nov. 10
Lambert, Kit: (d) April 7
Lamm, Robert: (b) Oct. 13
Lance, Major: (b) April 4
Lane, Ronnie: (b) April 1; Nov. 5,16
LBC: Oct. 8
Leadbelly: (d) Dec. 6
Leadbitter, Mike: (d) Nov. 16
Leadon, Bernie: (b) July 19
Le Bon, Simon (Duran Duran): (b) Oct. 27
Led Zeppelin: July 16,23; Oct. 18
Lee, Brenda: (b) Dec. 11
Lee, Curtis: (b) Oct. 28
Lee, Alvin: (b) Dec. 19
Lee, Dicky: (b) Sept. 21
Lee, Peggy: (b) May 6
Lee, Ric: (b) Oct. 20
Leeds, Gary: (b) Sept. 3
Leiber, Jerry: (b) April 25
Lennon, John: March 13,20,21,23; April 7,22,27; June 2,15,24; July 15,16; Aug, 13,20,23,30; Sept. 16; Oct, 2, (b) 9,18,24,25; Nov. 8,25,28,29; (d) Dec. 8,11,15,18
Lennon, Julian: (b) March 8
Lennon, Sean Ono: Oct. 9
Lenoir, J B: (b) March 5
Lesh, Phil: March 15
Lewie, Jona: (b) July 3
Lewis, Jerry Lee: May 24; June 30; July 10; (b) Sept. 29
Lewis, Ramsey: (b) May 27
Lewis, Smiley: July 5; (d) Oct. 7
Lewis, Walter: (d) Sept. 14
Leyton, John: (b) Feb. 17
Liebesit, Jackie: (b) May 26
Liggins, Joe: (b) July 9
Lightfoot, Gordon: (b) Nov. 17
Lightnin' Hopkins: (b) March 15
Lightnin' Slim: (d) July 27
Lindsay, John (Mayor, NYC): April 29
Lindsay, Mark: (b) March 9
Little Anthony: (b) Jan. 8
Little Eva: June 29
Little Junior Parker: (b) March 3; (d) Nov. 18
Little Milton: (b) Sept. 7
Little Richard: Sept. 14; Dec. 14, (b) 25
Little Walter: Feb. 15; (b) May 1
Little Willie John: (March 26; June 3; (b) Nov. 15
Littlefield, Little Willie: (b) Oct. 11
Lodge, John: (b) July 20
Loggins, Kenny: (b) Jan. 7
Loizzo, Gary: (b) Aug. 16
Loney, Ray: April 13
Longmuir, Alan (Bay City Rollers): (b) June 20
Lopez, Trini: (b) May 15
Lord, Jon: (b) June 9; Aug. 27
Love Me Tender: Aug. 22
Love, Mike: (b) March 15
Lovin' Spoonful: July 20
Lowe, Nick: Aug. 18
Lucas, Trevor: (b) Nov. 3
Lulu: (b) Nov. 3
Lwin, Annabella: (b) Oct. 31

Lydon, John: (b) Jan. 31; Feb. 13; Oct. 6
Lymon, Frankie: Feb. 28; (b) Sept. 30
Lynch, Tim: (b) July 18
Lyngstad-Fredriksson, Anni-Frid: (b) Nov. 15
Lynn, Barbara: (b) Jan. 16
Lynn, Loretta: (b) April 14
Lynn, Vera: July 4
Lynne, Jeff: (b) Dec. 30
Lynott, Philip: Feb. 13; (b) Aug. 20
Lynyrd Skynyrd: Oct. 27
Lyons, Leo: (b) Nov. 30

Mackay, Andy: (b) July 23
Madness: Aug. 23
Mestro, Johnny: (b) May 7
Magazine: Feb. 11; June 6
Magic Sam: (b) Feb. 14; (d) Dec. 1
Mallaber, Gary: (b) Oct. 11
Manilow, Barry: (b) July 18
Mann, Barry: (b) Feb. 9
Mann, Manfred: (b) Oct. 21
Manson, Charles: March 6; Aug. 9
Manzanera, Phil: (b) Jan. 31
Manzarek, Ray: (b) Feb. 12
March, Little Peggy: (b) March 8
Marconi: Dec. 12
Marsden, Gerry: (b) Sept. 24
Marsh, Ian Craig (Heaven 17): (b) Nov. 11
Martin, George: Jan. 3
Maresca, Ernie: (b) April 21
Marine Offences Act: Aug. 15
Marley, Bob: (b) Feb. 5; May 11; July 18; Oct. 8; Dec. 4
Marriott, Steve: (b) Jan. 30
Marvelettes: Sept. 16
Marvin, Hank B: (b) Oct. 28
Mar Y Sol Festival: April 1
Mason, Dave: (b) May 10
Mason, Nick: (b) Jan. 27
Matlock, Glen: Feb. 28; June 2; (b) Aug. 27
May, Brian: May 16; (b) July 19
May, Phil: (b) Sept. 11
Mayall, John: (b) Nov. 29
Mayfield, Curtis: (b) June 3
McCarty, Jim: (b) July 25
McCartney, Linda: (b) Sept. 24
McCartney, Paul: Jan. 16, Feb. 9,19,27; March 8,13; April 17,26; May 9; June 15, (b) 18,19; July 8; Aug. 3,10,28; Sept. 20,23; Dec. 25,30
McColl, Kirsty: Oct. 10
McCracklin, Jimmy: (b) Aug. 13
McCulloch, Ian (Echo & The Bunnymen): (b) May 5
McCulloch, Jimmy: (d) Sept. 28
McDaniels, Gene: (b) Feb. 12
McDonald, Country Joe: (b) Jan. 1; March 18
McDowell, Mississippi Fred: (d) June 3
McEwen, John: (b) Dec. 19
McGear, Mike: (b) Jan. 7
McGovern, Senator (Election Campaign): March 9
McGuinn, Jim: July 13
McGuinn, Roger: May 12
McGuinness, Tom: (b) Dec. 2
McGuire, Barry: Oct. 15
McIntosh, Robbie: (d) Sept. 23
McKenna, Hugh: (b) Nov. 28
McKenzie, Scott: (b) Oct. 1
McLagen, Ian: (b) May 12
McLaren, Malcolm: Feb. 22
McLymont, David (Orange Juice): (b) Nov. 30
McNally, John: Aug. 30
McPhatter, Clyde: (d) Nov. 15
McPherson, Donald: (d) July 4
McVie, John: (b) Nov. 25
MC5: April 16; Oct. 30
Meadon, Pete: (d) Aug. 5
Meatloaf: Feb. 20
Meaux, Huey: (b) March 10
Medley, Bill: (b) Sept. 19
Meek, Joe: (d) Feb. 3; May 7
Meisner, Randy: (b) March 8
Memphis Minnie: (d) Aug. 6
Memphis Slim: (b) Sept. 3
Mendes, Sergio: (b) Feb. 11
Mercury, Freddie: (b) Sept. 6
Messina, Jim: (b) Dec. 5
Meyer, Angie: (b) May 31
Miami Showband: July 31
Michaels, Lee: (b) Nov. 24
Midler, Bette: (b) Dec. 1
Milburn, Amos: (d) Jan. 3
Miles, Buddy: (b) Sept. 5
Miller, Glen: (b) Dec. 15
Miller, Jacob: Feb. 21
Miller, Steve: June 15
Million Dollar Quartet: Dec. 2
Mindbenders: Oct. 31
Miracles: Oct. 3; Dec. 18
Miss Christine: Nov. 5
Mitchell, Guy: (b) Feb. 21
Mitchell, Joni: Feb 17; (b) Nov. 7
Mitchell, Mitch: (b) July 9
Modern Records: April 21
Monkees: Sept. 12
Monroe, Charlie: (d) Sept. 25

THE ROCK DIARY 1983
BIBLIOGRAPHY

'Plagiarism's stealing from one source;
stealing from many, that's research.' — Anon.

1. GENERAL REFERENCE WORKS

BAGGELAAR, KRISTIN, & MILTON, DONALD, *The Folk Music Encyclopedia,* London, Omnibus Press, 1977.
CLARK, AL, ed. *The Rock Yearbook 1982,* London, Virgin, 1981.
GROSS, MICHAEL, & JAKUBOWSKI, MAXIM, eds. *The Rock Yearbook 1981,* London, Virgin, 1980.
HARDY, PHIL, &, LAING, DAVE, eds. *Encyclopedia Of Rock,* Vols. 1-3, London, Panther Books/Aquarius Books, 1976.
LOGAN, NICK, &, FINNIS, ROB, eds. *The New Musical Express Book Of Rock,* London, Star, 1975.
LOGAN, NICK, & WOFFINDEN, BOB, eds. *The Illustrated New Musical Express Encyclopedia Of Rock,* London, Salamander, 1977.
MARCHBANK, PEARCE, & MILES, *The Illustrated Rock Almanac,* London, Paddington Press, 1977.
MILLER, JIM, ed. *The Rolling Stone Illustrated History Of Rock & Roll,* New York, Rolling Stone Press/Random House, 1976.
SHESTACK, MELVIN, *The Country Music Encyclopedia,* London, Omnibus, 1977.
STAMBLER, IRWIN, *Encyclopedia Of Pop, Rock And Soul,* New York, St. Martin's Press, 1974.
STIKVOORT, JOS, ed. *Popzammelwerk 3,* Holland, 1972.

2. CHART LOGS

GILLETT, CHARLIE, ed. *Rock File,* London, New English Library, 1972.
GILLETT, CHARLIE, ed. *Rock File 2,* London, Panther, 1974.
GILLETT, CHARLIE, &, FRITH, SIMON, eds. *Rock File 3,* London, Panther, 1975.
GILLETT, CHARLIE, &, FRITH, SIMON, eds. *Rock File 4,* London, Panther, 1976.
GILLETT, CHARLIE, &, FRITH, SIMON, eds. *Rock File 5,* London, Panther, 1978.
REES, DAFYDD, *Star-File Annual,* London, Hamlyn, 1978.
RICE, JO & TIM; GAMBACCINI, PAUL, & READ, MIKE, *The Guinness Book of British Hit Singles,* London, Guinness Superlatives, 1979.
SOLOMON, CLIVE, *Record Hits,* Omnibus Press, 1977.
WHITBURN, JOEL, *Top Pop Artists And Singles 1955-78,* Menomonee Falls, Wisconsin. Record Research, 1979.

3. OTHER WORKS

BANGS, LESTER, *Blondie,* London, Omnibus Press, 1980.
BARNES, KEN, *The Beach Boys,* New York, Sire-Chappell, 1976.
BRAKE, MIKE, *The Sociology Of Youth Culture And Youth Subcultures,* London, Routledge & Kegan Paul, 1980.
BROVEN, JOHN, *Walking To New Orleans,* Bexhill-On-Sea, Sussex, Blues Unlimited, 1974.
CARR, ROY, *The Rolling Stones, An Illustrated Record,* London, New English Library, 1976.
CARR, ROY, &, TYLER, TONY, *The Beatles, An Illustrated Record,* London, New English Library, 1975.
CHAPPLE, STEVE, &, GAROFALO, REEBEE, *Rock'n'Roll Is Here To Pay,* Chicago, Nelson-Hall, 1977.
CHARLESWORTH, CHRIS, *David Bowie: Profile,* London, Proteus/Savoy, 1981.
CHARONE, BARBARA, *Keith Richards,* London, Futura, 1979.
CLARKE, SEBASTIAN, *Jah Music,* London, Heinemann Educational Books, 1980.
COHN, NIK, *Awopbopaloobop Alopbamboom,* London, Paladin, 1970.
COPPLE, CYNTHIA, ed. *Van Morrison: Reliable Sources,* Caledonia Productions, (undated).
CORTEZ, DIEGO, ed. *Private Elvis,* Stuttgart, Fey, 1978.
CROSTON, ERIC, ed. *Television & Radio 1979,* London, Independent Broadcasting Authority, 1978.
CUMMINGS, TONY, *The Sound Of Philadelphia,* London, Methuen, 1975.
DALTON, DAVID, *The Rolling Stones: The First Twenty Years,* London, Thames & Hudson, 1981.
DAVIES, HUNTER, *The Beatles: The Authorised Biography,* London, Mayfair, 1969.
FINNIS, ROB, *The Phil Spector Story,* London, Rockon, 1975.
FRAME, PETE, *Rock Family Trees,* London, Omnibus Press, 1980.
FRIEDMAN, MYRA, *Buried Alive: A Biography Of Janis Joplin,* London, Star, 1975.
FRITH, SIMON, *The Sociology of Rock,* London, Constable, 1978.
GILLETT, CHARLIE, *The Sound Of The City,* London, Sphere, 1971.
GILLETT, CHARLIE, *Making Tracks,* London, W.H. Allen, 1975.
GLEASON, RALPH J., *The Jefferson Airplane And The San Francisco Sound,* New York, Ballantine, 1969.
GOLDROSEN, JOHN J., *Buddy Holly,* London, Charisma, 1975.
GRAY, ANDY, *Great Pop Stars,* London, Hamlyn, 1973.
GRAY, MICHAEL, *Song And Dance Man: The Art Of Bob Dylan,* London, Abacus, 1973.
GURALNICK, PETER, *Feel Like Going Home: Portraits In Blues & Rock'n'Roll,* New York, Dutton, 1971.
GURALNICK, PETER, *Lost Highway: Journeys & Arrivals Of American Musicians,* Boston, David R. Godine, 1979.
HAWKINS, MARTIN, &, ESCOTT, COLIN, *Catalyst: The Sun Records Story,* London, Aquarius, 1975.
HAWKINS, MARTIN, & ESCOTT, COLIN, *Elvis Presley: The Illustrated Discography,* London, Omnibus Press, 1981.
HEBDIDGE, DICK, *Subculture: The Meaning Of Style,* London, Methuen, 1979.
HENNESSY, VAL, *In The Gutter,* London, Quartet, 1978.
HERMAN, GARY, *The Who,* London, Studio Vista, 1971.
HOGGARD, STUART, *David Bowie: An Illustrated Discography,* London, Omnibus Press, 1980.
HOLIDAY, BILLIE, with DUFTY, WILLIAM, *Lady Sings The Blues,* London, Sphere, 1973.
HOPKINS, JERRY, &, SUGERMAN, DANIEL, *No One Here Gets Out Alive,* New York, Warner Books, 1980.
JONES, LEROI, *Blues People,* New York, Morrow, 1963.
KALLYNDYR, ROLSTON, &, DALRYMPLE, HENDERSON, *Reggae, A People's Music,* London, Carib-Arawak, (undated).
KEIL, CHARLES, *Urban Blues,* Chicago, The University Of Chicago Press, 1970.
KELLEHER, ED, *David Bowie,* New York, Sire-Chappell, 1977.

KOFSKY, FRANK, *Black Nationalism And The Revolution In Music,* New York, Pathfinder Press, 1970.
KRIVINE, J., *Jukebox Saturday Night,* London, New English Library, 1977.
LAING, DAVE, *Buddy Holly,* London, Studio Vista, 1971.
LAZELL, BARRY, &, REES, DAFYDD, *The Illustrated Book Of Rock Records: A Book Of Lists,* London, Virgin, 1982.
LEADBITTER, MIKE, ed. *Nothing But The Blues,* London, Hanover, 1971.
LEADBITTER, MIKE, &, SLAVEN, NEIL, *Blues Records 1943-1966,* London/New York, Oak Publications, 1968.
LYNN, LORETTA, *Coal Miners' Daughter,* London, Panther, 1979.
McEWAN, JOE, *Sam Cooke: The Man Who Invented Soul,* New York, Sire-Chappell, 1977.
MARCUS, GREIL, *Mystery Train: Images Of America In Rock'n'Roll Music,* New York, Dutton, 1975.
MARCUS, GREIL, ed. *Stranded: Rock And Roll For A Desert Island,* New York, Alfred A. Knopf, 1979.
MARSH, DAVE, &, STEIN, KEVIN, *The Book Of Rock Lists,* London, Sidgwick & Jackson, 1981.
MELLY, GEORGE, *Revolt Into Style: The Pop Arts In Britain,* London, Penguin, 1972.
MILES, *Pink Floyd,* London, Omnibus Press, 1980.
MILES, *The Jam,* London, Omnibus Press, 1981.
MILES, *The Clash,* London, Omnibus Press, 1981.
MILES, *David Bowie Black Book,* London, Omnibus Press, 1980.
MILLAR, BILL, *The Drifters,* London, Studio Vista, 1971.
MILLAR, BILL, *The Coasters,* London, Star, 1975.
MORSE, DAVID, *Motown,* London, Studio Vista, 1971.
MURRELLS, JOSEPH, *The Book Of Golden Discs,* London, Barrie & Jenkins, 2nd edition, 1978.
NORMAN, PHILIP, *Shout! The True Story Of The Beatles,* London, Elm Tree Books, 1981.
NOLAN, TOM, *Jimi Hendrix,* New York, Sire-Chappell, 1977.
OBST, LYNDA ROSEN, *The Sixties,* New York, Random House/Rolling Stone Press, 1977.
PALMER, ROBERT, *Baby, That Was Rock & Roll: The Legendary Leiber & Stoller,* New York, Harvest/HBJ, 1978.
PEEBLES, ANDY, *The Lennon Tapes,* London, BBC Publications, 1981.
PELLAERT, GUY, &, COHN, NIK, *Rock Dreams,* London, Pan, 1974.
PIDGEON, JOHN, *Rod Stewart And The Changing Faces,* London, Panther, 1976.
PILE, STEPHEN, *The Book Of Heroic Failures,* London, Futura, 1980.
PROPES, STEVE, *Those Oldies But Goodies: A Guide To 50's Record Collecting,* New York, Collier Books, 1973.
PROPES, STEVE, *Golden Oldies: A Guide To 60's Record Collecting,* Radnor, Pennsylvania, Chilton, 1974.
REESE, KRISTA, *Elvis Costello,* London, Proteus, 1981.
RUSSELL, ROSS, *Bird Lives!,* London Quartet, 1973.
ROWE, MIKE, *Chicago Breakdown,* London, Eddison Press, 1973.
SCADUTO, ANTHONY, *Bob Dylan,* London, Abacus, 1972.
SHARPE, ROGER C., &, HAMILTON, JAMES, *Pinball!,* New York, Dutton, 1977.
SHAW, ARNOLD, *Honkers And Shouters,* New York, Collier, 1978.
SHAW, GREG, *New Wave On Record: England & Europe 1975-8,* Burbank, California, Bomp Books, 1978.
SMELTZER, DAVE, &, ABLETT, SHARON, *Rockola: Rock'n'Roll Trivia Quiz,* Toronto, Canada, Rockola Ent., 1978.
STEVENSON, RAY, *Sex Pistols Scrap Book,* London, R. Stevenson, (undated).
SUTCLIFFE, PHIL, &, FIELDER, HUGH, *The Police: L'Historia Bandido,* London, Proteus, 1981.
THOMAS, J.C., *Chasin' The Trane,* New York, Da Capo, 1976.
TOBLER, JOHN, *The Buddy Holly Story,* London, Plexus, 1979.
TOBLER, JOHN, *Abba: For The Record,* Knutsford, Cheshire, Stafford Pemberton, 1980.
TREMLETT, GEORGE, *The Slik Story,* London, Futura, 1976.
TREVANA, NIGEL, *Lou Reed & The Velvets,* Falmouth, Cornwall, Bantam, (undated).
VERMOREL, FRED AND JUDY, *The Sex Pistols,* London, Universal, 1978.
WERTHEIMER, ALFRED, *Elvis '56: In The Beginning,* London, Cassell, 1979.
WILLIAMS, RICHARD, *Out Of His Head: The Sound Of Phil Spector,* London, Abacus, 1974.
WILMER, VALERIE, *As Serious As Your Life,* London, Quartet, 1977.
YORK, PETER, *Style Wars,* London, Sidgwick & Jackson, 1980.
YORKE, RITCHIE, *Van Morrison: Into The Music,* London, Charisma/Futura, 1975.

4. PERIODICALS

UK
Blues Link, Blues Unlimited, The Face, The History Of Rock, Kicks, Melody Maker, New Musical Express, Pressure Drop, Record Mirror, Smash Hits, Sniffin' Glue, Sounds.

USA
Biff! Bang! Pow!, Creem, Goldmine, Rolling Stone, Time Barrier Express, Trouser Press, Who Put The Bomp.

5. ANYONE who has ever written album liner notes or contributed to a rock magazine. Thanks, we've stolen from you. (And double thanks to Fred Dellar, Pete Frame, Bill Millar, Ray Topping and Cliff White.)

HOME TAPING IS KILLING MUSIC

AND IT'S ILLEGAL

...it's also a relatively minor crime indulged in by a hell of a lot of people, including those who plaster the slogan above on the inner sleeve of all new albums, which, as a legal solution to combatting home-taping, stands about as much chance of sucess as the ancient prohibitions on adultery. What follows is a guide to more creative home-taping, how to get the very best out of your Walkman. Every tape recipe supplied fits *exactly* on to a C90. But remember, compiling these tapes, rather than just describing them, is a contravention of copyright laws — even if you do it from records you already own. The only way to put the tapes together without breaking the law is to acquire the permisson of *all* the copyright owners involved, both performers and composers. I suggest you make a start on getting that permission by writing to the following people:

Little Feat — Warner Brothers Records ın Burbank, California or London.
Elvis Costello — F-Beat Records, Executive Suite, 6 Horn Lane, Acton, London W3 9NJ.
Elvis Presley — Gracelands, Memphis or RCA Records in New York and London.
2 Tone — c/o, Chrysalis Records, 12 Stratford Place, London W1N 9AF.

COMPETITION!!!!!!!

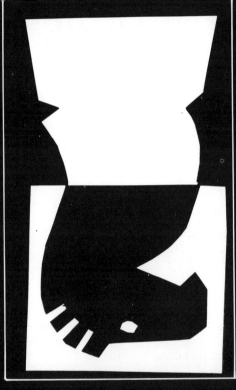

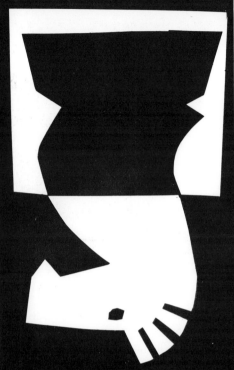

ROCKING RUSSIAN

'THE BEST OF 2 TONE'

'FOUR EYES, ONE VISION'
ELVIS COSTELLO

SIDE ONE

'BLITSKRIEG'

1. LIVING IN PARADISE (ACOUSTIC DEMOS)
2. WAVE A WHITE FLAG (RADIO LONDON DEMOS)
3. ALISON
4. (THE ANGELS WANNA WEAR MY) RED SHOES
5. WATCHING THE DETECTIVES
6. I JUST DON'T KNOW WHAT TO DO WITH MYSELF
7. NO ACTION
8. (I DON'T WANT TO GO TO) CHELSEA
9. PUMP IT UP
10. LITTLE TRIGGERS
11. NIGHT RALLY
12. THE BEAT (LIVE - WINTERLAND, SAN FRANCISCO, AUGUST 8 1978) *
13. RADIO RADIO
14. LESS THAN ZERO (LIVE 'AMERICAN' VERSION — WINTERLAND) *
15. WHAT'S SO FUNNY 'BOUT (PEACE, LOVE AND UNDERSTANDING)

*CAN BE REPLACED BY ORTHODOX VERSIONS ... WHICH WILL LEAVE ROOM FOR 'BLAME IT ON CAIN'. TRACK TWO CAN BE REPLACED BY 'WELCOME TO THE WORKING WEEK'

SIDE TWO

'BOP .... TO NASHVILLE'

1. ACCIDENTS WILL HAPPEN (LIVE VERSION)
2. GOON SQUAD
3. GREEN SHIRT
4. OLIVER'S ARMY
5. MY FUNNY VALENTINE
6. STRANGER IN THE HOUSE (DUET WITH GEORGE JONES)
7. I CAN'T STAND UP FOR FALLING DOWN
8. MOTEL MATCHES
9. TEMPTATION
10. I STAND ACCUSED
11. KING HORSE
12. CLOWNTIME IS OVER (SLOW VERSION)
13. CLUBLAND
14. HOOVER FACTORY
15. STRICT TIME
16. SHOT WITH HIS OWN GUN

SIDE ONE

'ALL THE HITS'

1. GANGSTERS
2. THE PRINCE (MADNESS)
3. ON MY RADIO (SELECTER)
4. A MESSAGE TO YOU RUDY
5. TEARS OF A CLOWN (BEAT)
6. TOO MUCH TOO YOUNG (LIVE)
7. MISSING WORDS (SELECTER)
8. RAT RACE
9. STEROTYPES PARTS ONE AND TWO (ALBUM VERSION)
10. DO NOTHING (SINGLE VERSION)
11. GHOST TOWN
12. THE BOILER (RHODA)

SIDE TWO

'..... AND MORE'

1. NITE KLUB
2. DOESN'T MAKE IT ALRIGHT
3. MONKEY MAN
4. STUPID MARRIAGE
5. SKINHEAD SYMPHONY
6. RUDER THAN YOU (BODYSNATCHERS)
7. RUDE BUOYS OUTTA JAIL
8. RUDE BUOYS OUTTA JAIL VERSION
9. MAN AT C & A
10. MAGGIE'S FARM
11. STAY OUT LATE (RICO)
12. YOU'RE WONDERING NOW

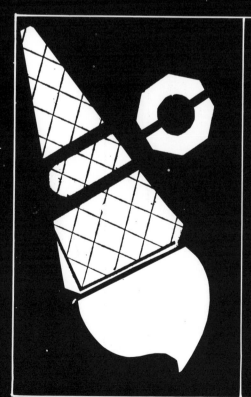

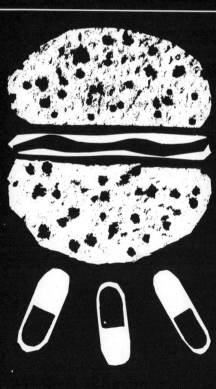

LYCANTHROPY.
THE BEST OF LITTLE FEAT ON RECORD.

'SAVE THE LAST CHEESEBURGER FOR ME'
ELVIS PRESLEY

SIDE ONE 'BEFORE'

1. THAT'S ALRIGHT (MAMA)
2. GOOD ROCKIN' TONIGHT
3. I'M LEFT' YOU'RE RIGHT', SHE'S GONE
4. BABY, LET'S PLAY HOUSE
5. MYSTERY TRAIN
6. TRYIN' TO GET TO YOU
7. INTERVIEW, WICHITA FALLS, 1956 (ON VOL 1. A LEGENDARY PERFORMER)
8. HEARTBREAK HOTEL
9. BLUE SUEDE SHOES
10. MY BABY LEFT ME
11. LAWDY MISS CLAWDY
12. HOUND DOG
13. DON'T BE CRUEL
14. (LET ME BE YOUR)
15. TEDDY BEAR
16. ALL SHOOK UP
17. JAILHOUSE ROCK
18. SANTA CLAUS IS BACK IN TOWN
19. DON'T
FAREWELL TO HIS FANS (ON VOL 1. A LEGENDARY PERFORMER)

SIDE TWO 'AFTER'

1. SUCH A NIGHT (FALSE START VERSION ON VOL 2. A LEGENDARY PERFORMER)
2. THE GIRL OF MY BEST FRIEND
3. MESS OF BLUES
4. RECONSIDER BABY
5. (MARIE'S THE NAME OF) HIS LATEST FLAME
6. LITTLE SISTER
7. SUSPICION
8. RETURN TO SENDER
9. TROUBLE/GUITAR MAN (TV SPECIAL)
10. BLUE CHRISTMAS/ONE NIGHT (TV SPECIAL)
11. IF I CAN DREAM
12. SUSPICIOUS MINDS
13. PROMISED LAND
14. LONG BLACK LIMOUSINE

SIDE ONE

1. WILLIN' (LITTLE FEAT)
2. 44 BLUES (HOY-HOY!)
3. TRUCKSTOP GIRL (LITTLE FEAT)
4. SAILIN' SHOES (SAILIN' SHOES)
5. TEENAGE NERVOUS BREAK DOWN (SAILIN' SHOES)
6. DIXIE CHICKEN (DIXIE CHICKEN)
7. TWO TRAINS (DIXIE CHICKEN)
8. ROLL UM EASY (DIXIE CHICKEN)
9. ROCK AND ROLL DOCTOR (HOY-HOY!)
10. OH! ATLANTA (FEATS DON'T FAIL ME NOW)
11. SPANISH MOON/SKIN IT BACK/FAT MAN IN THE BATHTUB(ELECTRIC LYCANTHROPE)
12. ROCKET IN MY POCKET (HOY-HOY!)

SIDE TWO

1. LONESOME WHISTLE (HOY-HOY!)
2. THE FAN (ELECTRIF LYCANTHROPE)
3. ON YOUR WAY DOWN (ELECTRIF LYCANTHROPE)
4. LONG DISTANCE LOVE (THE LAST RECORD ALBUM)
5. ONE LOVE STAND (THE LAST RECORD ALBUM)
6. NEW DELHI FREIGHT TRAIN (TIME LOVES A HERO)
7. ROCKET IN MY POCKET (TIME LOVES A HERO)
8. WHAT DO YOU WANT THE GIRL TO DO (THANKS I'LL EAT IT HERE — LOWELL GEORGE)
9. CHEEK TO CHEEK (THANKS I'LL EAT IT HERE — LOWELL GEORGE)
10. I CAN'T STAND THE RAIN (THANKS I'LL EAT IT HERE)
11. CHINA WHITE (HOY-HOY!)
12. FEATS DON'T FAIL ME NOW (HOY-HOY!)

BOOTLEG RECORDED LIVE AT ULTRASONIC FOR WLIR: REPUTEDLY MIXED BY GEORGE